STENDHAL

A COLLECTION OF CRITICAL ESSAYS

Edited

Victor Brombert

A SPECTRUM BOOK

Prentice-Hall, Inc., *Englewood Cliffs, N.J.*

© 1962

BY PRENTICE-HALL, INC.

ENGLEWOOD CLIFFS, N.J.

Second Printing .... June, 1962

LIBRARY OF CONGRESS CATALOG CARD NO.: 62-9306

Printed in the United States of America

84653-C

STENDHAL

For BETTINA

remembering piazza Rio di Janeiro

Foreword

A few words about this collection of critical essays. Its aim is to provide the reader with a representative variety of modern approaches and interpretations. The perspectives range from the strictly literary (Jean Prévost, Martin Turnell, Judd D. Hubert) to the psychological and philosophical (Jean Starobinski, Jean-Pierre Richard, Simone de Beauvoir). But whether the concern of the critics has been primarily social and political (Irving Howe, Raymond Giraud), biographical (Léon Blum), or that of the literary scholar and historian (Erich Auerbach), all of them cast light on the problems of the novel, all of them were drawn to Stendhal by a common love of literature.

It is only appropriate to pay tribute to the many scholars whose patient research has laid the foundations of Stendhal criticism. Paul Arbelet and Henri Martineau have been in the forefront of French scholarship. Their work, continued in our day by Vittorio del Litto (the editor of *Stendhal Club*), has been directly responsible for the fine books of Jean Prévost, Maurice Bardèche, Georges Blin, Francine Marill, and many others. Italian scholarship, under the guidance of the late Pietro Paolo Trompeo and Luigi Foscolo Benedetto, has also been extremely productive: Glauco Natoli, Carlo Cordié, Luigi Magnani, Mario Bonfantini are some of the names that come to mind. Jules Alciatore, in the United States, has done important and devoted research. All lovers of Stendhal owe them a debt.

The present collection, containing a number of texts heretofore unavailable in English, hopes to provide the reader with a balanced sampling of modern Stendhal criticism. It has obviously not been possible to include all the important critical studies. In particular, I regret the absence of Harry Levin's illuminating *Toward Stendhal*—too long for inclusion, and too good to be reproduced in part. Among the other distinguished names missing is that of Robert M. Adams, whose delightfully incisive *Stendhal: Notes on a Novelist,* written with zest and imaginative insight, should be in the hands of every Stendhalian.

V.B.

Table of Contents

INTRODUCTION—*Victor Brombert*   1

ON THE NOVELS

   LE ROUGE ET LE NOIR—*Martin Turnell*   15

   IN THE HÔTEL DE LA MOLE—*Erich Auerbach*   34

   LUCIEN LEUWEN—*Jean Prévost*   47

   ROMANTIC REALISM IN *LUCIEN LEUWEN*—
     Raymond Giraud   63

   STENDHAL: THE POLITICS OF SURVIVAL—
     Irving Howe   76

   THE DEVALUATION OF REALITY IN THE
     CHARTREUSE DE PARME—*Judd D. Hubert*   95

ON THE NOVELIST

   A THEORETICAL OUTLINE OF "BEYLISM"—
     Léon Blum   101

   TRUTH IN MASQUERADE—*Jean Starobinski*   114

   KNOWLEDGE AND TENDERNESS IN STENDHAL—
     Jean-Pierre Richard   127

   STENDHAL OR THE ROMANTIC OF REALITY—
     Simone de Beauvoir   147

   STENDHAL, ANALYST OR AMORIST?—
     Victor Brombert   157

Chronology of Important Dates   169

Notes on the Editor and Contributors   171

Bibliography   173

STENDHAL

Introduction

by Victor Brombert

I

Stendhal's irreverent mind, delighting in the paradoxical and the subversive, raised non-conformity to the level of a fine art. This achievement alone endears him to the modern reader. But non-conformity is never entirely a matter of choice. Stendhal's temperament condemned him to a precarious equilibrium. He seemed to thrive on tensions and inconsistencies. Born into the stolid provincial bourgeoisie, he saw himself as a volatile cosmopolitan. A timid dreamer, he wanted to become a cold-blooded analyst and a man of action. He yearned to open his heart, to confess himself in his writings, yet nothing delighted him so much as to disguise his emotion and mystify his readers. A Frenchman in proclaimed rebellion against France, a Bonapartist with a nostalgia for the Ancien Régime, a Republican with a strong distaste for the plebeian mentality, an inveterate free-lancer badly in need of approval and friendship—Stendhal appears indeed as the embodiment of paradox and insubordination. His refusal to submit extends to the imperatives of his own character.

Historical circumstances, or rather an acute responsiveness to the swift pace of contemporary events, account in large part for these alluring complexities. Stendhal was probably the first European writer to become irrevocably convinced that it was no longer possible to live on inherited values. Born in 1783, a few years before the Revolution, he grew up during a period of intense upheaval, went to school under the Directory, became an adolescent with the Consulate, reached manhood under the Empire, participated in the Napoleonic débâcle in Russia, wrote half of his books under the Restoration and the other half during the July Monarchy, and died, in 1842, only a few years before another revolutionary storm was to shake France. His life, one might say, was lived out under the very sign of Revolution. Moreover, he bridged two centuries—two worlds—in a way none of his "contemporaries" did: Balzac, Hugo, Vigny, all the Romantic writers in fact, were born after the Revolu-

tion and were still boys when Napoleon fell. Being their elder, close to
them in terms of literary history, yet distant in terms of age and experience, only increased his sense of homelessness and his tragic awareness
of Time and Change.

The eminently "modern" quality of Stendhal's writings owes much
to this awareness of an historical *fatum*. For history, in his day, could
no longer be treated with archeological detachment, as a form of tourism
in time. It had become an explosive and corrosive force, a current that
sweeps nations and individuals, and pits them against each other. The
rapid succession of political regimes in his lifetime made Stendhal the
witness to an extraordinary acceleration of history. Together with his
generation, he became haunted, and no doubt exhilarated also, by the very
principles of instability, evanescence, and transformation. His keen
temporal perspective made him an unusually sharp observer of all moral
and social phenomena. Repeatedly—in the *Courrier anglais* it is a real
leitmotiv—he commented on the coexistence of several generations quite
near each other in time, but irremediably alienated from each other by
dissimilar educations and experiences. And between these generations
the dialogue had become almost impossible. Fathers and sons: the novels
of Stendhal constantly dramatize this theme of conflicting generations.
Even brothers have become estranged. And with this theme Stendhal was
broaching one of the major concerns of our time.

Political affairs held an endless fascination for Stendhal. He could
view them both as a comic choreography and as a dramatic force. No
matter with what hypnotic intensity his characters indulge in their
private dreams and in the subtle dialectics of love, the political contingency always forms the substructure of his novels. Although he quipped
that politics in a novel were as incongruous as a pistol shot in a concert
hall, he suspected that in that incongruity lay a deeper truth. Stendhal's
originality as a "realist" lies indeed primarily in his understanding that
no individual destiny can be detached from the events and currents that
victimize it. The pistol shot, he felt, was part of the concert.

Stendhal's achievement as a journalist and political commentator
has not always received the attention it deserves. He was unusually well
informed. An avid newspaper reader, he also cultivated friends such
as the baron de Mareste (an important official at the Préfecture de
Police) and Joseph Lingay (personal assistant to the Minister of the
Interior, Decazes) who provided him with political tidbits with which he
seasoned the innumerable articles he wrote anonymously for various
British publications. These articles, gathered by Henri Martineau in the
five volumes of the *Courrier anglais,* constitute a pungent chronicle in
which the future author of *Le Rouge et le noir* diagnoses the multiple
ills of the Restoration and provides an astute, if not always impartial,
portrayal of various classes and professional groups: the ultra-royalists, the

liberals, the new financial aristocracy, the merchant class, the magistracy, the army, the clergy, the provincial power groups. Even his books on tourism and on the arts are focused on social and political problems. *Rome, Naples et Florence* (characteristically the first book to be signed by the pseudonym of Stendhal) is in reality largely concerned with a satirical denunciation of a post-Napoleonic Italy dominated by the Church and by a vengeful, reactionary Austria.

Stendhal's tragic sense of History and Politics goes, however, far beyond satire. It is uncannily prophetic of the most pressing dilemmas of our own day. Julien Sorel's war with society is not merely the surface quarrel that pits a young man's pride against all forms of philistinism; it foreshadows the bitter war of the classes ("Je n'ai point l'honneur d'appartenir à votre classe," he ironically tells his jury) and explains why Marxist critics, whose emphasis is of course one-sided, may well consider Stendhal's novels as outstanding examples of "critical realism." Stendhal's entire work seems to echo Napoleon's pronouncement that modern writers would seek in politics a sense of fate no less despotic than that which inspired the Greek tragedians. Yet there is here no mystique of History—quite to the contrary. As Erich Auerbach reminds us, Stendhal is immune to romantic Historism. Indeed, he seemed to intuit how easily history could become a form of tyranny.

The images of this tyranny fill the pages of his books. Some of them—the somber plots, the spies, the infinite precautions, and secret messages—may at first appear like the private games of an imagination that enjoys scaring itself and that seeks pleasure in dreams of persecution. Yet they all point to a significant obsession: the permanent terror of the police state. They all point to a world in which denunciation and repression have already become a daily reality—a world in which an all-probing and all-intruding political eye has invaded, or is about to invade, the individual conscience. The Farnese tower, in the *Chartreuse,* is not at all a sheer fairytale invention. Stendhal could not forget that men like Silvio Pellico and Maroncelli were rotting in the *carcere duro* of prisons such as the feared Spielberg. In fact the Spielberg fortress casts its ominous shadow across the otherwise sunny *Chartreuse.* And Parma, "that country of secret threats," is clearly symbolic of a world that endangers the very dignity of man. For the political tragi-comedy is a steady warning of the dangers of human degradation. The *Te Deum* in celebration of their jailer's recovery, sung voluntarily (and at their own expense!) by the prisoners of the citadel, reveals the depth to which man can debase the very image of man, and foreshadows some of the horrors of our own tortured era.

In the face of such tyranny, the real problem—as the title of Irving Howe's important essay suggests—becomes one of survival. If Stendhal speaks with such directness to the modern reader, it is no doubt because, in one way or another, his entire work is an effort at salvaging the notion of the individual from the bankruptcy of Humanism. The overwhelming question is how an elite of heart and mind can save itself against the encroachments of any form of despotism without at the same time abdicating its values and surrendering to absolutes. Stendhal was unquestionably one of the first European writers to diagnose the disease of power and absolutism. And he was one of the first also, as Irving Howe well puts it, to speak for an increasingly marginal and "homeless" intelligentsia. *Estrangement* should indeed be a key word in dealing with Stendhal. There is more than a chance coincidence in the parallel prison-destinies of Julien Sorel and of Camus's *étranger*, Meursault. Society has condemned them, yet they have found their dignity and their salvation in not playing the game of this society and in accepting their private "cell." Stendhal's characters are "strangers" all: Octave (in *Armance*), Lucien Leuwen, Fabrice, Lamiel—all of them, including the proud women who find refuge in their *pudeur* and liberation in love, and who all learn the hard way to resist the ignominious pressures of the world.

In that struggle for independence and for survival, the alienated hero of Stendhal has only a few weapons. They are not always noble weapons, but he must use them in self-defense. And the art of hypocrisy, the art of conscious and controlled dissembling, is the most efficacious. Here too Stendhal has been prophetic. The Stalins and Hitlers of our time have persecuted the intellectuals, but this is largely because they knew that intellectuals—as Brice Parain tersely puts it—are those who know best how to say *yes* while meaning *no*. In *The Captive Mind,* one of the most revealing books of our time, the Polish writer Czeslaw Milosz refers to the practice of *Ketmân* as the only method for maintaining a private life and heretical views under an oppressive regime. And *Ketmân,* as Gobineau had described it in his study of central Asian philosophies and religions, is the art of protecting one's deepest faith by openly renouncing one's true opinion, by paying lip service to the infidel and by performing the required rites with the perfection and malicious pleasure of an actor. Stendhal, like Julien Sorel, sometimes slips and forgets to play his role. But most often he and his heroes practice a "Beyliste" form of *Ketmân* with consummate artistry. Ultimately, they even learn to love all that which impinges on their inner freedom, for obstacles and shackles bring out the best in them.

II

The very *tone* of Stendhal is provocative. Unconstrained and impertinent, it draws the reader into a state of complicity. His style and his technique proclaim a subversive temperament. A sworn enemy of clichés and sentimentalism, he suspects every form of fakery and wages steady war on all the manifestations of cant and conventionality. His literary technique is no less "modern" than his intuition about History as the villain of our time. He is the master of the short cut, the understatement, the ellipsis. The rapidity of his transitions flatters the intelligence. His dialectics of sentiment and analysis, of precision and enthusiasm, masterfully explored by Jean-Pierre Richard, create a climate of ambiguity in which surrender to emotion is perpetually kept in check by the exigencies of a self-conscious mind. Such inner tensions give little comfort to the reader who likes an unequivocal viewpoint. Stendhal offers no respite. Above all, he has developed the modern technique of the limited field of vision, and not only in the famous battle of Waterloo, which is seen through a single consciousness (and not through the historian's all-knowing and all-ordering mind), but in every one of his novels which evoke the protagonists' direct experience of a world bounded by their own horizon. The characters of Stendhal are thus at the same time highly "aware" and capable of great blindness, but this very immurement within their own consciousness protects their inner life and grants them the freedom to pursue their private dream.

This existential freedom of his characters is probably the most striking originality of Stendhal. One finds here none of those definitions whereby a novelist, playing at god or at tyrant, freezes a living psychological reality. If a Julien Sorel or a Fabrice del Dongo appear from the outset so naïve and unstable, it is because the author refuses to make them the prisoners of their supposed essence. Unlike Balzac, whose characters are almost always the dynamic embodiment of an abstraction, Stendhal does not create predetermined types and situations. He seems to proclaim, a century ahead of Malraux, that man is what he does, not what he hides. It is no surprise that the writers of our Existentialist generation have been so drawn to him. For his main theme is also that of *freedom,* political to be sure, but primarily metaphysical and psychological: freedom discovered in love, in prison, and above all in the very act of living. Stendhal, who never *defines* his characters, allows them (compels them, one might say) to discover themselves. His literary devices (his ironic intrusions, his commentaries, his pretense at being surprised, the capricious rhythms of his narration, his apparent improvisations), far from ensnaring them, seem to accord his fictional creatures the freedom to discover themselves. And indeed, Stendhalian heroes constantly make discoveries of this sort. Free from prejudice, they too have not defined themselves. They observe themselves, they judge themselves, they watch themselves live and act, but they do not know themselves as yet. Hence also an underlying feeling of anguish, the urge to set out on a quest.

The quest for freedom is thus intimately bound up with the quest for identity and the disturbing riddle of the personality. A riddle and a quest which account in large part for Stendhal's compelling auto-biographic urge. Numerous texts discovered and published posthumously attest to his assiduous self-observation and self-assessment. From his adolescent days in Paris, he scribbled endless diaries, "psychological" notes, personal accounts, analyses and "consultations"—displaying an al-most obsessive tendency to view himself both as subject and object which culminated in two autobiographic masterpieces, *Souvenirs d'égotisme* and *Vie de Henry Brulard*. In these two books the auto-biographer rises to the level of artist. Their real interest lies not, how-ever, in the many vivid details, peppery anecdotes, and memories they provide, nor even in the subtle nuances with which Stendhal diagnoses his sensibility. What counts here is the *manner* of the exploration, the state of innocence with which Stendhal faces himself, the problematical nature of his approach. Influenced by Rousseau's *Confessions*, these texts differ sharply, however, in their fundamental angle of vision: they are written not to justify a man, but to discover him. The telescoping of past and present, the almost Proustian insistence on an uncontrolled and uncerebral memory, are all aimed at a discovery *in time* of a fluid psychic reality.

Puzzled by the mystery of his personality, nettled by the conflicting images he projects into the minds of others, Stendhal constantly asks himself the double question: "What am I?"—"What have I been?" With sadness he recognizes that the eye cannot see itself: "L'œil ne se voit pas lui-même." Much like his fictional characters, Stendhal feels compelled to search for the severest judges. But *Souvenirs d'égotisme* and *Vie de Henry Brulard* also show to what extent their author is trapped between the need to reveal himself and the fear of being penetrated by another con-science. The eye thus comes to play a crucial metaphoric role. Not to be discovered becomes as important as to discover oneself. And through a strange but deeply meaningful paradox, the wearing of a mask, the art of intellectual disguise, the lie which is to protect the inner being, function simultaneously as means of self-defense and means of self-dis-covery. All the characters of Stendhal are obsessed by the need to unveil their conscience to themselves, if need be by changing their lives and even their identity. Octave, the hero of *Armance*, thirsts for *incognito*. Mina de Vanghel goes so far as to alter the color of her skin. "I would wear a mask with pleasure," confesses Stendhal in *Souvenirs d'égotisme*.

This puzzled search for the self is perhaps nowhere more evident than in the case of Lucien Leuwen who knows that he can be sure of nothing about himself. Unable to "foresee" his emotions, perpetually surprised by his own reactions, he tries out all sorts of roles. But Lucien's instability and self-imposed obstacles are typical of all the characters of Stendhal. The theme of the father-search which runs through all his novels is a symptom of this quest for identity. Stendhal thus creates a multiplicity of fathers for his heroes (the Abbés Chélan and Pirard, the marquis de La Mole for Julien; Abbé Blanès and count Mosca for Fabrice)—but the pseudo-father at best becomes an instrument of emancipation from the imprisonment of real paternity; he will not offer the hero a clear picture of himself. This picture no external authority can provide for him. Such responsibility cannot be transferred. The solipsistic nature of the Stendhalian hero is not merely a form of egotism; it is the proud awareness that each conscience must seek itself, and as it were *create* itself in this pursuit. The act of creation and the act of knowledge are thus closely bound up with each other. The only method whereby Stendhal's heroes can discover themselves is by "trying themselves out" in an almost histrionic sense. On this relationship between masquerade and self-discovery Jean Starobinski has written some superb pages.

III

This ironic and self-conscious pursuit of self, this play-acting in the service of truth, explain in part why Stendhal has been so often misunderstood. Fencing with his own shadows, he seems to be fencing also with his readers. Each generation has created for itself a partial image. The readers of 1830 saw him as a master cynic. Taine and his friends of the École Normale admired in him the rationalist heir to the eighteenth-century Idéologues. Zola and the naturalist school praised him for his realism. To the generation of Bourget and Barrès he appeared as the great professor of energy, the supreme egotist whose brand of analytical romanticism and biting impertinences seemed to initiate them into a private cult. Tender and yet sarcastic, lyrical and yet obsessed with fact, sophisticated and at the same time naïve—the protean image conjured up in the minds of his readers owes a great deal to Stendhal's anguished awareness that the author is involved not only with his own characters and with himself, but with his reader—and that this involvement is highly ambiguous. Here too a mask was necessary.

The ambiguities of Stendhal's tone can easily unsettle the unsophisticated reader. The staccato lyricism of his novels never allows the mind to immobilize constantly shifting meanings. Prosaic precision and poetic vagueness, illusion and disenchantment, cynicism and idealism, negation and affirmation of values, parody and sentimental commitment—all coexist, clash, and somehow merge in a mercurial synthesis. Even the vocabulary of Stendhal remains ambivalent: terms of praise often assume a derogatory function. The perspective is constantly ironic, but ironic in the deepest sense of the word. For there is nothing frivolous about Stendhal's irony. All may seem a game—even politics and passion. Yet no one has used his wit more effectively to protect his joy and his sadness. And this irony which avenges Stendhal for his heart's bondage while rejoicing in it, which dissembles in order better to suggest and reveal, is ultimately as dreamy and smilingly melancholic as the autumnal light that falls on the terrible and marvelous citadel of Parma.

Few writers have practiced more assiduously the art of dissimulation or felt more keenly the urge to cover up their tracks. It is as though Stendhal were afraid of his emotions. The typical intrusions in his novels represent not so much a histrion's desire to be on stage as a form of camouflage whereby he disguises his enthusiasm through apparent disclaimers and perfidious asides. These ironic interventions range from the jovial sally to the most insolent banter. They include a variety of "attitudes": the paternal and patronizing tone, pretended surprise, false pity and false naïveté, the detached clinical observation, the worldly maxim and urbane scorn. Stendhal seems to betray his fictional world—but he only betrays it in order better to shield it. A fundamental timidity lies at the heart of this strategy: the desire to communicate clashes at every moment with the distressing awareness of incommunicability. Isolated and withdrawn, the author has recourse to the ironic mode. He splits and multiplies himself so as not to be alone. He thus comes to assume a role, and finds his consolation in a provisional betrayal of precisely that which he holds most dear.

These baffling inner tensions are no doubt a key factor in the genesis of his works—a factor more important by far than all the models, plots, and literary sources. The unconscious desire to check and even punish himself constitutes a powerful creative force. Thus, side by side with dashing young heroes whom he exposes to humiliations and defeats that recall his own, he also creates unflattering images of middle-aged men who are obvious caricatures of himself. Dr. Sansfin, the witty hunchback seducer in the unfinished novel *Lamiel*, is only the most extreme example of a permanent tendency on Stendhal's part to punish and humiliate himself through his fiction. As author, Stendhal has this in common with his characters: he indulges in his mortifications and exaggerates his defeats. Holding himself guilty toward himself, he bitterly ruminates over his vexations to the point of transforming his remorse into an *idée fixe*. But curiously, this obsessive rumination stimulates the imagination into transcending reality by toying with what "might have" happened. Self-deprecation thus, paradoxically, proposes a hypothetical action. In *Vie de Henry Brulard*, Stendhal himself has acutely diagnosed the creative and compensatory nature of his "ruminations": "I ruminate ceaselessly on that which concerns me; by dint of looking at it from various *positions of my soul*, I end up by seeing something new, I make it *change its aspect*." It is exciting to observe the intimate links which connect the omniscience of the novelist with his speculative search for compensations. The mind of Stendhal is a theater where the same gestures are reenacted with infinite variations of mood.

Equally disconcerting to the uninitiated reader are the unpredictable changes of pace and mixtures of tone. No episode is, in this respect, more characteristic than the pages describing Fabrice's participation in the battle of Waterloo. Much praise has been lavished on Stendhal for having been the first to describe a battle from a "realistic" point of view —that is, with all its confusion and from the strictly limited viewpoint of a single character. We are far removed here from traditional epic accounts where every participant, every weapon, every skirmish, and every wound is catalogued and described by the omniscient author. There is something comical and contingent in Fabrice's very presence on the battlefield. This romantic Candide, thirsting for sensations and for the din of war, is in fact a heroic parasite. And as the author leads him from surprise to surprise, from blunder to blunder, from one humiliating experience to another, it becomes quite clear that these pages have little to do with a realistic account, but that they are in fact a mock-heroic episode, a parody of epic attitudes and epic conventions.

And indeed, the situation does seem to contain some of the essential elements of the epic: a tremendous spectacle, great crowds, a hero who travels far and who throws himself into a series of actions filled with obstacles, mysterious omens, battles in which entire armies clash, the weight of destiny—for the entire future of Europe is at stake. It is not surprising that Fabrice, who has read precisely those books that would overheat his imagination, dreams that he is living a tale of high romance and that his fellow soldiers are heroic companions straight out of the pages of Tasso and Ariosto. But alas, reality bears little resemblance to the epic dream. What he discovers is not sublime courage and generosity, but stupidity, selfishness, and the confusion of an abject rout. It is this conflict between the dreamed reality and the lived reality which provides the dramatic tension. Stendhal, who seems to take a malicious pleasure in exposing Fabrice to every indignity (including the theft of his horse!), shows how reality forces his "hero" to undo one by one every dream of chivalrous friendship. The soldiers of the Grande Armée have decidedly little in common with Tasso's *Gerusalemme liberata*. It is as though the entire Waterloo episode were only a therapy for curing Fabrice of his illusions.

Nothing could be more misleading, however, than to interpret the interlude at Waterloo as a simple return to lucidity. Fabrice may remind one of Candide, but he has also something of Don Quixote. And dreams are not cured that easily. War may no longer be that noble enthusiasm of souls in love with glory, but if the world is not what it might or should be, this does not prevent Don Quixote from living up to himself. Alternating lyricism and mockery, creating a caustic mixture of bitter-sweet, Stendhal brings into sharp focus the poetic temperament of his hero. Fabrice's romantic and idealistic nature stands out in high relief

against this background of parody and insignificance. Ariosto and Tasso
are in fact not at all pretexts for irony. From the earliest pages of the
Chartreuse, they are symbols of lofty poetry. Countess Pietranera dreams
near the lake of Como to the mental accompaniment of their tender
lines. In his own autobiography, Stendhal associates Ariosto with love-
nostalgia and with the vast silence of magic forests. And the wistful,
slightly melancholic smile of the author of the *Chartreuse* is not without
resemblance to the smile of the poet who sang:

> Le Donne, i Cavalier, l'arme, gli amori,
> Le cortesie, l'audaci imprese. . . .

The elements of parody, far from disrupting the lyrical illusion, serve
here as a protection and reveal an over-sensitive hero whom the world's
coarseness forces into exile within himself.

It is a surprising fictional world in which laughter and sarcasm serve
the highest exigencies of the heart. Stendhal's chronic reversal of values
is perhaps even more unsettling in the basic "immorality" that reigns
in the *Chartreuse*. Charles Maurras called it "a charming primer in
political knavery." This *coquinologie* is, however, not limited to politics.
From the very outset, every worldly success appears as a form of turpitude.
Count Mosca, an admirable professor of cynicism, knows of course that
politics are only a game. But he also knows that power sanctifies everything, that sentiments are mere dupery. Yet he is the willing victim of
his own illusions. He not only loves and suffers with the timidity of an
adolescent, but is eager to give up his own power to follow into exile
the woman he loves.

Thus behind the apparent immorality of the novel, a personal ethics
is evolved—a special ethics which has its foundation in the very conventions and hypocrisies it challenges. For it is precisely the Moscas of
this world—those who proclaim themselves to be cynical and incapable
of gravity—who refuse to live according to a comfortable and profitable
morality, and who are the true creators of moral values: the ones to forge
for themselves a rigorous moral code. But this moral code remains a
private affair and only confirms the bankruptcy of collective values.
Mosca does not set store by the "liberal" formulas of his day. The claim
to seek the greatest good for the greatest number seems to him sheer
folly, if not downright charlatanism. (Mosca believes first and foremost
in the greatest good of count Mosca!) But Stendhal also makes it very
clear that Mosca is a man of unimpeachable *personal* honor—the brand
of honor that exists only between equals, and in a privileged relationship.
In short, it is the code of the *happy few*. And the first law of this code
is not to cheat with oneself, not to fall in one's own esteem. Stendhal
makes this revealing comment about the duchess Sanseverina: "She was

a woman honest with herself." It is this same ethics of good faith and severity toward oneself (this fear of intellectual fraud) which explains why, after the battle of Waterloo—unlike the many immorally moral people who never question anything—Fabrice wants to know whether he has really been in a battle and whether he has really fought.

Perhaps it is because of this subversive morality that the most ardent Stendhalians, whatever their devotion to *Le Rouge et le noir, Lucien Leuwen,* or *Vie de Henry Brulard,* are above all fanatical *"Chartreusistes."* For in this novel they find the very essence of "Beylisme" which teaches that true passion is the appanage of an elite. The novel is indeed dedicated TO THE HAPPY FEW—those "happy few" who, together with the author, value passion (and the *pudeur* of passion which is its mask), who know how not to be dupes and yet prefer to be the victims of their illusions, who know above all—as André Suarès suggested—that it is divine to be taken in by the beauty of one's dreams.

IV

What is this beauty and what are those dreams? Much of the answer can be found in Stendhal's swan song, *La Chartreuse de Parme.* A peculiar autumn light, a late afternoon sun ever so slightly sad, bring out all contours with softness and precision. Strange combination of mellowness and recaptured youth! The typical climate of his novels is one of youthful drive. But nowhere is this feverish exaltation more contagious than in the *Chartreuse.* This army of soldiers, all under twenty-five, invading Milan, this atmosphere of slight inebriation, this contempt for all that is powdered and bewigged and that is old in spirit—all this initiates us into a world where the term *impossible* seems incongruous, where boredom is the one unredeemable sin.

Equally inebriating are the landmarks evoked in the *Chartreuse.* The Lombardy countryside, Grianta and the lake of Como, the palace in Parma, the Farnese citadel, the tower of Abbé Blanès: imaginary places and real places which all suggest the Italy that Stendhal had, for his own private usage, transfigured into a world of revery and energy. As epigraph he had chosen the famous lines of Ariosto:

> Gia mi fur dolci inviti a empir le carte
> I luoghi ameni.

These *luoghi ameni*—these enchanting spots of Stendhal's mental geography—all participate in the same giddiness of the mind and of the senses. With lyrical joy he conjures up the starry sky, the feeble light of dawn outlining the chain of the Alps, the noble architecture of palazzi, the two branches of the lake Fabrice admires from the belfry, the sound of the bells, the rhythmical beat of the oars, and these *mortaretti* fire-works during the feast of San Giovita, whose irregular explosions symbolize the carefree spontaneity which is probably the "Italian" virtue Stendhal admires most.

"Italian"—for it is obvious that this "Italy" has been metamorphosed into resembling the inner landscape of Stendhal. His Italy thus becomes the very world of poetic estrangement and grants access to the author's most permanent dreams. Blending invention and reality, this projected landscape serves to impose a vision. Every eccentricity, every unconventional move of his characters enjoys the immunity of a transalpine never-never land. The veiled shapes of an enchanted region and the climate of a fairy tale (but a fairy tale for adults) allow for all extravagances.

The importance of this Italian myth is crucial in the work of Stendhal. It is bound up with his sentimental education in Milan, with his early memories of Rousseau, with the discovery of art, with Napoleonic glory and an adolescent need for emancipation. Italy, Stendhal felt, had liberated him from family constraints and national prejudice. The list of his works in which Italy plays a central role is impressive. The *Journal* of 1811 already prefigures *Rome, Naples et Florence* (of which there exist two versions). *L'Histoire de la peinture en Italie,* and *Vies de Haydn, Mozart et Métastase* were directly influenced by his long stay in Milan. Two unfinished lives of Napoleon evoke the Italian adventure with gusto. Add to that the *Vie de Rossini, Promenades dans Rome,* and the most dithyrambic pages of *Vie de Henry Brulard* and it becomes clear that the *Chroniques italiennes* and *La Chartreuse de Parme* were not the result of chance discoveries of dusty old manuscripts, but that they were slowly matured in a life-long genesis. And this explains why the *Chroniques italiennes,* though literally hardly more than a skillful adaptation of melodramatic chronicles, carry some of Stendhal's most insistent poetic themes: the rebellion of the outlaw, the double point of view on morality, the ambiguous clash of private virtues with public vices, the themes of tragic happiness, of love as a *coup de foudre* and as an impossibility, of the immurement of the beloved.

This fundamental unity of Stendhal's poetic vision makes him a particularly apt subject for existential criticism. It is indeed difficult to speak of any given novel without referring to the recurrent patterns of his imagination. The artistic activity, in his case, is no less interesting than the artistic result. Few novelists have built their fictional universes more consistently around a few central preoccupations. Underneath all the surface noise about passion and energy, behind the game of politics and the tensions of society, three closely related themes support the Stendhalian edifice: the poetry of the privileged moment, the poetry of the inaccessible, the poetry of the prison cell.

The almost religious exaltation of the privileged moment ("Pour un tel moment il vaut la peine d'avoir vécu") owes much to Rousseau. Like the author of *La Nouvelle Héloïse,* Stendhal has a real cult of those rare, ineffable, evanescent hours which make man forget his contingency and allow him, sometimes retrospectively, to see into the life of things: moments such as the precious evenings Julien spends with Mme de Rênal in the garden at Vergy—and which, alas, he will learn to value too late; moments of innocence and of "naturel," when suddenly the voice of the world is still. *De l'Amour,* his novels, his autobiographical writings are all punctuated by these fragile and indescribable moments. Even the act of writing has its moments of grace: rare, elated moments when the joy of creating is fused with the joy of remembering. Stendhal's most moving pages are perhaps those where he confesses to the inadequacy of language. "I would like to write in a sacred tongue," he sadly remarks in *Promenades dans Rome,* as he once more suffers from the urge to communicate the incommunicable. "How to describe happiness?" he asks in the *Vie de Henry Brulard* which, significantly, ends on a note of silence.

This poetic inadequacy of language has its counterpart in the poetry of the *inaccessible* which colors, and further deepens, the most beautiful human experiences in his novels. The most desired joys are condemned to remain unattainable. But this is how they preserve their purity. Something elusive and unfulfilled protects all beauty from corrosion. Stendhal's affection for his heroes can be measured by the "incompleteness" of their earthly destiny. He grants them a fleeting vision of their promised land, never the right to take possession of it. Their meteoric course protects them from the snares of time and disillusionment. They remain pure: compromises they know, but never the surrender to baseness. Events may defeat them, but not the act of living.

The prison theme is clearly related to this poetry of the unattained. The prison cell where Mme de Rênal and Julien meet again, the cell where Clélia and Fabrice love each other, are symbolic of the intimate bond between those who seek and find each other beyond the reach of the common herd. But they also symbolize the *impossibility* of their love. For this myth of the "impossible" love is at the very heart of Stendhal's work. Hence all the amorous conquests *à distance* and all the women imprisoned by timidity or prejudice. Hence also the poetics of the glance, that typical Stendhalian intimacy by means of distant signs. For in Stendhal's mythology of love, what matters is not intimacy and gratification of the senses, but inner tension and desire. Love is for Stendhal's characters the *"grande affaire"* of their lives. But this *"affaire"* has value only because it implies the profound energies of the soul, because it involves the entire human being and projects him into existence. Love, according to Stendhal, is thus never a possession. His characters remain free: neither possessed, nor humiliated, nor subjugated, nor betrayed.

The prison cell where Fabrice and Clélia know love points forward to the monastic cell into which Fabrice finally withdraws. It also recalls the cell where Julien Sorel meditated on his imminent death. In every case it represents the highest form of escape, escape within the self. Prison, in fact, assumes a protective and purifying role. It is in prison that Julien discovers his freedom. His only complaint is that he cannot lock his door from the inside. All the characters of Stendhal are thus secretly drawn to one form or another of imprisonment. This prison-wish is closely related to a yearning for altitude and vast panoramas. Marcel Proust once described the entire world of Stendhal as "a feeling of altitude linked with the spiritual life." The image conjures up all the elevated and lonely places where Stendhalian heroes find moments of serenity: the rock of Julien, the gothic dungeon of Besançon, the tower of Abbé Blanès, the cell in the Farnese fortress. Altitude and isolation mark the moments of the most exalted poetic fervor: a "solitude aérienne" which allows only for a view of the sky. The four walls of the prison cell become the very symbol of a private dream-world.

Stendhal's quest for self-knowledge thus comes full circle. The urge to solve the riddle of his personality drives him back into himself. Condemned to the freedom of self-discovery, he cannot escape solipsistic confinement. But confinement here does not imply stasia. Stendhal, together with his heroes, carries the prison image along with him. For his is not the paralyzing self-analysis of a Benjamin Constant, but a restless apprenticeship of self. This self, perpetually elusive, draws him into the obsessive mirror-game of thought and into the anguished awareness of his own liberty. "I do not know myself, and this—whenever I think of it at night—distresses me," he confesses in *Souvenirs d'egotisme*. But all of his heroes suffer from this same form of insomnia; all of them experience the same anxious self-questioning. Precisely because they all know that the eye cannot see itself, they all seek and at the same time fear the glance of "others."

This desired terror of the glance is no doubt responsible for the intriguing chiaroscuro of his novels. Ultimately, the metaphysics of human freedom are perhaps the true source of tragedy in Stendhal's work. For it is impossible not to sense, beyond his courageous smile, beyond the fervor of his characters, the tragic dilemma of a man who is in turn seduced and awed by his own freedom, and who finds it difficult to watch himself live in a mirror other than that of literary creation.

Le Rouge et le noir

by Martin Turnell

The opening chapters of a novel by Stendhal must be read with the same care as the opening scenes of a comedy by Molière. They contain the essential clues to the understanding of the whole book. *Le Rouge et le noir* begins with a description of the little town of Verrières in which the novelist displays his admirable sensibility:

> La petite ville de Verrières peut passer pour l'une des plus jolies de la Franche-Comté. Ses maisons blanches avec leurs toits pointus de tuiles rouges s'étendent sur la pente d'une colline, dont les touffes de vigoureux châtaigniers marquent les moindres sinuosités. Le Doubs coule à quelques centaines de pieds au-dessous de ses fortifications, bâties jadis par les Espagnols, et maintenant ruinées.

> [The small town of Verrières may be regarded as one of the most attractive in the Franche-Comté. Its white houses with their high pitched roofs of red tiles are spread over the slope of a hill, the slightest contours of which are indicated by clumps of sturdy chestnuts. The Doubs runs some hundreds of feet below its fortifications, built in times past by the Spaniards and now in ruins.]

The little town nestling among the hills, with its "habitants plus paysans que bourgeois" and its "jeunes filles fraîches et jolies" who work in the mills, gives and is intended to give an impression of peacefulness. We must not overlook the "fortifications." In an earlier period, they had marked the limit reached by the invader. Nor is it without significance that they are "ruined." For Verrières will suffer from an "invader" of another kind whose incursions will cause a considerable disturbance.

The novelist goes on to describe the industries of the place: the sawmills, the manufacture of "painted tiles" and nails. Then we are introduced to M. de Rênal, Mayor of Verrières:

At the sight of him every hat is quickly raised. His hair is turning grey, and he is dressed in grey. He is a Companion of several Orders, has a high forehead, an aquiline nose, and on the whole his face is not wanting in a certain regularity: indeed, the first impression formed of it may be that it combines with the dignity of a village mayor that sort of charm which may still be found in a man of forty-eight or fifty. But soon the visitor from Paris is annoyed by a certain air of self-satisfaction and self-sufficiency mingled with a suggestion of limitations and want of originality. One feels, finally, that this man's talent is confined to securing the exact payment of whatever is owed to him and to postponing payment till the last possible moment when he is the debtor.

It is not simply the portrait of an individual; it is the portrait of a class. For M. de Rênal is the symbol of the privileged classes—genteel on the surface, hard as nails underneath—in their ruthless struggle with the unprivileged.

No one who has read Stendhal's principal works will have failed to notice that he was obsessed with prisons, secret police and spies. The casual reference to "fortifications" in the first paragraph of the book is caught up three pages later by a reference to "walls":

> You must not for a moment expect to find in France those picturesque gardens which enclose the manufacturing towns of Germany; Leipsic, Frankfort, Nuremberg, and the rest. In the Franche-Comté, the more walls a man builds, the more he makes his property bristle with stones piled one above another, the greater title he acquires to the respect of his neighbours.

Walls is one of the focal words of the novel. They are in the first place the ramparts which separate the two worlds of the privileged and the unprivileged. They are also the "fortifications" which preserve the bourgeois world from the incursions of peasants and workers. In spite of their gentility and respectability, the privileged are far from being idle behind their fortifications; they wage a ceaseless war against those outside and are constantly thrusting their ramparts further forward and acquiring fresh territory:

> M. de Rênal's gardens, honeycombed with *walls*, are still further admired because he bought, for their weight in gold, certain minute scraps of ground which they cover. For example that sawmill, whose curious position on the bank of the Doubs struck you as you entered Verrières, and on which you noticed the name *Sorel* inscribed in huge letters on a board which overtops the roof, occupied, six years ago, the ground on which at this moment they are building the *wall* of the fourth terrace of M. de Rênal's gardens.

At this point the two worlds represented by M. de Rênal and Sorel—Julien's father—face one another directly. The Mayor's victory was hardly

won. He had to pay Sorel a fat price to move his factory, but, adds
Stendhal ironically, he also had to pull strings in Paris to have the *public*
stream which fed the sawmill turned.

The theme is pursued in the second chapter:

> Fortunately for M. de Rênal's reputation as an administrator, a *huge
> retaining wall* [1] was required for the public avenue which skirts the hillside
> a hundred feet above the bed of the Doubs. To this admirable position
> it is indebted for one of the most picturesque views in France. But, every
> spring, torrents of rainwater made channels across the avenue, carved deep
> gullies in it and left it impassable. This nuisance, which affected everybody
> alike, placed M. de Rênal under the fortunate obligation to immortalize
> his administration by a *wall* twenty feet in height and seventy or eighty yards
> long.

Although the Mayor appears to be performing a public duty in constructing his "huge retaining wall," it is not without substantial advantages to himself:

> The sun is extremely hot in these mountains; when it is directly overhead,
> the traveller's rest is sheltered on this terrace by a row of magnificent planes.
> Their rapid growth, and handsome foliage of a bluish tint are due to the
> artificial soil with which the Mayor has filled in the space behind his *im-
> mense retaining wall,* for, despite the opposition of the town council, he
> has widened the avenue by more than six feet. . . .

One of the central themes of *Le Rouge et le noir* is the "class war."
Stendhal's conception of it was much wider than that of modern political
theorists, but his book is the story of a parvenu who succeeds in penetrat-
ing the "walls" which protect the privileged and in attaching himself to
a class to which he does not belong. He penetrates not only the walls of
M. de Rênal's estate, but the walls of the seminary and of the Hôtel de
La Mole. In the end, society takes its revenge. With the same ease with
which it casts the simple Abbé Chélan outside its walls, it finally shuts
Julien behind prison walls and executes him not for slaying, or attempting
to slay, one of its members, but for trying to usurp its privileges.

We must turn now to the character of the parvenu. Stendhal uses a
number of different methods of creating character, but one of the most
important is the description of his chief character's effect on other people.
We are told of Julien at the seminary:

> Julien avait beau se faire petit et sot, il ne pouvait plaire, il était trop
> différent.

[1] Italics in the text.

[In vain might Julien make himself small and foolish, he could not give satisfaction, he was too different.]

The Abbé Pirard says to him:

Avec ce je ne sais quoi d'indéfinissable, du moins pour moi qu'il y a dans votre caractère, si vous ne faites pas fortune, vous serez persécuté; il n'y a pas de moyen terme pour vous.

[With this something indefinable that there is in your character, at any rate for me, if you do not make your fortune you will be persecuted. There is no middle way for you.]

He fares no better in his own family:

Objet du mépris de tous à la maison, il haïssait ses frères et son père; dans les jeux du dimanche, sur la place publique, il était toujours battu.

[An object of contempt to the rest of the household, he hated his brothers and father; in the games on Sundays, on the public square, he was invariably beaten.]

The Marquis de La Mole says of him:

Mais au fond de ce caractère je trouve quelque chose d'effrayant. C'est l'impression qu'il produit sur tout le monde, donc il y a là quelque chose de réel.

[But at the bottom of this character I find something frightening. It's the impression that he makes on everybody, so there must be something real about it.]

These observations reveal Julien from a number of different angles. We see him as he appeared to his proletarian family, to his fellow-seminarists, to his confessor and to aristocratic conservatives like M. de La Mole; but they have one thing in common. The *reader's* reactions are almost identical with those of the other *characters*. We, too, find Julien "different," "indefinable," "difficult to place," "frightening." Stendhal certainly intended that we should, and he himself completes the evidence by describing him as "un homme malheureux, en guerre avec toute la société." For Julien is an *étranger* or "outsider" in the society of his time.[2]

Now this conception of character is of capital importance in Stendhal's work and something must be said of the *étranger* type and of the age which produced him. It is commonly assumed that there are resemblances

[2] The word *étranger* is Stendhal's own.

between the Napoleonic age and our own, but it is easy to exaggerate them. In spite of revolution, war and devastation, the Europe which emerged from the Napoleonic wars was on the threshold of a great age of peace and plenty. At the same time, to a contemporary observer, it must have presented an appearance of considerable confusion. The Revolution had petered out in dictatorship; and dictatorship led not simply to monarchy, but to an extremely sordid, conventional and repressive monarchy. In politics, France was divided between conservatives and liberals, but we often find it difficult to distinguish between their policies which appear equally confused.

A sensitive observer like Stendhal was struck by the muddle and lack of vitality of this society—it is the constant burden of his writings—and it is precisely in these conditions that the *étranger* makes his appearance. He is the Janus-face who emerges in periods when the sensitive individual cannot identify himself with any of the different groups of which society is composed. For the *étranger* has *no recognized mode of feeling*. In spite of his intelligence and his extraordinary calculations, he is continually swinging from one extreme of feeling to another and back again. "Chez cet être singulier," said Stendhal, "c'était presque tous les jours tempête."

The *étranger* is essentially an individualist at odds with society, but it must be recognized that he is an entirely new type in European fiction. He has little in common with the Romantic outcast or Flaubert's *ratés,* with Gide's *immoraliste* or Camus's "outsider," who are all manifestations of a much more personal attitude. Stendhal's characters are the direct product of their age and are only comprehensible when seen in relation to it. They are left to work out their destiny in a chaotic society and their only supports are their own immense force of character and their own genius. In spite of their shortcomings, the way in which they set about their task stamps their attitude as an heroic one. I think that we can go further than this and say that Julien Sorel is "the modern hero."

Stendhal's conception of character is an example of the way in which he discarded philosophical theories when they came into conflict with his artistic vision. The materialism implicit in the work of the philosophers whom he admired led logically to determinism, to the belief that character is nothing but the product of environment. It would be an understatement to say that Stendhal did not accept this view. *Le Rouge et le noir* is based on the contrary view—on the view that genius is absolute and inexplicable. Stendhal took his "plot" from a newspaper account of a peasant who was executed for shooting his mistress and proceeded to transform it in the light of his own experience.[3] There is nothing in Julien's upbringing or environment to account for his gifts. His instruction has been limited to a few Latin lessons with the *curé*

[3] On the genesis of the novels, see M. Henri Martineau's admirable study, *L'Œuvre de Stendhal: Histoire de ses livres et de sa pensée* (Paris, 1945).

and reading a life of Napoleon given to him by an old soldier. He has been bullied and obstructed in every possible way by his family, but when his chance comes he is ready to seize it with both hands. The lesson is obvious. The genius will either turn into Napoleon or be executed as a common criminal. The answer depends on the sort of society in which he finds himself and on the use he makes of his opportunities. In other words, environment does not determine a man's *character,* but it does determine his *fate.*

When this is grasped, it is easy to see what *Le Rouge et le noir* is "about." Julien's character is not, perhaps, drawn with the firmness of Fabrice's and there are moments when Stendhal slips into melodrama or reveals the unfortunate influence of Romanticism; but these are minor flaws in his great achievement. The book is a profound study of the impact of genius on a corrupt society.

When Sainte-Beuve said that Stendhal "forms his characters with two or three ideas," he was certainly right; but when he added that "they are not living beings but ingeniously constructed automata," he showed that he had failed to understand his aims. Julien has a good deal in common with his creator. He had lost his mother when a child and loathes his father and family. All his actions are prompted by two feelings: anxiety at having no place in his own world and a consciousness of his genius. He is, as Taine remarked, *un esprit supérieur,* and he is determined to use his gifts to win a great position for himself. He has spent his youth brooding over the *Mémorial de Sainte-Hélène* and *Tartuffe.*[4] The first of these books is the story of a parvenu who, starting like Julien from nothing, had made himself master of Europe, and it represents the goal to be attained. The second is a handbook which explains the means which Julien must use in order to realize his ambitions. In this sense, and this sense only, Stendhal "forms his characters with two or three ideas."

It follows from this that the first step in Julien's career is to discover not merely what sort of a man he is, but what sort of a man he must become in order to succeed. When we read the novels, we find that all Stendhal's principal characters are tormented by the novelist's own question: "Qu'ai-je été, que suis-je?" They are perpetually interrogating themselves about their own feelings, wondering what they really feel for this woman, why that woman leaves them cold or asking themselves whether or not some defect in their make-up renders them incapable of loving at all.

---

[4] "In the provinces, a performance of *Tartuffe* had the same significance for the 'left' as the setting up of a mission cross had for the 'right.' . . . *Tartuffe* had become to the same extent as *Athalie,* but in the opposite sense, a religious play." (A. Thibaudet, *Stendhal,* Paris 1931, p. 108.)

Il est dans l'essense de cette âme à la fois d'agir et de se regarder agir, de sentir et de se regarder sentir.[5]

Paul Bourget's comment draws attention to an important difference between Stendhal and all his predecessors. Self-knowledge is not destructive as it was for Mme de La Fayette and Constant; it is not merely a prelude to action as it was for Laclos; in Stendhal action and analysis are simultaneous. All his characters realize that they can only exploit their genius by becoming something, by discovering some principle of unity within themselves. They must first of all rid themselves of the gnawing sense of anxiety which dogs them and become integrated personalities, and they can only become integrated personalities by observing their feelings at the actual moment of action. *Logique* and *espagnolisme* play a big part in the drama. The function of *logique* is to integrate personality, to control and direct the blind forces of *espagnolisme*. It is *logique* which is continually pulling them up, making them pause and ask themselves what they feel and why they feel as they do.

Although *Le Rouge et le noir* deals with the class war, I think that it will be apparent that the term *étranger* is not primarily a *social,* but a *psychological* distinction. The "walls" are barriers between the different classes, but they also stand for the psychological barriers which cut the "outsider" off from the rest of humanity. For the book is much more than a conflict between two social classes. It is a conflict between two irreconcilable ways of life. Julien would have been an "outsider" in any class of society, and he is equally out of place in the world of his father, of the Rênals and the La Moles. The fact that he belongs socially to the proletariat simply provides a particular setting for the study of a much wider problem and creates an additional obstacle to Julien's success. There was not the slightest chance of his exercising his peculiar talents in his father's world, and a rise in the social scale is necessary to start him on his career.

He does not make the first breach in the "walls" himself. M. de Rênal is prompted by vanity to engage a tutor for his children in order to score off his fellow-bourgeois. He approaches M. Sorel, knowing that he has a son who enjoys a certain reputation for learning. The bourgeois thus makes the first breach in his own walls which lets the outsider in. From this moment Julien's fortunes depend on himself. His attack is twofold. He has to impress the bourgeois, and he has to overcome his own feeling of anxiety by a personal success. There could be no better way than to persuade the bourgeois that he is a prodigy of learning and to seduce his employer's wife. Everything goes according to plan. The bourgeois, astonished by Julien's extraordinary verbal memory, treat

[5] *Essais de psychologie contemporaine,* I, p. 298.

him as though he were a performing monkey; and Mme de Rênal, whose maternal instincts are awakened by his youth and good looks, allows her feelings to turn into something very different.

Julien's success with Mme de Rênal is a form of apprenticeship in which for the first time he puts his theories into practice, and the account of his feelings is instructive:

> Cette main se retira bien vite; mais Julien pensa qu'il était de son *devoir* d'obtenir que l'on ne retirât pas cette main quand il la touchait. L'idée d'un devoir à accomplir, et d'un ridicule on plutôt d'un sentiment d'infériorité à encourir si l'on n'y parvenait pas, éloigna sur-le-champ tout plaisir de son cœur.

> [The hand was hurriedly withdrawn; but Julien decided that it was his duty to secure that the hand should not be withdrawn when he touched it. The idea of a duty to be performed, and of making himself ridiculous, or rather being left with a sense of inferiority if he did not succeed in performing it, at once took all the pleasure from his heart.]

In the French analysis of emotion, said Rivière, "la morale même devient un élément psychologique." [6] Stendhal's use of the word *devoir* is an excellent example. It is the focal word of the passage and he underlines it to make sure that its significance shall not escape us. It means something very different from Corneille's *devoir*. It is not a disinterested "duty"; the imperative comes from Julien's subjective need to bolster up his own inner morale or, as Stendhal, very much in advance of his time, suggests, to rid himself of a *sentiment d'infériorité*.

This is how Stendhal describes his feelings after he has made a conquest of Mme de Rênal:

> Le lendemain on le réveilla à cinq heures; et, ce qui eût été cruel pour Mme de Rênal si elle l'eût su, à peine lui donna-t-il une pensée. Il avait fait *son devoir, et un devoir héroïque*. Rempli de bonheur par ce sentiment, il s'enferma à clef dans sa chambre, et se livra avec un plaisir nouveau à la lecture des exploits de son héros.

> [Next morning he was called at five o'clock, and (what would have been a cruel blow to Madame de Rênal had she known of it) he barely gave her a thought. He had done *his duty, and a heroic duty*. Filled with joy by this sentiment, he turned the key in the door of his bedroom and gave himself up with an entirely new pleasure to reading about the exploits of his hero.]

The words in italic were underscored by Stendhal. Julien's feelings are no longer purely subjective and selfish. His experience has modified his whole outlook and the feelings which accompany his success are

[6] *Le Français* (Paris, 1928), p. 27.

something entirely new for him. The *sentiment d'infériorité* has, at any rate for the time being, been exorcized and has been replaced by satisfaction over accomplishing "son devoir, et un devoir héroïque." There is an immense relief behind the words, a sense of release from something which was imprisoning him and preventing the development of his personality. Instead of being eaten up by a subjective feeling of inferiority, he has broken the vicious circle and identifies himself with the *public* figure of Napoleon.

II

"In contrast to the naturalness of the Rênal estate at Vergy," writes Mr. Harry Levin of the love-affair with Mathilde de La Mole, "her love has ripened in a library, nourished on the chronicles of Brantôme and Aubigné and the novels of Rousseau and Prévost." [7]

It is a suggestive remark, but I find it difficult to accept Mr. Levin's conclusions. The contrast between the "naturalness" of Vergy and the atmosphere of the "library" in Paris is certainly intentional and the meaning of the whole novel depends on a correct interpretation of it. Stendhal chose the Franche-Comté because it was on the outskirts of France and geographically remote from the sophisticated capital to which Julien will eventually graduate. It is the start of his career, the place at which the forward bastions of civilization are breached to admit the intruder.

Julien's career is a journey to the interior. When he leaves Verrières, we have the impression that he is entering a long, dark tunnel and that the "fresh, deep valleys" which surround the "little town" are the daylight receding behind him as he penetrates further and further into it. We are aware of a feeling of claustrophobia as the seminary doors close on him. Henceforth, the drama takes place not in the open air, but in the oppressive, airless seminary, in the library of M. de La Mole and at the secret session amid the candles and the sealing wax, the papers and the serious anonymous faces of the conspirators.

The physical journey is at the same time *a journey to the interior of the mind*. It is accompanied by a deepening of experience, a growing complexity of feeling. The outer world loses its importance; the "action" shifts to the world within. The change is well illustrated by an encounter between Julien and Mathilde when she comes into the library and asks him to fetch a book for her:

Julien avait approché l'échelle; il avait cherché le volume, il le lui avait remis, sans encore pouvoir songer à elle. En remportant l'échelle, dans sa

[7] *Toward Stendhal* (Murray, Utah, 1945), p. 48.

précipitation, il donna un coup de coude dans une glace de la bibliothèque; les éclats, en tombant sur le parquet, le réveillèrent enfin.

[He brought the ladder; he found the volume, he handed it to her, still without being able to think of her. As he carried back the ladder, in his preoccupation, his elbow struck one of the glass panes protecting the shelves; the sound of the splinters falling on the floor at length aroused him.]

The characters live in a dream world, entirely preoccupied with what is going on inside their own minds; and the movement of this passage reflects the mechanical movements of a sleep-walker. From time to time a violent incident in the external world—the breaking of the pane in the bookcase or the smashing of the Japanese vase—brings them back to earth with a shock. It is the striking of a clock which recalls the dreamer from the timeless world to the world of time and chance.[8]

"Il a de l'imprévu," remarks the Marquis in speaking to his daughter of Julien. It is his way of recognizing Julien's "otherness," and it must be distinguished from the reactions of the bourgeois of Verrières who gape open-mouthed while he recites chapter after chapter of the New Testament from memory. The Marquis de La Mole is not interested in his looks or his parlour tricks, but in his intellectual attainments and his character. Julien's qualities are also recognized by Mathilde, but her reactions are quite different from her father's. For here like calls to like. Mathilde, too, is an *étrangère* in nineteenth-century society, and it is because she has failed to meet anyone like herself that, until Julien arrives, she spends her time in a private world of her own reading about the heroic exploits of her sixteenth-century ancestors. She is desperately bored and desperately out of place in a society of which she can say with some truth: "Je ne vois que la condamnation à mort qui distingue un homme . . . c'est la seule chose qui ne s'achète pas."

Her criticism is reinforced by an observation of the Comte Altamira's:

Il n'y a plus de passions véritables au XIXe siècle: c'est pour cela que l'on s'ennuie tant en France. On fait les plus grandes cruautés, mais sans cruauté.

[There are no longer any genuine passions in the nineteenth century; that is why people are so bored in France. We commit the greatest cruelties, but without cruelty.]

[8] One of the most striking examples of this preoccupation is the occasion when Julien seizes an old sword from the wall of the library and is on the point of attacking Mathilde who is delighted to think that she was almost killed by her lover. The sword is a talisman which transports them both to a different age, to the age to which spiritually they belong.

It used to be fashionable at one time to debate the respective merits of *Le Rouge et le noir* and *La Chartreuse de Parme*. The *Chartreuse de Parme* may be the greater novel, but I do not think that Stendhal ever surpassed the account of the love affair between Julien and Mathilde:

> Rien [we are told] ne fut plaisant comme le dialogue de ces deux amants; sans s'en douter ils étaient animés l'un contre l'autre des sentiments de la haine la plus vive.

> [Nothing could be more entertaining than the dialogue between these young lovers; unconsciously they were animated by a mutual sentiment of the keenest hatred.]

Their attraction-and-repulsion sounds at first like an episode in the sex war; but Stendhal's interpretation of this fundamental antipathy is much more profound than Laclos' in the *Liaisons dangereuses*. In the *Liaisons* it is inspired by a desire to dominate the opposite sex; in *Le Rouge et le noir* it is part of a larger war against society seen collectively. In spite of the violent conflict between them and the savage delight that they experience in humiliating one another's pride—always the vulnerable spot—Julien and Mathilde are allies against society and are united by a bond which goes far deeper than their antipathy. The words *singulier—singularité* must occur a hundred times in the second part of the novel, and they describe the link which unites Julien and Mathilde and separates them from everyone else.[9]

The forty-sixth chapter, which describes the seduction of Julien by Mathilde, illustrates some of Stendhal's most remarkable qualities—his insight into conflicting and contradictory feelings, his blend of tenderness and irony and also his use of the Romantics' stock-in-trade to express an anti-romantic attitude. Julien has just climbed into Mathilde's bedroom:

> "Vous voilà, monsieur," lui dit Mathilde avec beaucoup d'émotion; "je suis vos mouvements depuis une heure."
> Julien était fort embarrassé, il ne savait comment se conduire, il n'avait pas d'amour du tout. Dans son embarras, il pensa qu'il fallait oser, il essaya d'embrasser Mathilde.

[9] It is a quality which is recognized by members of Mathilde's entourage even when they do not like it: "Mathilde a de la singularité, pensa-t-il [M. de Croisenois]; c'est un inconvénient, mais elle donne une si belle position sociale à son mari . . . cette singularité de Mathilde peut passer pour du génie. Avec une haute naissance et beaucoup de fortune, le génie n'est point un ridicule, et alors quelle distinction!"
It is an example of the way in which Stendhal's criticism is dissolved into the novel. Her "genius" is a threat to a precarious social order, but it can be neutralized, or so her admirer hopes, by a great position and great wealth.

"Fi donc!" lui dit-elle en le repoussant.

["Here you are, sir," Mathilde said to him with deep emotion; "I have been following your movements for the last hour."
Julien was greatly embarrassed, he did not know how to behave, he did not feel the least vestige of love. In his embarrassment, he decided that he must show courage, he attempted to embrace Mathilde.
"Fie, sir!" she said, and thrust him from her.]

They are both extremely embarrassed, but for different reasons. Their mutual attraction is deeper than they realize, but Julien has engaged in the escapade largely out of bravado and because he is flattered by the invitation to visit the daughter of the house in the small hours. A Romantic hero would certainly have worked himself up into a fine frenzy by a torrent of words. Julien does his best, but Stendhal shows us with his customary lucidity that in reality he feels nothing and has no idea what to do.

Mathilde, too, is anxious for a "big scene," but she is paralyzed by the conflict between what is really admirable in her—her boldness and *singularité*—and the conventional feelings against which she rebels:

> Elle souffrait étrangement; tous les sentiments de retenue et de timidité, si naturels à une fille bien née, avaient repris leur empire, et la mettaient au supplice. . . .
> Si elle l'eût pu. elle eût anéanti elle et Julien. Quand par instants la force de sa volonté faisait taire les remords, des sentiments de timidité et de pudeur souffrante la rendaient fort malheureuse. Elle n'avait nullement prévu l'état affreux où elle se trouvait.

> [She was strangely ill at ease; all the feelings of reserve and timidity, so natural to a young girl of good family, had resumed their sway and were keeping her on tenterhooks. . . .
> Had it been possible, she would have destroyed herself and Julien. Whenever, for an instant, the strengtth of her will made her remorse silent; feelings of shyness and outraged modesty made her extremely wretched. She had never for a moment anticipated the dreadful plight in which she now found herself.]

Stendhal is remorseless in his exposure of their embarrassment:

> Mathilde faisait effort pour le tutoyer, elle était évidemment plus attentive à cette étrange façon de parler qu'au fond des choses qu'elle disait. . . .
> "Il faut cependant que je lui parle," dit-elle à la fin, "cela est dans les convenances, on parle à son amant."

> [Mathilde made an effort to use the more intimate form; she was evidently more attentive to this unusual way of speaking than to what she was saying. . . .

"I must speak to him, though," she said to herself, finally, "that is laid down in the rules, one speaks to one's lover."]

Then comes the final criticism of the Romantic attitude:

Après de longues incertitudes, qui eussent pu paraître à un observateur superficiel l'effet de la haine la plus décidée . . . Mathilde finit par être pour lui une maîtresse aimable.

A la vérité, ces transports étaient un peu voulus. L'amour passionné était encore plutôt un modèle qu'on imitait qu'une réalité.

[After prolonged uncertainties, which might have appeared to a superficial observer to be due to the most decided hatred . . . Mathilde finally became his mistress.

To tell the truth their ardours were a little artificial. Passionate love was still more of a model to be imitated than a reality.]

And the final exposure:

Mlle de La Mole croyait remplir un devoir envers elle-même et envers son amant. "Le pauvre garçon," se disait-elle, "a été d'une bravoure achevée, il doit être heureux, ou bien c'est moi qui manque de caractère. Mais elle eût voulu racheter au prix d'une éternité de malheur la nécessité cruelle où elle se trouvait.

[Mademoiselle de La Mole believed that she was performing a duty towards herself and towards her lover. "The poor boy," she told herself, "has been the last word in daring, he deserves to be happy, or else I am wanting in character." But she would gladly have redeemed at the cost of an eternity of suffering the cruel necessity to which she found herself committed.]

The whole incident is related in a tone of ironic comedy, but we continually have the impression that Stendhal's words are *doing* more than they *say*. The hot, prickly embarrassment of the lovers is contagious and communicates itself to us; but we are aware of the underlying seriousness and we see far more deeply into the real impulses of the characters than they do themselves.

Stendhal's prose is, indeed, seen at its most impressive in the encounters between Julien and Mathilde. The conflict goes on at two levels. It begins with their unspoken thoughts. Suddenly there is a violent eruption and they denounce one another with the ferocity of Racine's characters. One of them is temporarily "knocked out," and with equal suddenness the tumult subsides, as they revert to a sort of silent, hostile dialogue:

Il lui semblait qu'une chose apporterait à sa douleur un soulagement infini: ce serait de parler à Mathilde. Mais cependant qu'oserait-il lui dire?

C'est à quoi un matin, à sept heures, il rêvait profondément, lorsque tout à coup il la vit entrer dans la bibliothèque.

"Je sais, monsieur, que vous désirez me parler."

"Grand Dieu! qui vous l'a dit?"

"Je sais, que vous importe?"

"Si vous manquez d'honneur, vous pouvez me perdre ou du moins le tenter; mais ce danger, que je ne crois pas réel, ne m'empêchera certainement pas d'être sincère. Je ne vous aime plus, monsieur, mon imagination folle m'a trompée."

A ce coup terrible, éperdu d'amour et de malheur, Julien essaya de se justifier. Rien de plus absurde. Se justifie-t-on de déplaire? Mais la raison n'avait plus aucun empire sur ses actions. Un instinct aveugle le poussait à retarder la décision de son sort. Il lui semblait que tant qu'il parlait, tout n'était pas fini. Mathilde n'écoutait pas ses paroles, leur son l'irritait, elle ne concevait pas qu'il eût l'audace de l'interrompre.

[It seemed to him that one thing would supply boundless comfort to his grief: namely to speak to Mathilde. And yet what could he venture to say to her?

This was the question upon which one morning at seven o'clock he was pondering deeply, when suddenly he saw her enter the library.

"I know, sir, that you desire to speak to me."

"Great God! Who told you that?"

"I know it, what more do you want? If you are lacking in honour, you may ruin me, or at least attempt to do so; but this danger, which I do not regard as real, will certainly not prevent me from being sincere. I no longer love you, sir; my wild imagination misled me."

On receiving this terrible blow, desperate with love and misery, Julien tried to excuse himself. Nothing could be more absurd. Does one excuse oneself for failing to please? But reason no longer held sway over his actions. A blind instinct urged him to postpone the decision of his fate. It seemed to him that so long as he was still speaking, nothing was definitely settled. Mathilde did not listen to his words, the sound of them irritated her, she could not conceive how he had the audacity to interrupt her.]

Stendhal's prose bears a marked resemblance to eighteenth-century prose, but this resemblance is deceptive. It was certainly founded on the classic syntax, but though the structure of his sentences is often similar, the movement of his paragraphs is sometimes quite different. The difference has been well expressed by M. Gide. "With Stendhal," he writes, "one sentence never calls the next into being, nor is it born of the one that went before. Each of them stands perpendicularly to the fact or idea." [10] His prose does not move steadily forward from one fixed point to another. It has greater density and greater range. Each sentence or each clause in a sentence corresponds to what the French call a *fait psychique*,

---

[10] *Journal des Faux-Monnayeurs* (Paris, 1927), pp. 28-29.

and their relation to one another forms the pattern of his style. A passage like this is not the direct expression of emotion; it is rather a geometrical construction, a configuration of feelings, which enables us to perceive with startling clarity what is happening inside the characters' minds and to follow the clash of contradictory impulses. For this reason, instead of being a logical progression, Stendhal's prose is continually twisting and turning, changing direction and producing startling juxtapositions between the "perpendicular" sentences. The outcome is that it seems to be moving in several directions at once and to touch us simultaneously in different places. The first two sentences are a series of sorties and retreats which lead up to the final assault on the position. At each sortie, Mathilde strikes Julien in a different place—his honour, his pride, his belief in himself, his emotional stability—then withdraws in order to deliver a still heavier blow. The total effect is of an attack which is at once very widespread and very concentrated. Then, suddenly, Mathilde seems to gather the whole of her energy for the final smashing blow: "I no longer love you, sir; my wild imagination misled me."

The first paragraph reveals Mathilde's complete command of the situation, the second the effect of her onslaught on Julien. When Stendhal writes, "A ce coup terrible," we hear the sickening thud as the blow lands. In the French classic writers, *éperdu* always stands for complete mental and emotional disorientation, and in this passage it registers the devastating effect of Mathilde's attack. Julien is dazed, but makes a feeble and belated attempt to justify himself. The two short sentences—"Rien de plus absurde. Se justifie-t-on de déplaire?"—are the mocking reverberation of her words in his stunned mind. Instead of recovering, his pain increases. The attempt to justify himself is the last glimmer of sense before he becomes incoherent. The words, "La raison n'avait plus aucun empire sur ses actions," are a sign of disintegration and collapse; and the *plus* makes us feel the mechanism of personality falling apart. When reason fails, he is thrown back on "un instinct *aveugle*." He struggles blindly on, persuaded that if only he can keep going, if only he can keep on talking, something must happen to save him.

These and similar passages have won for Stendhal the reputation of being one of the greatest psychologists among modern novelists. Beneath its dry sparkle, his prose has tentacular roots which thrust downwards into the hidden places of the mind. He possessed the *vue directe* into the complexity of the human heart, the power of seizing feelings at the moment of their formation and translating them with an admirable lucidity:

Ce tutoiement, dépouillé du ton de la tendresse, ne faisait aucun plaisir à Julien, il s'étonnait de l'absence du bonheur; enfin, pour le sentir, il eut recours à sa raison. Il se voyait estimé par cette jeune fille si fière, et qui n'accordait jamais de louanges sans restriction; avec ce raisonnement il parvint à un bonheur d'amour-propre.

[This use of the singular form, stripped of the tone of affection, ceased, after a moment, to afford Julien any pleasure, he was astonished at the absence of happiness; finally, in order to feel it, he had recourse to his reason. He saw himself highly esteemed by this girl who was so proud, and never bestowed unrestricted praise; by this line of reasoning he arrived at a gratification of his self-esteem.]

Once again the prose performs the actions that it describes. The novelist suggests a feeling to us, then proceeds to peel away the outer layers in order to show us that it is not at all what it appears to be. The *tutoiement* should be a sign of *tendresse,* but is not. It gives Julien no "pleasure," and he is "astonished" at the absence of a *bonheur* which is normally a product of *tendresse* and *plaisir. Enfin* marks the characteristic change of direction. Julien sets to work to produce a substitute feeling of "happiness" by the use of "reason." He tells himself that if there is no "tenderness" in Mathilde's tone, at least this person who is proud and not given to overpraising anyone "esteems" him. This argument, this manipulation of ideas, produces a fresh combination of feelings. We have watched the whole process from the beginning, have seen the feelings transformed. With the *bonheur d'amour-propre* everything suddenly falls neatly into place.

In other places Stendhal writes:

Deux mois de combats et de sensations nouvelles renouvelèrent pour ainsi dire tout son être moral.

Ce cruel soupçon changea toute la position morale de Julien. Cette idée trouva dans son cœur un commencement d'amour qu'elle n'eut pas de peine à détruire.

Ces souvenirs de bonheur passé s'emparaient de Julien et détruisaient bientôt tout l'ouvrage de la raison.

Son mot si franc, mais si stupide, vint tout changer en un instant: Mathilde, sûre d'être aimée, le méprisa parfaitement.

[Two months of struggle and of novel sensations had so to speak altered her whole moral nature.

This cruel suspicion completely changed Julien's moral attitude. The idea encountered in his heart a germ of love which it had no difficulty in destroying.

These memories of past happiness took possession of Julien, and rapidly undid all the work of reason.

This speech, so frank but so stupid, altered the whole situation in an instant: Mathilde, certain of being loved, despised him completely.]

In all these examples, the operative words are the verbs *changer,*
renouveler, détruire. The verb—usually a transitive verb—is the pivot
of Stendhal's most characteristic sentences because he is much more
interested in mental *activity* than in mental *states.* These three verbs
indicate the field of experience. His characters' feelings are constantly
"changing," are engaged in a continual process of "renewal" and
"destruction." They are not superficial changes of mood; they go to the
roots of the "moral being." A sudden shock "destroys" their moral
stability; they set to work slowly and painfully to rebuild it. Another
shock undoes the work of "reason," and the whole process starts all over
again. A final sentence completes the picture:

> Mathilde était alors dans l'état où Julien se trouvait quelques jours
> auparavant.

> [Mathilde was at that time in the state in which Julien had been a few
> days previously.]

Although they are bound to one another in the innermost depths of
being, Julien and Mathilde are practically never both in the same mood
on the same day, and this produces the clash. It is a psychological obstacle
race in which they take it in turns to be pursuer and pursued, executioner
and victim.

One of the most interesting things about Stendhal's characters is the
impression that they give that the whole of their lives, the whole of their
being, is engaged in every action:

> Le courage était la première qualité de son caractère [we are told of
> Mathilde]. Rien ne pouvait lui donner quelque agitation et la guérir d'un
> fond d'ennui sans cesse renaissant que l'idée *qu'elle jouait à croix ou à pile*
> *son existence entière.*[11]

> [Courage was the fundamental quality in her character. Nothing was
> capable of giving her any excitement and of curing her of an ever present
> tendency to boredom but the idea *that she was playing heads or tails with*
> *her whole existence.*]

It is this that makes the encounters between Julien and Mathilde so
dramatic and such a strain on their personalities. We may sometimes
wonder why they could not go on indefinitely, but Stendhal gives the
answer in a sentence:

> Elle [Mathilde] tomba tout à fait évanouie.
> "La voilà donc, cette orgueilleuse à mes pieds," se dit Julien.

---

[11] Italics mine.

[She fell to the ground in a dead faint.
"There she is then, the proud thing, at my feet," Julien said to himself.]

The life of Stendhal's characters is a process of *extension* which finally reaches the point at which not merely something, but *everything* gives way. It is because they are "outsiders" that they can find no proper outlet for their great gifts. Their incredible calculations and their immensely sharpened sensibility, which result from this position, subject their personalities to an intolerable strain until they are driven to abandon the world of action and to withdraw completely into the world of contemplation.

Julien's imprisonment and death have been variously interpreted. One writer, comparing him with Meursault, the hero of M. Camus's *L'Etranger,* suggests that he is a "social" rather than a "metaphysical martyr." [12] An American critic speaks of "the alienated libido and the expiating martyr 'in love with death.' " [13] For reasons that I have already given, I think that it is easy to misinterpret the "social" factor; and though the desire for "martyrdom" and "the death-wish" are present, I do not believe that they are decisive. When Julien reaches the prison at Besançon his sensibility is exhausted. The extended personality has reached the point at which it can no longer carry on, when there is nothing left for it in life. This explains Julien's attitude to Mathilde and Mme de Rênal. He cannot face the prospect of life together with Mathilde and he turns to the more restful figure of Mme de Rênal. She is of course the mother-image and the prison itself a symbol of the womb to which he wishes to return. Once in prison, he can give himself up to *rêverie.* The last thing he wants is to be acquitted or to escape or even to return to the world of action after a term of imprisonment. Mathilde's attempts to save him are simply exasperating and he takes good care that they fail.

I think we must add that the prison episode is also a profound study of the psychology of heroism. Julien appears to stick to his ideals, to go heroically to his death. In fact, he commits suicide; but he does not do so for the reasons suggested by his critics. The "hero" lives at a far greater pitch of intensity than the general run of men, and what appears to be an heroic death in battle is probably in many instances a case of suicide dictated by an unconscious realization that he is "finished."

The account of the execution is a masterly example of Stendhal's power of understatement:

Tout se passa simplement, convenablement, et de sa part sans aucune affectation.

[12] H. A. Mason, "M. Camus and the Tragic Hero" in *Scrutiny,* Vol. XIV, No. 2, p. 83.
[13] Matthew Josephson, *Stendhal or The Pursuit of Happiness* (New York, 1946), p. 346.

[Everything passed simply, decorously, and without affection on his part.]

The last scene, in which Mathilde follows the funeral cortège with Julien's severed head on her knees, has perplexed Stendhal's critics. It seems to me to be a deliberately macabre piece of comedy. His admiration for the sixteenth century was deep-rooted, and he certainly approved this final display of Mathilde's *singularité,* which could only have appeared odd to an effete age. It was Stendhal's parting shot at the men of 1830.

In the Hôtel de La Mole

by *Erich Auerbach*

Julien Sorel, the hero of Stendhal's novel *Le Rouge et le noir* (1830), an ambitious and passionate young man, son of an uneducated petty bourgeois from the Franche-Comté, is conducted by a series of circumstances from the seminary at Besançon, where he has been studying theology, to Paris and the position of secretary to a gentleman of rank, the Marquis de La Mole, whose confidence he gains. Mathilde, the Marquis's daughter, is a girl of nineteen, witty, spoiled, imaginative, and so arrogant that her own position and circle begin to bore her. The dawning of her passion for her father's *domestique* is one of Stendhal's masterpieces and has been greatly admired. One of the preparatory scenes, in which her interest in Julien begins to awaken, is the following, from volume 2, chapter 4:

> Un matin que l'abbé travaillait avec Julien, dans la bibliothèque du marquis, à l'éternel procès de Frilair:
>
> —Monsieur, dit Julien tout à coup, dîner tous les jours avec madame la marquise, est-ce un de mes devoirs, ou est-ce une bonté que l'on a pour moi?
>
> —C'est un honneur insigne! reprit l'abbé, scandalisé. Jamais M. N. . . l'académicien, qui, depuis quinze ans, fait une cour assidue, n'a pu l'obtenir pour son neveu M. Tanbeau.
>
> —C'est pour moi, monsieur, la partie la plus pénible de mon emploi. Je m'ennuyais moins au séminaire. Je vois bâiller quelquefois jusqu'à mademoiselle de La Mole, qui pourtant doit être accoutumée à l'amabilité des amis de la maison. J'ai peur de m'endormir. De grâce, obtenez-moi la permission d'aller dîner à quarante sous dans quelque auberge obscure.
>
> L'abbé, véritable parvenu, était fort sensible à l'honneur de dîner avec un grand seigneur. Pendant qu'il s'efforçait de faire comprendre ce sentiment par Julien, un léger bruit leur fit tourner la tête. Julien vit made-

moiselle de La Mole qui écoutait. Il rougit. Elle était venue chercher un livre et avait tout entendu; elle prit quelque considération pour Julien. Celui-là n'est pas né à genoux, pensa-t-elle, comme ce vieil abbé. Dieu! qu'il est laid.

A dîner, Julien n'osait pas regarder mademoiselle de La Mole, mais elle eut la bonté de lui adresser la parole. Ce jour-là on attendait beaucoup de monde, elle l'engagea à rester. . . .

[One morning while the Abbé was with Julien in the Marquis's library, working on the interminable Frilair suit:

"Monsieur," said Julien suddenly, "is dining with Madame la Marquise every day one of my duties, or is it a favor to me?"

"It is an extraordinary honor!" the Abbé corrected him, scandalized. "Monsieur N., the academician, who has been paying court here assiduously for fifteen years, was never able to manage it for his nephew, Monsieur Tanbeau."

"For me, Monsieur, it is the most painful part of my position. Nothing at the seminary bored me so much. I even see Mademoiselle de La Mole yawning sometimes, yet she must be well inured to the amiabilities of the guests of this house. I am in dread of falling asleep. Do me the favor of getting me permission to eat a forty-sou dinner at some inn."

The Abbé, a true parvenu, was extremely conscious of the honor of dining with a noble lord. While he was trying to inculcate this sentiment into Julien, a slight sound made them turn. Julien saw Mademoiselle da La Mole listening. He blushed. She had come for a book and had heard everything; she began to feel a certain esteem for Julien. He was not born on his knees, like that old Abbé, she thought. God, how ugly he is!

At dinner Julien did not dare to look at Mademoiselle de La Mole, but she condescended to speak to him. A number of guests were expected that day, she asked him to stay. . . .]

The scene, as I said, is designed to prepare for a passionate and extremely tragic love intrigue. Its function and its psychological value we shall not here discuss; they lie outside of our subject. What interests us in the scene is this: it would be almost incomprehensible without a most accurate and detailed knowledge of the political situation, the social stratification, and the economic circumstances of a perfectly definite historical moment, namely, that in which France found itself just before the July Revolution; accordingly, the novel bears the subtitle, *Chronique de 1830.* Even the boredom which reigns in the dining room and salon of this noble house is no ordinary boredom. It does not arise from the fortuitous personal dullness of the people who are brought together there; among them there are highly educated, witty, and sometimes important people, and the master of the house is intelligent and amiable. Rather, we are confronted, in their boredom, by a phenomenon politically and ideologically characteristic of the Restoration period. In the seventeenth century, and even more in the eighteenth, the corresponding salons were anything but boring. But the inadequately implemented attempt which the Bourbon regime made to restore conditions long since made obsolete by events, creates, among its adherents in the official and ruling classes, an atmosphere of pure convention, of limitation, of constraint and lack of freedom, against which the intelligence and good will of the persons involved are powerless. In these salons the things which interest everyone—the political and religious problems of the present, and consequently most of the subjects of its literature or of that of the very recent past— could not be discussed, or at best could be discussed only in official phrases so mendacious that a man of taste and tact would rather avoid them. How different from the intellectual daring of the famous eighteenth-century salons, which, to be sure, did not dream of the dangers to their own existence which they were unleashing! Now the dangers are known, and life is governed by the fear that the catastrophe of 1793 might be repeated. As these people are conscious that they no longer themselves believe in the thing they represent, and that they are bound to be defeated in any public argument, they choose to talk of nothing but the weather, music, and court gossip. In addition, they are obliged to accept as allies snobbish and corrupt people from among the newly-rich bourgeoisie, who, with the unashamed baseness of their ambition and with their fear for their ill-gotten wealth, completely vitiate the atmosphere of society. So much for the pervading boredom.

But Julien's reaction, too, and the very fact that he and the former director of his seminary, the Abbé Pirard, are present at all in the house of the Marquis de La Mole, are only to be understood in terms of the actual historical moment. Julien's passionate and imaginative nature has from his earliest youth been filled with enthusiasm for the great ideas of the Revolution and of Rousseau, for the great events of the Napoleonic period; from his earliest youth he has felt nothing but loathing and scorn for the piddling hypocrisy and the petty lying corruption of the classes in power since Napoleon's fall. He is too imaginative, too ambitious, and too fond of power, to be satisfied with a mediocre life within the bourgeoisie, such as his friend Fouquet proposes to him. Having observed that a man of petty-bourgeois origin can attain to a situation of command only through the all-powerful Church, he has consciously and deliberately become a hypocrite; and his great talents would assure him a brilliant intellectual career, were not his real personal and political feelings, the direct passionateness of his nature, prone to burst forth at decisive moments. One such moment of self-betrayal we have in the passage before us, when Julien confides his feelings in the Marquise's salon to the Abbé Pirard, his former teacher and protector; for the intellectual freedom to which it testifies is unthinkable without an admixture of intellectual arrogance and a sense of inner superiority hardly becoming in a young ecclesiastic and protégé of the house. (In this particular instance his frankness does him no harm; the Abbé Pirard is his friend, and upon Mathilde, who happens to overhear him, his words make an entirely different impression from that which he must expect and fear.) The Abbé is here described as a true parvenu, who knows how highly the honor of sitting at a great man's table should be esteemed and hence disapproves of Julien's remarks; as another motive for the Abbé's disapproval Stendhal could have cited the fact that uncritical submission to the evil of this world, in full consciousness that it is evil, is a typical attitude for strict Jansenists; and the Abbé Pirard is a Jansenist. We know from the previous part of the novel that as director of the seminary at Besançon he had had to endure much persecution and much chicanery on account of his Jansenism and his strict piety which no intrigues could touch; for the clergy of the province were under the influence of the Jesuits. When the Marquis de La Mole's most powerful opponent, the Abbé de Frilair, a vicar-general to the bishop, had brought a suit against him, the Marquis had made the Abbé Pirard his confidant and had thus learned to value his intelligence and uprightness; so that finally, to free him from his untenable position at Besançon, the Marquis had procured him a benefice in Paris and somewhat later had taken the Abbé's favorite pupil, Julien Sorel, into his household as private secretary.

The characters, attitudes, and relationships of the dramatis personae, then, are very closely connected with contemporary historical circumstances; contemporary political and social conditions are woven into the action in a manner more detailed and more real than had been exhibited in any earlier novel, and indeed in any works of literary art except those expressly purporting to be politico-satirical tracts. So logically and systematically to situate the tragically conceived life of a man of low social position (as here that of Julien Sorel) within the most concrete kind of contemporary history and to develop it therefrom—this is an entirely new and highly significant phenomenon. The other circles in which Julien Sorel moves—his father's family, the house of the mayor of Verrières, M. de Rênal, the seminary at Besançon—are sociologically defined in conformity with the historical moment with the same penetration as is the La Mole household; and not one of the minor characters—the old priest Chélan, for example, or the director of the *dépôt de mendicité,* Valenod—would be conceivable outside the particular historical situation of the Restoration period, in the manner in which they are set before us. The same laying of a contemporary foundation for events is to be found in Stendhal's other novels—still incomplete and too narrowly circumscribed in *Armance,* but fully developed in the later works: in the *Chartreuse de Parme* (which, however, since its setting is a place not yet greatly affected by modern development, sometimes gives the effect of being a historical novel), as also in *Lucien Leuwen,* a novel of the Louis Philippe period, which Stendhal left unfinished. In the latter, indeed, in the form in which it has come down to us, the element of current history and politics is too heavily emphasized: it is not always wholly integrated into the course of the action and is set forth in far too great detail in proportion to the principal theme; but perhaps in a final revision Stendhal would have achieved an organic articulation of the whole. Finally, his autobiographical works, despite the capricious and erratic "egotism" of their style and manner, are likewise far more closely, essentially, and concretely connected with the politics, sociology, and economics of the period than are, for example, the corresponding works of Rousseau or Goethe; one feels that the great events of contemporary history affected Stendhal much more directly than they did the other two; Rousseau did not live to see them, and Goethe had managed to keep aloof from them.

To have stated this is also to have stated what circumstance it was which, at that particular moment and in a man of that particular period, gave rise to modern tragic realism based on the contemporary; it was the first of the great movements of modern times in which large masses of men consciously took part—the French Revolution with all the consequent convulsions which spread from it over Europe. From the Reformation movement, which was no less powerful and which aroused the masses no less, it is distinguished by the much faster tempo of its spread, its mass effects, and the changes which it produced in practical daily life within a comparatively extensive territory; for the progress then achieved in transportation and communication, together with the spread of elementary education resulting from the trends of the Revolution itself, made it possible to mobilize the people far more rapidly and in a far more unified direction; everyone was reached by the same ideas and events far more quickly, more consciously, and more uniformly. For Europe there began that process of temporal concentration, both of historical events themselves and of everyone's knowledge of them, which has since made tremendous progress and which not only permits us to prophesy a unification of human life throughout the world but has in a certain sense already achieved it. Such a development abrogates or renders powerless the entire social structure of orders and categories previously held valid; the tempo of the changes demands a perpetual and extremely difficult effort toward inner adaptation and produces intense concomitant crises. He who would account to himself for his real life and his place in human society is obliged to do so upon a far wider practical foundation and in a far larger context than before, and to be continually conscious that the social base upon which he lives is not constant for a moment but is perpetually changing through convulsions of the most various kinds.

We may ask ourselves how it came about that modern consciousness of reality began to find literary form for the first time precisely in Henri

Beyle of Grenoble. Beyle-Stendhal was a man of keen intelligence, quick and alive, mentally independent and courageous, but not quite a great figure. His ideas are often forceful and inspired, but they are erratic, arbitrarily advanced, and, despite all their show of boldness, lacking in inward certainty and continuity. There is something unsettled about his whole nature: his fluctuation between realistic candor in general and silly mystification in particulars, between cold self-control, rapturous abandonment to sensual pleasures, and insecure and sometimes sentimental vaingloriousness, is not always easy to put up with; his literary style is very impressive and unmistakably original, but it is short-winded, not uniformly successful, and only seldom wholly takes possession of and fixes the subject. But, such as he was, he offered himself to the moment; circumstances seized him, tossed him about, and laid upon him a unique and unexpected destiny; they formed him so that he was compelled to come to terms with reality in a way which no one had done before him.

When the Revolution broke out Stendhal was a boy of six; when he left his native city of Grenoble and his reactionary, solidly bourgeois family, who though glumly sulking at the new situation were still very wealthy, and went to Paris, he was sixteen. He arrived there immediately after Napoleon's *coup d'état;* one of his relatives, Pierre Daru, was an influential adherent of the First Consul; after some hesitations and interruptions, Stendhal made a brilliant career in the Napoleonic administration. He saw Europe on Napoleon's expeditions; he grew to be a man, and indeed an extremely elegant man of the world; he also became, it appears, a useful administrative official and a reliable, cold-blooded organizer who did not lose his calm even in danger. When Napoleon's fall threw Stendhal out of the saddle, he was in his thirty-second year. The first, active, successful, and brilliant part of his career was over. Thenceforth he has no profession and no place claims him. He can go where he pleases, so long as he has money enough and so long as the suspicious officials of the post-Napoleonic period have no objection to his sojourns. But his financial circumstances gradually become worse; in 1821 he is exiled from Milan, where he had first settled down, by Metternich's police; he goes to Paris, and there he lives for another nine years, without a profession, alone, and with very slender means. After the July Revolution his friends get him a post in the diplomatic service; since the Austrians refuse him an exequatur for Trieste, he has to go as consul to the little port of Civitavecchia; it is a dreary place to live, and there are those who try to get him into trouble if he prolongs his visits to Rome unduly; to be sure, he is allowed to spend a few years in Paris on leave —so long, that is, as one of his protectors is Minister of Foreign Affairs. Finally he falls seriously ill in Civitavecchia and is given another leave in Paris; he dies there in 1842, smitten by apoplexy in the street, not yet sixty. This is the second half of his life; during this period, he acquires the reputation of being a witty, eccentric, politically and morally unreliable man; during this period, he begins to write. He writes first on music, on Italy and Italian art, on love; it is not until he is forty-three and is in Paris during the first flowering of the Romantic movement (to which he contributed in his way) that he publishes his first novel.

From this sketch of his life it should appear that he first reached the point of accounting for himself, and the point of realistic writing, when he was seeking a haven in his "storm-tossed boat," and discovered that, for his boat, there was no fit and safe haven; when, though in no sense weary or discouraged, yet already a man of forty, whose early and successful career lay far behind him, alone and comparatively poor, he became aware, with all the sting of that knowledge, that he belonged nowhere. For the first time, the social world around him became a problem; his feeling that he was different from other men, until now borne easily and proudly, doubtless now first became the predominant concern of his consciousness and finally the recurring theme of his literary activity. Stendhal's realistic writing grew out of his discomfort in the post-Napoleonic world and his consciousness that he did not belong to it and had no place in it. Discomfort in the given world and inability to become part of it is, to be sure, characteristic of Rousseauan romanticism and it is probable that Stendhal had something of that even in his youth; there is something of it in his congenital disposition, and the course of his youth can only have strengthened such tendencies, which, so to speak, harmonized with the tenor of life of his generation; on the other hand, he did not write his recollections of his youth, the *Vie de Henry Brulard,* until he was in his thirties, and we must allow for the possibility that, from the viewpoint of his later development, from the viewpoint of 1832, he overstressed such motifs of individualistic isolation. It is, in any case, certain that the motifs and expressions of his isolation and his problematic relation to society are wholly different from the corresponding phenomena in Rousseau and his early romantic disciples.

Stendhal, in contrast to Rousseau, had a bent for practical affairs and the requisite ability; he aspired to sensual enjoyment of life as given; he did not withdraw from practical reality from the outset, did not entirely condemn it from the outset—instead he attempted, and successfully at first, to master it. Material success and material enjoyments were desirable to him; he admires energy and the ability to master life, and even his cherished dreams (*le silence du bonheur*) are more sensual, more concrete, more dependent upon human society and human creations (Cimarosa, Mozart, Shakespeare, Italian art) than those of the *Promeneur Solitaire.* Not until success and pleasure began to slip away from him, not until practical circumstances threatened to cut the ground from under his feet, did the society of his time become a problem and a subject to him. Rousseau did not find himself at home in the social world he encountered, which did not appreciably change during his lifetime; he rose in it without thereby becoming happier or more reconciled to it, while it appeared to remain unchanged. Stendhal lived while one earthquake after another shook the foundations of society; one of the earthquakes jarred him out of the everyday course of life prescribed for men of his station, flung him, like many of his contemporaries, into previously inconceivable adventures, events, responsibilities, tests of himself, and experiences of freedom and power; another flung him back into a new everyday which he thought more boring, more stupid, and less attractive than the old; the most interesting thing about it was that it too gave no promise of enduring; new upheavals were in the air, and indeed broke out here and there even though not with the power of the first.

Because Stendhal's interest arose out of the experiences of his own life, it was held not by the structure of a possible society but by the changes in the society actually given. Temporal perspective is a factor of which he never loses sight, the concept of incessantly changing forms and manners of life dominates his thoughts—the more so as it holds a hope for him: In 1880 or 1930 I shall find readers who understand me! I will cite a few examples. When he speaks of La Bruyère's *esprit* (*Henry Brulard,* chapter 30), it is apparent to him that this type of formative endeavor of the intellect has lost in validity since 1789:

> L'esprit, si délicieux pour qui le sent, ne dure pas. Comme une pêche passe en quelques jours, l'esprit passe en deux cents ans, et bien plus vite, s'il y a révolution dans les rapports que les classes d'une société ont entre elles.

The *Souvenirs d'égotisme* contains an abundance of observations (for the most part truly prophetic) based on temporal perspective. He foresees (chapter 7, near the end) that "at the time when this chapter is read" it will have become a commonplace to make the ruling classes responsible for the crimes of thieves and murderers; he fears, at the beginning of chapter 9, that all his bold utterances, which he dares put forth only with fear and trembling, will become platitudes ten years after his death, if heaven grants him a decent allowance of life, say eighty or ninety years; in the next chapter he speaks of one of his friends who pays an unusually high price for the favors of an "honnête femme du peuple," and adds in explanation: "cinq cents francs en 1832, c'est comme mille en 1872"— that is, forty years after the time at which he is writing and thirty after his death.

It would be possible to quote many more passages of the same general import. But it is unnecessary, for the element of time-perspective is apparent everywhere in the presentation itself. In his realistic writings, Stendhal everywhere deals with the reality which presents itself to him:

"Je prends au hasard ce qui se trouve sur ma route," he says not far from the passage just quoted: in his effort to understand men, he does not pick and choose among them; this method, as Montaigne knew, is the best for eliminating the arbitrariness of one's own constructions, and for surrendering oneself to reality as given. But the reality which he encountered was so constituted that, without permanent reference to the immense changes of the immediate past and without a premonitory searching after the imminent changes of the future, one could not represent it; all the human figures and all the human events in his work appear upon a ground politically and socially disturbed. To bring the significance of this graphically before us, we have but to compare him with the best-known realistic writers of the pre-Revolutionary eighteenth century: with Lesage or the Abbé Prévost, with the preeminent Henry Fielding or with Goldsmith; we have but to consider how much more accurately and profoundly he enters into given contemporary reality than Voltaire, Rousseau, and the youthful realistic work of Schiller, and upon how much broader a basis than Saint-Simon, whom, though in the very incomplete edition then available, he read assiduously. Insofar as the serious realism of modern times cannot represent man otherwise than as embedded in a total reality, political, social, and economic, which is concrete and constantly evolving—as is the case today in any novel or film—Stendhal is its founder.

However, the attitude from which Stendhal apprehends the world of event and attempts to reproduce it with all its inter-connections is as yet hardly influenced by Historism—which, though it penetrated into France in his time, had little effect upon him. For that very reason we have referred in the last few pages to time-perspective and to a constant consciousness of changes and cataclysms, but not to a comprehension of evolutions. It is not too easy to describe Stendhal's inner attitude toward social phenomena. It is his aim to seize their every nuance; he most accurately represents the particular structure of any given milieu, he has no preconceived rationalistic system concerning the general factors which determine social life, nor any pattern-concept of how the ideal society ought to look; but in particulars his representation of events is oriented, wholly in the spirit of classic ethical psychology, upon an *analyse du cœur humain,* not upon discovery or premonitions of historical forces; we find rationalistic, empirical, sensual motifs in him, but hardly those of romantic Historism. Absolutism, religion and the Church, the privileges of rank, he regards very much as would an average protagonist of the Enlightenment, that is as a web of superstition, deceit, and intrigue; in general, artfully contrived intrigue (together with passion) plays a decisive role in his plot construction, while the historical forces which are the basis of it hardly appear. Naturally all this can be explained by his political viewpoint, which was democratic-republican; this alone sufficed to render him immune to romantic Historism; besides which the emphatic manner of such writers as Chateaubriand displeased him in the extreme. On the other hand, he treats even the classes of society which, according to his views, should be closest to him, extremely critically and without a trace of the emotional values which romanticism attached to the word "people." The practically active bourgeoisie with its respectable money-making, inspires him with unconquerable boredom, he shudders at the *vertu républicaine* of the United States, and despite his ostensible lack of sentimentality he regrets the fall of the social culture of the *ancien régime*. "Ma foi, l'esprit manque," he writes in chapter 30 of *Henry Brulard*," chacun réserve toutes ses forces pour un métier qui lui donne un rang dans le monde." No longer is birth or intelligence or the self-cultivation of the *honnête homme* the deciding factor—it is ability in some profession. This is no world in which Stendhal-Dominique can live and breathe. Of course, like his heroes, he too can work and work efficiently, when that is what is called for. But how can one take anything like practical professional work seriously in the long run! Love, music, passion, intrigue, heroism—these are the things that make life worth-while. . . .

Stendhal is an aristocratic son of the *ancien régime grande bourgeoisie,* he will and can be no nineteenth-century bourgeois. He says so himself time and again: My views were Republican even in my youth but my family handed down their aristocratic instincts to me (*Brulard,* ch. 14); since the Revolution theater audiences have become stupid (*Brulard,* ch. 22); I was a liberal myself (in 1821), and yet I found the liberals "outrageusement niais" (*Souvenirs d'égotisme,* ch. 6); to converse with a "gros marchand de province" makes me dull and unhappy all day (*Égotisme,* ch. 7 and *passim*)—these and similar remarks, which sometimes also refer to his physical constitution (La nature m'a donné les nerfs délicats et la peau sensible d'une femme," *Brulard,* ch. 32), occur plentifully. Sometimes he has pronounced accesses of socialism: in 1811, he writes, energy was to be found only in the class "qui est en lutte avec les vrais besoins" (*Brulard,* ch. 2). But he finds the smell and the noise of the masses unendurable, and in his books, outspokenly realistic though they are in other respects, we find no "people," either in the romantic "folk" sense or in the socialist sense—only petty bourgeois, and occasional accessory figures such as soldiers, domestic servants, and coffee-house mademoiselles. Finally, he sees the individual man far less as the product of his historical situation and as taking part in it, than as an atom within it; a man seems to have been thrown almost by chance into the milieu in which he lives; it is a resistance with which he can deal more or less successfully, not really a culture-medium with which he is organically connected. In addition, Stendhal's conception of mankind is on the whole preponderantly materialistic and sensualistic; an excellent illustration of this occurs in *Henry Brulard* (ch. 36):

> J'appelle *caractère* d'un homme sa manière habituelle d'aller a la chasse du bonheur, en termes plus clairs, mais moins qualificatifs, *l'ensemble de ses habitudes morales.*

But in Stendhal, happiness, even though highly organized human beings can find it only in the mind, in art, passion, or fame, always has a far more sensory and earthy coloring than in the romanticists. His aversion to philistine efficiency, to the type of bourgeois that was coming into existence, could be romantic too. But a romantic would hardly conclude a passage on his distaste for money-making with the words: "J'ai eu le rare plaisir de faire toute ma vie à peu près ce qui me plaisait" (*Brulard*, ch. 32). His conception of *esprit* and of freedom is still entirely that of the pre-Revolutionary eighteenth century, although it is only with effort and a little spasmodically that he succeeds in realizing it in his own person. For freedom he has to pay the price of poverty and loneliness and his *esprit* easily becomes paradox, bitter and wounding: "une gaité qui fait peur" (*Brulard*, ch. 6). His *esprit* no longer has the self-assurance of the Voltaire period; he manages neither his social life nor that particularly important part of it, his sexual relations, with the easy mastery of a gentleman of rank of the *ancien régime;* he even goes so far as to say that he cultivated *esprit* only to conceal his passion for a woman whom he did not possess—"cette peur, mille fois répétée, a été, dans le fait, le principe dirigeant de ma vie pendant dix ans" (*Égotisme,* ch. 1). Such traits make him appear a man born too late who tries in vain to realize the form of life of a past period; other elements of his character, the merciless objectivity of his realistic power, his courageous assertion of his personality against the triviality of the rising *juste milieu,* and much more, show him as the forerunner of certain later intellectual modes and forms of life; but he always feels and experiences the reality of his period as a resistance. That very thing makes his realism (though it proceeded, if at all, to only a very slight degree from a loving genetic comprehension of evolutions—that is, from the historistic attitude) so energetic and so closely connected with his own existence: the realism of this *cheval ombrageux* is a product of his fight for self-assertion. And this explains the fact that the stylistic level of his great realistic novels is much closer to the old great and heroic concept of tragedy than is that of most later realists—Julien Sorel is much more a "hero" than the characters of Balzac, to say nothing of Flaubert.

That the rule of style promulgated by classical aesthetics which excluded any material realism from serious tragic works was already giving way in the eighteenth century is well known. Even in France the relaxation of this rule can be observed as early as the first half of the eighteenth century; during the second half, it was Diderot particularly who propagated a more intermediate level of style both in theory and in practice, but he did not pass beyond the boundaries of the bourgeois and the pathetic. In his novels, especially in the *Neveu de Rameau,* characters from everyday life and of intermediate if not low station are portrayed with a certain seriousness; but the seriousness is more reminiscent of the moralistic and satirical attitudes of the Enlightenment than of nineteenth-century realism. In the figure and the work of Rousseau there is unmistakably a germ of the later evolution. Rousseau, as Meinecke says in his book on Historism (2, 390), was able "even though he did not attain to complete historical thinking, to help in awakening the new sense of the individual merely through the revelation of his own unique individuality." Meinecke is here speaking of historical thinking; but a corresponding statement may be made in respect to realism. Rousseau is not properly realistic; to his material—especially when it is his own life—he brings such a strongly apologetic and ethico-critical interest, his judgment of events is so influenced by his principles of natural law, that the reality of the social world does not become for him an immediate subject; yet the example of the *Confessions,* which attempts to represent his own existence in its true relation to contemporary life, is important as a stylistic model for writers who had more sense of reality as given than he. Perhaps even more important in its indirect influence upon serious realism is his politicizing of the idyllic concept of Nature. This created a wish-image for the design of life which, as we know, exercised an immense power of suggestion and which, it was believed, could be directly realized; the wish-image soon showed itself to be in absolute opposition to the established historical reality, and the contrast grew stronger and more tragic the more apparent it became that the realization of the wish-image was miscarrying. Thus practical historical reality became a problem in a way hitherto unknown—far more concretely and far more immediately.

In the first decades after Rousseau's death, in French preromanticism, the effect of that immense disillusionment was, to be sure, quite the opposite: it showed itself, among the most important writers, in a tendency to flee from contemporary reality. The Revolution, the Empire, and even the Restoration are poor in realistic literary works. The heroes of preromantic novels betray a sometimes almost morbid aversion to entering into contemporary life. The contradiction between the natural, which he desired, and the historically based reality which he encountered, had already become tragic for Rousseau; but the very contradiction had roused him to do battle for the natural. He was no longer alive when the Revolution and Napoleon created a situation which, though new, was, in his sense of the word, no more "natural" but instead again entangled historically. The next generation, deeply influenced by his ideas and hopes, experienced the victorious resistance of the real and the historical, and it was especially those who had fallen most deeply under Rousseau's fascination, who found themselves not at home in the new world which had utterly destroyed their hopes. They entered into opposition to it or they turned away from it. Of Rousseau they carried on only the inward rift, the tendency to flee from society, the need to retire and to be alone; the other side of Rousseau's nature, the revolutionary and fighting side, they had lost. The outward circumstances which destroyed the unity of intellectual life, and the dominating influence of literature in France, also contributed to this development; from the outbreak of the Revolution to the fall of Napoleon there is hardly a literary work of any consequence which did not exhibit symptoms of this flight from contemporary reality, and such symptoms are still very prevalent among the romantic groups after 1820. They appear most purely and most completely in Sénancour. But in its very negativeness the attitude of the majority of pre-romantics to the historical reality of their time is far more seriously problematic than is the attitude of the society of the Enlightenment. The Rousseauist movement and the great disillusionment it underwent was a prerequisite for the rise of the modern conception of reality. Rousseau, by passionately contrasting the natural condition of man with the existing reality of life determined by history, made the latter a practical problem; now for the first time the eighteenth-century style of historically unproblematic and unmoved presentation of life became valueless.

Romanticism, which had taken shape much earlier in Germany and England, and whose historical and individualistic trends had been long in preparation in France, reached its full development after 1820; and, as we know, it was precisely the principle of a mixture of styles which Victor Hugo and his friends made the slogan of their movement; in that principle the contrast to the classical treatment of subjects and the classical literary language stood out most obviously. Yet in Hugo's formula there is something too pointedly antithetical; for him it is a matter of mixing the sublime and the grotesque. These are both extremes of style which give no consideration to reality. And in practice he did not aim at understandingly bestowing form upon reality as given; rather, in dealing both with historical and contemporary subjects, he elaborates the stylistic poles of the sublime and the grotesque, or other ethical and aesthetic antitheses, to the utmost, so that they clash; in this way very strong effects are produced, for Hugo's command of expression is powerful and suggestive; but the effects are improbable and, as a reflection of human life, untrue.

Lucien Leuwen

by Jean Prévost

Lucien Leuwen, though the longest of Stendhal's novels, remains uncompleted. We have both its preliminary outlines and those reworked during the writing. We have several successive versions of the first completed part. And finally, we have notes—the last of which annul the first—for the conclusion which the author never wrote. This then is a work which offers us the almost unique occasion (as was noted by Henri Martineau) to examine Stendhal's work in the process of creation.

We must, however, ask if the same reasons that prevented the author from finishing his novel were not responsible for the hesitations, numerous projects, and reworkings so characteristic of his work.

In *Le Rouge et le noir*, the author began with an exterior *datum*, a lowly one that had to be ennobled, but that guided the plot up to the end. In the *Chartreuse*, the basic elements of the story were again external, but this time they had to be made more contemporary and more familiar.

In *Lucien Leuwen*, Stendhal does not have to respect the basic elements supplied him by Mme Jules Gaulthier's novel. These elements are not real but fictional, and Beyle rightfully considers himself an altogether different novelist from Mme Jules Gaulthier. Above all, in the two other great novels, he was supplied with the plot and then later invented the characters. In *Lucien Leuwen*, the characters are what he invents and possesses first of all. He does indeed foresee an ending, but a simple, remote and expected one: the marriage of the young lovers. The task of the plot and the true invention will thus lie in delaying the dénouement rather than provoking it. In *Lamiel* as well, the characters appeared to the author before the plot. And *Lamiel*, like *Lucien Leuwen*, was to remain unfinished.

The manuscript of Mme Jules Gaulthier, contrary to the set accounts

"Lucien Leuwen." Translated by Ann Bayless. From *La Création chez Stendhal* by Jean Prévost (Paris: Mercure de France, 1951). All rights reserved. Reprinted by permission of Mercure de France. The translation reflects the elliptic style of the original.

of the seminarist Berthet for the *Rouge* and of Vandozza Farnese for the *Chartreuse,* at first excited Stendhal's imagination precisely because of what it lacked. He started out by writing a letter to the author on the defects of the book. The following night, as we know from a note in his own hand, he had the idea of reworking the subject himself. The defects were of a kind to stimulate him.

II

In *Lucien Leuwen* there is a lack of simplicity, refinement and humor, too much vagueness in the characterization. Most certainly, from his first outline, Stendhal put something of himself into Lucien. There is more than one way of putting oneself into a character. Beyle was able to draw upon his own character three times (even four if one counts *Lamiel*) without ever repeating himself. In Julien, he transposed himself by exalting his powers and his desires, adding only beauty. Lucien emerges rather from a dream of wish fulfillment: the author endows him right from the start with everything he himself had wanted to possess but could not by then hope to obtain. Until the end of his life Stendhal indulged in dreams of wish fulfillment. We have an example of this in the charming badinage of *Privilèges,* reprinted in *Mélanges Intimes.* Lucien is thus from the outset extremely rich without even concern for the management of his fortune. His mother is alive and loves him; his father understands him and supports him, as Beyle's father always refused to do. Lucien even has that natural grace and refinement that Beyle lacked and withheld from Julien. Lucien is a man who has everything, the dream of a man ungraced by nature and fortune. Finally, Bathilde de Chasteller is Métilde Dembowska even more completely than Mathilde de La Mole. Mathilde was made up of Méry and Giulia, and Stendhal in that instance transposed only the memory of separation and pain. Bathilde de Chasteller, on the contrary, loves Lucien from the moment she sets eyes on him, and as deeply as he loves her. Beyle thought himself loved by Métilde but separated from her. A hero, however, blessed from the beginning with that which even a fairy tale hero does not attain until the end of the story makes the plot of a novel fairly difficult to maintain. The hero's happiness cannot dwindle; a *decrescendo* is unpleasant in literature. It is thus necessary to accumulate material obstacles. This is what Stendhal beautifully compares to the wilful retardation that Haydn provides for the conclusion of his symphonies. In such a case a continuous plot line is impossible. What is needed is a series of distinct episodes, and to avoid monotony, a change of scene, environment, and secondary characters. The provinces (a somewhat undefined Nancy or an imaginary Montvallier) with a military career;

Paris with a political career; finally, perhaps Rome with a diplomatic career. The hero, in the peripeteia, can fall to the lowest point through the death of his father, the loss of his fortune and position, at the very moment he attains happiness and the hand of the woman he loves.

III

All this would not have accounted for Lucien's moral life. To understand the structure of the novel, one must first recognize to what degree he is occupied with moral concerns. If the *Rouge* developed an ethics of energy, Lucien develops one of conscience.

What to do to esteem oneself? This is the central problem of the book. This is in fact the true moral problem that faces a man endowed with everything. This is finally the problem that faces Beyle himself in 1835. Rebellious, jacobite, despising Louis-Philippe, he enjoys, however, one favor—his consulate.

In order to esteem himself, the exigent Lucien is never content with that which comes to him. Fortune's favors even become obstacles for him. He is not content with duels and worldly success. He requires proof of his moral stamina. He needs to dirty his hands, wilfully suffer humiliation, even in his own eyes. In fact, he always seeks, for his conduct, the most demanding judges.

A number of secondary characters, invented through somewhat the same method as the confidants in the *Rouge,* play considerably different roles in *Lucien Leuwen*. Together they serve as an exterior conscience for the principal character. One of them, Ernest Develroy (patterned after a contemporary of Stendhal's—professor Lherminier—and similar to Julien but lacking his sensitivity) represents the morality of personal success. Far inferior to Lucien, who despises him for his baseness, Develroy nevertheless hurts him deeply by his reproaches and even by his envy: "What can you do by yourself, what would you be able to achieve on your own? Are you capable of arousing love except by contagion, tears, by 'la voie humide'?"

Later, the jacobite Coffe intervenes, much more the confidant, whose ideas are closer to the secret morality of the author. Intrepid, almost cruel for the sake of the public weal, like Beyle, he despises even more than Beyle any sensibility that conflicts with principles. He completes the hero by contrast. And finally, Madame de Chasteller (despite the grievances Lucien thinks he holds against her) becomes for him the supreme judge in matters of honor and intelligence—an imaginary judge like the ladies of medieval knights.

At every decisive moment Lucien wonders "What would she think of me?"

IV

The case of the father is somewhat different, and even more curious in the study of literary creation. At first he represents success, solid and substantial—his money obtained through merit, his success in society obtained through wit. In the Paris episode (the intrigues surrounding the Ministry) the outline was bound to give greater importance to Monsieur Leuwen, who in a sense was to pull the strings. Stendhal, however, as he progressed, took a further interest in this character. In his youth, Stendhal dreamed of becoming an epicurean, a wealthy banker and a man of wit. His practical philosophy was the same as Monsieur Leuwen's.

The author, wherever father and son appear together, ceases to identify with Lucien. He transposes only his literary ambition (that he had even when he wanted to be a banker) into the more recent political ambition that he had discovered in 1830. It is through the eyes of Monsieur Leuwen that we see the underside of ministerial politics, Louis-Philippe, and the development of the Grandet episode. At that moment, instead of remaining an incarnation (or rather a compensation for Beyle) Lucien is treated as the son of the author, with tenderness and offhanded amusement. This transposition would not have been possible with Julien Sorel. But just as many fathers seek in their sons the fulfillment of their own lives, a character that compensates for the youth of the author may be seen and described as though by a father.

V

All the other secondary characters play a double role. They serve to describe France in 1835, and are or should be comical. They also serve to distract us from the love story and to delay the ending. The many outlines that Stendhal experimented with as he proceeded, the numerous additions that he made to the original story (and that do or do not appear in the text, according to the edition) all point to the same direction. Rather than a concern for a tightly knitted plot, all these plans indicate a taste for an episodic construction. All these independent episodes make of *Lucien Leuwen* a vast comedy on the order of Molière's *Les Fâcheux*.

Two other influences are strongly felt in the composition of the secondary characters. The first is the one produced by the criticism of the *Rouge* that the author suffered or himself formulated. Contrary to the critics, he was pleased with the characterization of Julien, Mme de Rênal, and Mathilde. He was less pleased with the rest. He subsequently counted on secondary characters to provide greater density, more description, more gaiety, and less tension. Greater density? It was for that reason that he added secondary characters in his reworkings. For example, there was a dearth of ordinary people and soldiers, and so he later invented the story of the lancer Ménuel, which he was unable to work sufficiently into Lucien's stay in Nancy.

In everything that followed in the wake of those tales sketched out during the years preceding *Lucien Leuwen,* he thought it necessary to provide a physical portrait of the characters. But usually he postponed this task that he found so loathsome.

We know by what slightly abstract methods the secondary characters of the *Rouge* were delineated, and that the palest of them were merely repetitions or reflections of others. In *Lucien Leuwen,* on the other hand, the secondary characters are copied, even and above all physically, after living models, generally named by the author in his marginal notes. Since we hardly know most of these models, it is impossible to compare the portraits with their originals. Suffice it to note that these sketches were made at a distance of a thousand miles and five years. Memory has therefore made a choice among their traits and retained only the most distinctive, the most singular, and the most comical. For an author as experienced as Stendhal was by 1835, memory was the first of his aesthetic sifting processes. According to a law of the novel, secondary characters should be better drawn than protagonists, painted in fewer but bolder strokes.

For this kind of composition Stendhal had a model to avoid—La Bruyère, analyst and moralist like himself, whose overly refined and inert portraits had no purpose other than themselves. Such portraits should therefore never appear in a novel in which everything must encourage action and serve as part of the whole.

VI

The other model, though highly remote from *Lucien Leuwen,* that Stendhal has in mind constantly is the Fielding of *Tom Jones.* Out of love for Fielding, he always presented the protagonist while placing the reader at the heart of the hero's thoughts, though in his own manner. "Outside of genius," he commented in a marginal note, "the chief difference between Fielding and Dominique is that Fielding *at the same time* described the sentiments and actions of a *number* of characters, while Dominique describes those of *only one.* Where does this technique of Dominique lead? I don't know. Is it an improvement? Is it the first stage of art, or rather the frigid type of the philosophical character?" In addition to analysis, he thus accepted, without anticipating a satisfactory result, this aspect of a moral problem that we earlier indicated. In the margin of chapter 25, on the subject of the fake quarrel between Mme de Chasteller and Lucien, he writes with greater uneasiness this time: "This is certainly different and perhaps far inferior in interest compared to the plan of *Tom Jones*. Interest, instead of being heightened by all these characters, rests solely on Lucien." Whereupon he corrected himself: "One never goes so far as when one does not know where one goes. This does not resemble Julien; so much the better." In the margin of chapter 23, there are two notes, one dated May first, the other September 1834. The first advises "the physical portrayal of all secondary and boring characters"; the second, "a more flowery and less arid style, witty and gay." He adds, "Not like the *Tom Jones* of 1750, but like the same Fielding as he would be in 1834."

Beginning with that chapter, in fact, what he does write is different from what he set out to write.

VII

It is very rare for an author to do exactly *what he wanted to do* according to his outlines. And those pages completely worked out in advance are rarely the best. The broad perspectives in Buffon's *Epoques de la nature,* the scenes in Chateaubriand's *Les Martyrs* that take place in heaven or hell, the serious pages in *Bouvard et Pécuchet* are just such fully executed outlines with nothing added. These selections give the reader the impression of a vast field of amplification measured out by a ruler. The movement is uniform; one is no longer even aware of it. There is no proper movement in a book without an over-all plan, but a plan of detail is always immobilizing; it paralyzes the execution. This kind of plan is suitable for abstract ideas and descriptions for which the greatest of authors require the accumulation of many layers of successive inventions. Stendhal at the beginning of *Lucien Leuwen* had *intentions* rather than a *plan,* but very firm intentions. He quickly saw that his chapters deviated from these intentions. He had to compromise with himself and come to terms with these differences.

As an author who already knew himself, he sought those qualities that he lacked. But he would not have agreed to give up those he already possessed. An outline does not select among the qualities of an author. In the process of writing, it is the author who must select. Or rather the temperament of the author chooses for him, and the work itself makes certain demands that carry him far from projects and intentions.

VIII

The first chapter shows us Lucien and his uniform. It is keenly felt and well thought out in advance as are all the early chapters. In its lightness, humor, refinement of description, it coincides thoroughly with the author's intentions. However, Stendhal could not continue in the same key. That kind of light humor slows down the action to the point where *Lucien Leuwen* would have required twenty volumes. And all through those twenty volumes the hero, always seen from the outside, would seem like a puppet or at best an eccentric.

The chapter is amusing but followed by twenty like it would result in a tiresome novel. Stendhal cannot display humor and at the same time make his characters act. To reveal them he must see them from within, identify with them, or make us identify with them, which eliminates continuous humor. All that can remain is a marginal humor when the author intervenes for a few lines, or, what he called "Italian humor," when the hero pokes fun at himself. These are variations of wit, rich in comedy and the unexpected, but they are not always suitable. In the *Rouge* the humorous or rather amusing chapters—Géronimo, the conversation in the stage coach, or the dinner at the bishop's palace in Besançon—stopped all action short. On the other hand, action carried the author far from humor.

With the second chapter of *Lucien Leuwen,* the wilful frivolity of the beginning gives way to the more incisive and more sweeping style of the *Rouge.* The author's intention is certainly to connect humor to action, as Fielding does. But it is the ordinariness of their adventures and the simplicity of his heroes that permit Fielding the luxury of humor. Stendhal, when he composes the actions and thoughts of his characters, wants neither to vulgarize nor to simplify them. He must then compromise and seek humor through other means. In Nancy, the timidity and charming clumsiness of blossoming love make of Lucien a rather ludicrous character. In the second part, when he is no longer ludicrous at all, the quality of humor has to be sustained around him through characters like his father or Coffe, or through a trip that recalls the bitter satire of the *Rouge.* We cannot even guess at what the humor might have been directed in the last part that was to have been set in Rome. A satire on diplomatic circles might have furnished one or two chapters, but would hardly have sufficed.

IX

The humor afforded by the blunders of the young lancer lieutenant and the witticisms of his father provided none of the picturesque quality Stendhal was seeking. The book, consequently, had to be written in two stages: first the plot, then the background. Only the beginning of the book was recast in this manner and it is the most slowly paced of all of Stendhal's writing. The beginning is exquisite in its perfection of detail and in the beauty of the dream of Mme de Chasteller shared by Lucien, the author, and the reader. A slow tempo is fine for the beginning of a novel. The author, however, thought of interjecting still other episodes

like the one about the lancer Ménuel. It is a question whether further
additions might not have dulled the novel. He may well have sensed it,
which is perhaps why he left the work dormant. The whole of *Lucien
Leuwen* could not have resembled *Le Chasseur vert*.

Furthermore, the episodes to be added (or those that play no part in the
major action, like the account of the strike and the repression) required
of the author a new kind of humor like that of Fielding or Cervantes,
which is practically the opposite of his own. He abounds in irony on the
subject of those in power: the juste-milieu prefects under Louis-Philippe,
the ministers, the rich woman who permits herself every right are all
inexhaustible subjects for him. His heroes have the kind of irony that
ridicules itself, which is another sign of strength. But Stendhal is at
the antipodes of the picaresque. When he paints the poor and miserable
he cannot push the picturesque quality of their misfortunes to the
point of buffoonery. Picturesque humor requires a plastic verve, a decision
to remain *outside* the individual, which relates Cervantes to Velasquez,
Scarron or Molière to Callot. In order to make a picturesque character
of Ménuel, Stendhal required him to be robust, handsome, swaggering,
and gay, with nothing in him to provoke pity. The Cortis scandal, the
hospital and electoral scenes of the second part are overdrawn, but
as remote from humor as Daumier's *Rue Transnonain* is from caricature.
The book is only the better for it, but it is no longer what the author
had in mind. His natural bent won out while the work was in progress.

X

This taste for light humor, for *whipped cream* as he said of Rossini,
altered dialogues more easily than the actual story. Stendhal was also
better prepared for this. His theatrical training had already served him
well for the dialogues in the *Rouge,* which, however, are short, filled
with the vitality of the characters, and like the distant rumblings that
precede a storm. Eighteenth century comedy reappears in the long
conversations in *Lucien Leuwen* which are gratuitous games like scenes
in Marivaux.

Leaving aside the moral disputations of Lucien and his exterior consciences, much in the novel reminds us of Regnard as well as of Marivaux
and the lighter Molière of *La Princesse d'Elide, L'Amour peintre,* or
Zerbinette in *Les Fourberies de Scapin:* the skirmishes over the Tuileries
moat, the frivolous conversations in the salon of Mme d'Hocquincourt,
the comments of Dr. Du Poirier—converted to the doctrines of Lamennais
but not to courage—Monsieur Leuwen's manipulation of his southern
deputies, and finally the fencing that goes on between Lucien and Mme
Grandet. What sometimes matters more than the characters expressing
themselves or revealing themselves to each other is the exchange of

words that bounces back and forth between them with a drollery that is deliberate with some and unintentional with others.

This superabundance of peppery dialogue is never sought or added as are the material details of the story. It simply flows, and this inner well-spring is not hard to understand. Stendhal, when he wrote this book, had no one with whom to converse in Civitavecchia. One feels in the letters of his early years as consul how much he yearned for conversation. Letter-writing could not satisfy him because of the long delay before receiving an answer. He thus found greater pleasure in his characters and in his imaginary conversations.

This impression is further verified by an examination of the manuscripts of *Lucien Leuwen* at the library of Grenoble, particularly in the case of the first volume.

Conversations and dialogues, in fact, abound in the manuscripts, more so than in the three texts edited by Debraye for Champion, by Henri Rambaud for Brossard, and by Henri Martineau for the *Divan,* or in the *Pléiade* edition. If these individual editions disagree somewhat (which is almost inevitable, considering the extreme complexity of the manuscript and the number of variants), they naturally agree in the elimination of everything Stendhal crossed out and deliberately rejected.

There are many developments (particularly Lucien's entry into Nancy society) that Stendhal discarded with the notation "True, but drawn out" (chapters XI, XII, XIII in the *Pléiade* edition).

These developments are at times completely eliminated (chapter XI), at others summarized (chapter XIII). The summary, which recaptures the subject and mood, is added to other complete conversations and creates a feeling of density. At times, he summarized even Lucien's thoughts in a few lines of indirect discourse. The auther in rereading himself was troubled by the abundance of material and had to reduce it any way he could. He added other episodes, like the Ménuel story, but he still needed to show more of the common people and the army. He could well feel that he had devoted too much attention to Nancy's upper classes. It is rather a question of proportion than brevity that prompted his editing. On each reading, Stendhal's keen awareness of the whole scene led him to sacrifice detail for the general effect.

He was right, and his later editors did well in respecting his judgment. But we nonetheless regret the omission of those many successful pages that scintillate with the ridicule of drawing room sots and with Lucien's vivacity, which Stendhal graced with his own verve. One of the editors, Henri Rambaud, transcribed all of these passages in his notes. But these two volumes of notes have as yet not appeared. Few readers would probably be interested. However, the publication of these texts under the title *Conversations en 1835* would surely add to our understanding of Stendhal, his fame, and his vivacity. For him, mirth is a matter of detail. "Laughter," he writes in the margin of one of his outlines, "will grow from the outer epidermis."

XI

Une Position sociale, a piece that preceded *Lucien Leuwen* and was to have formed the core of the next-to-the-last part, was more a conversation than a book, but a conversation with only one person and almost exclusively on one subject, religion. Certainly there is greater variety in *Lucien Leuwen.* But whether Lucien debates with his exterior consciences or with his father, it remains Stendhal, through an aspect of either his personality or his thinking, who provides the answers and the questions. His characters have conversations that are somewhat overdrawn. They become foils for his wit. This kind of teasing humor is in the style of a Regnard or other comic writers of the eighteenth century. In addition, the writers of epigrammatic comedies may have brought this style into fashion. Musset, writing his comedies at that time, was influenced by the same sources. If anything reminds us of the conversations in *Lucien Leuwen* it is the dialogues in *Il ne faut jurer de rien.*

Humor sought in the minute detail, subtly overdrawn characters who converse with incarnations of the author, episodes given considerable breadth without any obligation on the part of the author to provide development—this artistic formula, a compromise between Stendhal's *temperament* and his *intentions,* is very similar to that developed by Proust. The same causes (autobiographic or burlesque characters, events, and conversations imagined by a recluse whose art is compensatory, voluminous additions to the first draft) produced the same effects, but without any imitation, since Proust could have read only one abridged and unfaithful edition of *Lucien Leuwen.*

XII

A further consequence of this need to compensate through writing for the silence of seclusion is that interior monologues no longer have the superb movement to be found in the *Rouge.* Fortunately, the first draft of the character was better adapted for slower monologues. Just as Julien is habitually carried away, so Lucien wavers in his thinking. He can and should be more critical of himself. It is doubtless the first monologues that guided Stendhal's development of his hero. *In the end, these long monologues came to be essential to the character.* This novel was in danger of being less solidly constructed around the hero than the *Rouge* around Julien. Not that Lucien appears less frequently, but his will is less often responsible for the events in the story. He is acted upon

more often than he acts. His appointment as second lieutenant, his separation from Mme de Chasteller, his actions and trips as first secretary, his
financial ruin, and his nomination to Rome are brought about by his
enemies, his father, his superiors.

The scope of these interior monologues makes up for his lack of
initiative. And above all, except for Mme de Chasteller during the
awakening of her love, and a few supernumeraries (whose grotesque attitudes—like Du Poirier's timorousness—do not arouse our sympathies), all
are seen from the outside.

XIII

Monsieur Leuwen, who at times is the center of the story, acts or
speaks, he does not deliberate with himself; his age and irony make him
somewhat remote. A character with whom we might have sympathized to
the point of neglecting the hero, such as the exquisite and delightful
Mme Leuwen, is summarily sketched. Mme Grandet is given to endless
self-deliberation, but of a nature that leads our sympathies rather to
Lucien. So that our interest, even if slightly less intense, is better directed
to the hero. Another difficulty: unless it is a simple episodic novel such
as *Gil Blas,* any fictional story should be constructed for the progression of
the effect. In this case, the central plot, the naïve love relation between
Lucien and Mme de Chasteller, is insufficient for such a progression.

When the interest lags, the author senses it even more keenly than the
reader, through his difficulty and slowness in inventing what follows.
The commonest measure at such a moment is the very one taken by the
man who is bored and leaves on a trip: the hero is placed in a new
setting and the action starts afresh. As in the uprooting of trees, trans-
plantation provides a plot with renewed vigor and freshness. *Le Rouge
et le noir* has three locations: Verrières, the seminary in Besançon, Paris.
Lucien Leuwen was also to have been set in three cities: Nancy, Paris,
then Rome. But here the change of scene was to cause the author even
graver problems.

Toward the middle of the *Rouge* (according to page count), Julien
Sorel is in Paris. He will be able to love again. In *Lucien Leuwen,* on the
other hand, when we have emerged from the political intrigue (which in
its bitterness and somberness corresponds to the seminary episode), we
are two-thirds through the novel. The hero's heart has been given once
and for all to Mme de Chasteller. The author can no longer create a
true heroine who will involve us in a new setting. Mme Grandet is little
better than a figure. She has the pretensions of an ennobled bourgeois,
such as Mme de Fervaques, and the intense defeated pride of Mathilde de
La Mole. But we can be no more interested in her than is Lucien. Will
the author have to construct a whole new society and provide the hero

with another fake love affair in order to create an episode in the last
quarter of the book? This change of scene would have been more trouble
than it was worth.

Stendhal was well aware of this. Henri Martineau has already underlined the importance of the notation dated April 28, 1835: "I am
eliminating the third volume for the reason that it is only in the first
excitement of youth and love that exposition and new characters can be
swallowed. After a certain age, this is impossible. And so, no duchesse
de Saint-Mégrin and no third volume. It will be for another novel."

"The first excitement of youth" must not be applied to the author,
nor does it mean that he wishes only eighteen-year old readers. The soul
of a reader in the course of a book passes, as it does in life, through in-
fancy when it discovers the world, then through youth when it is impassioned. Later it matures; knowledge replaces experience, and fatigue
—playing the role of old age—slows it down. The soul of a reader,
whether eighteen or sixty, is no longer young enough to change its habits
and be transplanted three-quarters through the book.

XIV

Before deciding to make this sacrifice, the author tried to link together
his different sections. For example, in several projects for rearrangement,
Mme Grandet was to have appeared in the first part and an unhappy
writer was to have committed suicide over her. Dr. Du Poirier, in Paris,
was to have played the role of a turncoat deputy and a coward. And
since all wealthy families have country estates, nothing could have
been simpler than to give a chateau near Nancy to the Saint-Mégrins
whom Lucien would have met again later on as ambassadors to Madrid
or Rome.

Such would certainly have been Balzac's method; it is by means of
such links that he unifies his *Comédie humaine*. Stendhal, concerned this
time with all the refinements of his craft, added other equally important
details, for example the Ménuel episode. The addition to his first
draft of gratuitous and picturesque episodes amused him. But the
laborious insertion of purely functional fragments designed to prepare for
later developments ran the risk of boring him and his reader. Only Balzac
knew how to derive beauty from these fastidious preparations.

Finally, as we have seen, this fourth part was to have taken up an
earlier work—*Une Position sociale*—the beginning of a novel he abandoned in 1832. There was no difficulty at all in this linking of opening
sections. The hero of *Une Position sociale* was, as he recognized in a note,
Dominique idealized, which is to say himself.

Lucien Leuwen also resembles Dominique, but these two likenesses are incompatible.

Lucien is a sentimental compensation for Stendhal. Roizand, on the other hand, although curious and passionate, is considerably older and somewhat maladroit. His is more a life of the mind. At the beginning of the story, he seems spiritually idle and risks falling under the spell of the duchess. Lucien, on the contrary, obsessed with Mme de Chasteller, only seeks distraction elsewhere. For Roizand (as for Beyle in 1832 after the cruel moment of Austria's denial of his *exequatur*[1]), loss of position means total loss. Lucien Leuwen loses, one after the other, his happiness in love, his father, and his fortune. The additional loss of his secretaryship at the embassy is for him only an insignificant one, incapable of further-ing the plot or maintaining the reader's interest.

It would have been better to forget Roizand. But Stendhal clung to this curious subject. To attempt through divine terror and the perusal of the *Apocalypse* the seduction of a woman seemed to Stendhal a splendid complexity. Roizand gave up after the first few steps, but the subject deserved to be taken up again one day. In this way, the final decision to separate the two plots is justified.

Two episodes are missing. All that remains of them are the blank spaces on the manuscript pages.

Lucien's abrupt departure from Nancy is not enough to mark his rupture with Mme de Chasteller. She might have tried to justify herself or send her friend and confident after Lucien. The reader, however, might well have forgotten her had he lost sight of her for one whole volume.

It was, therefore, necessary to insert chapters of regret, of attempts to renew the relationship, that would contrast in tone with the satire of Paris and the political intrigue. This is precisely why the author was unable to write them. In order to continue and to aggravate this painful mis-understanding between the young lovers, he was in need of an emotion and a pathos that his description of Paris could not ressuscitate.

Consequently, he skipped over this part while awaiting the inspiration of tenderness. "While in a dry vein I am creating Mme Grandet." Variety always grew of itself in his other works through a natural need for change of tone or subject. He was to find this spontaneous variety in the *Chartreuse*. But in *Lucien Leuwen*, which he wrote more slowly, he did not. For he invents the plot as he goes along, and, in the tone, discovers new ideas for it. This freedom in the course of the story inhibits rather then helps the pace that Stendhal maintains when he knows in advance where he is going.

---

[1] Stendhal, having been appointed consul to Trieste in 1830, was not granted the *exequatur* (official authorization) by Austria because of his political views. [Ed. note.]

XV

The reworked plans in the margins indicate the hesitations over certain chapters, over the dimension to give certain episodes. In some cases there are calendar investigations to ascertain the verisimilitude of factual material. But these are not the plans or *guideposts* that direct the author.

Contrasted with these awkward and almost shapeless plans are *perfectly written fragments* that establish in advance the tone of a later chapter in its subtlest nuance. These fragments, produced in moments of genius, serve as landmarks, as stimulants, when he writes the chapter. The problem is to remain at this level. The last of these notes, according to the sequence of the plot, and the most exquisite in form, was like a beacon in the harbor toward which he was navigating:

> "You are mine," she told him covering him with kisses. "Leave for Nancy. Immediately, sir, immediately. You know only too well how much my father hates me. Question him, question anyone, and write me. When your letters reveal conviction (you know that I am a good judge), then return, but only then. I shall know perfectly well how to distinguish between the philosophy of a sensible man who forgives a misdeed committed prior to his tenure, or the impatience born of the love you naturally have for me, and the sincere conviction of this heart that I adore."—Lucien returned at the end of eight days.—End of novel.

He wrote this note below the first great love chapter of the book. It has the same verve, the same enthusiasm as the chapter itself. Most certainly this is almost word for word how he would have ended the book. He could have found no better way to thrust his protagonists, as well as his reader's imagination, into the realm of happiness. In the course of all the detours that a long novel requires, the memory of this ending leads him ahead, permits him contrasts of dullness and sadness, prevents him from getting lost or bored.

These perfect fragments, written in advance, differ from a plan. They have, according to Stendhal's method of writing, greater importance than a plan. These notes are as stimulating to his imagination as his plans are torturing. A plan is a thing to respect, to follow while adding detail, a thing that requires constant reference to memory and stifles the imagination. A plan has no nuances; it is a heavy shapeless mass that has to be modeled. The perfect fragment provides detail, summons other details; it creates about itself a crystallization.

To start with a few perfect fragments, then to unite them in a continuous work that from beginning to end must be on the same level, this is *par excellence* the method of the poet. The perfect fragments in the notes to *Lucien Leuwen* are like the *vers donnés* that Paul Valéry has at the beginning of a poem, lines that he found as soon as he decided to write the poem (perhaps determined by them). Poets whose incompleted fragments have survived, André Chénier for example, suggest the same method. The problem is to construct the poem around these fragments in order to connect them; they will provide the poem with its tone and pitch. Robert Frost tells me that he works in exactly the same way.

One might call this method of composing "poetic," a method that consists in uniting the first spontaneous and truly inspired ideas. Stendhal himself, in his early notebooks, when he toyed with poetry, noted here and there a line of verse. This same method, rediscovered in his fictional composition, gives his writing the spontaneity of great moments, the delightful madness that makes up its own personal logic, the enchantment thanks to which this logician, this mocker, this realist, can, when he wishes, make us rise far above the level of ordinary existence.

XVI

When he completed *Le Rouge et le noir* he was embarrassed by the scantiness of certain parts of the outline, and the necessity—as he said, of *adding substance*. In *Lucien Leuwen* he planned to over-amplify and later edit. In appraising himself as he went along, he discovered that in fact he was changing his whole style, that the *Rouge* was a "fresco" and *Lucien Leuwen* a "miniature." It is unlikely that he would have cut much more. Many of the notes made during his re-readings speak rather of adding than of abridging.

What must have diminished his desire to please the reader, as he progressed, was the certainty of not publishing soon enough. As he continued, he sought to please himself. Through the political satire and the fantasy of certain details, he let himself wander further and further away from this novel for which he had, at first, wished success. Finally, while his satiric verve lasted, he put off writing the sentimental parts for a time when he would be better disposed to do so. Elsewhere, he postponed the purely functional sections until the last moment. All that follows the completed parts, all that goes beyond the *Chasseur vert,* must be assessed as improvisation dictated by the mood of the moment.

It is unlikely, however, that Monsieur Leuwen's death, which we do not witness, was for Stendhal an episode to be developed. Literary euthanasia—the sudden elimination of a character—which is too surprising to the reader to distress him, successfully attenuated a terrible end in the *Rouge* and made of it a poem. In the same way it was to have eliminated a character in *Lucien Leuwen* who had become the protagonist and who interfered with the main plot. However, this character was attractive. The story, as we know it, suddenly whisks Monsieur Leuwen away. This abruptness was necessary and would doubtless have remained.

On the other hand, Stendhal planned to make of Mme Grandet, herself disappointed in love, an avowed enemy of Lucien's happiness. These somber machinations do not emerge from the *plan*. No fragment indicates any such clear intention on the part of the author. One can suppose that this part of his project disturbed him. The last allusion to Mme Grandet is sober, almost too brief. This unpleasant woman, in the great scene during which she throws herself at Lucien, demonstrates her capacity for a deep love that is hopeless and uncalculated. It became difficult to make of her a nasty character. In attempting to write the ending (which was so close now that he abandoned the fourth section in Rome), Stendhal suddenly found himself deprived of two resources: he could no longer use *Une Position sociale;* the two lovers were no longer separated by anything, neither a real obstacle nor an evil demon. They had nothing left but to fall into each other's arms. It would have made one chapter, or two at the most, and the easiest chapter to write for the average novelist.

But not for Stendhal. He needed one last and serious obstacle to place between Lucien and Mme de Chasteller in order to avoid blandness and the slow arrival of happiness. It would have been necessary to replace obstacles in which he was no longer interested. He already had the vision, the end of this chapter. All that remained was to find the *résistance* that would have given it conflict and substance. It was because of his inability to find a real obstacle to interpose between the lovers that he left unfinished a book so close to its end, a book for which he had already written the closing lines.

Romantic Realism
in *Lucien Leuwen*

by Raymond Giraud

Lucien at Blois—A Moral Comedy

In October 1835 the Comte de Vaize, Minister of the Interior for Louis-Philippe, sends Lucien Leuwen, then his confidential assistant, on a delicate and important political mission. In two localities in which the government's candidates for the Chamber of Deputies are weak, Lucien is expected to assure the defeat of the opposition by whatever tactics he sees fit to use. On the way to the first of the threatened area Lucien and his helper, Coffe, stop at Blois for dinner. Having left a carriage-load of defamatory pamphlets outside the inn, they are peacefully seated at table when they hear the sounds of a mob assembling in the street. Their frightened host enters to tell them that their carriage is being pillaged. At the door, Lucien is greeted by a deafening shout: "Down with the spy! Down with the police official!"

Although aware that the activity in which he is engaged is not regarded with universal approval, Lucien's first reaction is neither fear nor dismay, but a shocked and outraged feeling of indignation: "Red as a rooster, he did not deign to reply and tried to get to his carriage. The crowd separated a bit. As he opened the carriage door, an enormous shovelful of mud fell on his face and then down on his neckerchief. As he was speaking to M. Coffe just then, some of the mud even got into his mouth." To cap this humiliation, so precisely and objectively narrated, a tall, red-whiskered clerk, observing the mud on Lucien's face, cries out to the crowd: "See how dirty he is; you have put his soul upon his face." This is indeed the cruelest blow of all. (Conceivably, this line may have been a reminiscence from the *Liaisons dangereuses,* a novel Stendhal had admired as much as the *Nouvelle Héloïse*. The last comment about Mme de Merteuil, after smallpox had disfigured her beauty at the end of the book, was that "her disease had turned her inside out and now her soul was on her face.")

Lucien is clearly unprepared to meet this situation. He is sincerely indignant, tries to get his saber out of the carriage and would defy the crowd with military courage if Coffe, a cooler head, were not at hand to stifle his protests and hustle him out of town. Once they are on the highway, Coffe analyzes the episode for Lucien's benefit and offers him some observations that fill the young hero with rage and shame.

> "Well," Coffe answered coldly, "the minister offers you his arm when you leave the Opera. Your fortune is envied by magistrates on duty at the State Council, by prefects on leave and deputies handling warehouses of tobacco. This is the other face of the coin. It's that simple."
>
> "Your composure is enough to drive me mad," said Lucien, beside himself with rage. "These indignities! That atrocious remark: 'His soul is on his face'! That mud!"
>
> "That mud is for us the noble stain of the field of honor. That public uproar will weigh in your favor. These are the shining deeds of the career you have chosen and into which my poverty and gratitude have moved me to follow you."
>
> "You mean that you would not be here if you had an income of 1200 francs."
>
> "If I had only three hundred, I should not be serving a minister who keeps thousands of poor devils locked up in the dungeons of Mont-Saint-Michel and Clairvaux."

There can be no doubt that Coffe's voice is Stendhal's own. In it are reflected the irony, bitterness, and detachment that color not only the author's personal view of contemporary politics, but all the political incidents of *Lucien Leuwen*. This does not contradict the fact that Lucien is the "hero" of the novel and of this episode as well. It signifies rather that Stendhal has identified himself partially with two points of view, that of Lucien, the subjective or sentimental hero, and that of Coffe, the objective or rational observer or *raisonneur*.

The interest of the above text resides not so much in its exposure of the eternal techniques of scheming politicians, or the revelation of Stendhal's well-known estimation of certain ministers of the July Monarchy, as in the curious kind of comical humiliation to which the author has subjected his hero. Lucien, his face covered by "an enormous shovelful of mud," is in a mortifying situation that was, if not exactly dear to Stendhal, at least something of an obsession with him. He had long before used a similar incident to illustrate his definition of the comic in *Racine et Shakespeare*. An elegantly attired person, leaving his carriage, falls flat on his face in a puddle of mud. According to Stendhal's analysis, the comedy in this is not merely the result of the contrast between the *before* and the *after;* the spectator senses that the victim has put himself into an embarrassing and inferior position, feels a momentary superiority, and cruelly laughs.

Both this incident and the episode at Blois can of course be viewed in a number of different ways. There is the point of view of the spectator in the narration—crude, vulgar persons in both stories; there is the humiliated protagonist, sensitive to the laughter, inwardly sure of some kind of superiority, but furious that the tables have been turned; and, omitting the unknown quantity represented by the reader, there is the author himself, deliberately plotting his hero's discomfiture, ironically, perhaps even with some intention of tormenting himself and hoping that the sympathetic happy few will see through the jest.

Of the several other such incidents in Stendhal's writings, incorporating falls, mud-splattering, the laughter of onlookers, and injured pride on the part of the subject, perhaps the cruelest and the most injurious to a character's self-esteem is the fall taken by Dr. Sansfin in *Lamiel.* His frightened horse rears and throws the little hunchback head first into half a foot of mud, in full view of a group of jeering washerwomen. When Sansfin raises his muddy face, he too confronts a chorus of vulgar laughter. He then leaps furiously back on his horse and gallops away. Some of these details were also put into the account of Lucien's fall from a horse in Nancy before the window of Mme de Chasteller. There, it is true, Lucien escaped a mud-bath. Not so with Julien Sorel, who early in his stay in Paris fell from a horse and "covered himself with mud," as had the unfortunate M. de Moirod, a timid man, "fearful of both falls and ridicule." Stendhal himself confessed in the *Souvenirs d'égotisme* that he had spent his life falling from horses, and in the *Vie de Henry Brulard* he tells how he almost was thrown into the Lake of Geneva and barely escaped being humiliated before his groom.

Surely, then, with all these examples from reality and fiction, this matter of humiliation, this horrible and cruel experience of having to present a mud-splattered face to a laughing crowd, was as much "pour Dominique" as the sagest reflections on love and courtship. One might say that this experience stamps Lucien unmistakably with the mark of the Stendhalian hero. Yet, at a moment when the hero threatens to merge with the writer, Stendhal retreats. He seeks partial refuge in Coffe's coolly analytical personality and at the same time maintains an aloof objectivity. Despite his sympathy for Lucien, Stendhal amusedly watches the young hero turning "red as a rooster" and finds a perverse and ironic intellectual pleasure in pricking Lucien's sensibility to the quick.

There is not a breath of overt anti-bourgeois sentiment in this episode, but it is nevertheless a literary application of Heine's belief that, in the bourgeois nineteenth century, heroic ideas and feelings either perish or become ridiculous. (*De la France,* 1838, pp. 275-276.) In Lucien we have a man who might have behaved "heroically" in another age, under another government or even, for that matter, under Louis-Philippe, if the ambitions proper to his class, his education, and his family had not led him into a situation where heroism was absurd. Lucien's role is falsified from the start of this electoral adventure. He may behave intelligently, competently, courageously; but heroism is impossible. Once again, we might think of Don Quixote, especially as Arnold Hauser describes him, that is, as a seriocomic combination of saint and fool, humorous in a new ironic way because of his ambiguity. (*Social History of Art,* I, 398-401.) But this temptation should be resisted. Stendhal's writing is not "manneristic." He was too seriously sad and too personally involved with his age and his hero to be capable of the decorative, theatrical, and sophisticated baroque irony. There was plenty of irony, to be sure; Stendhal was outstandingly ironic, but romantically, passionately, sentimentally, even bitterly so.

The deeper moral comedy implicit in the Blois episode is confirmed and defined in two almost identical marginal comments Stendhal jotted down in the manuscript. The first is opposite the beginning of the episode: "Source of the comic, the following absurdity: Lucien wants to combine the profits from his ministerial position and the fine sensibility of a man of honor." A bit below, the comment is expanded as follows: "*General plan.*—I am constructing the backbone around which the animal will be built. The laughter will come when I get to the outermost layer of the skin. *Source of humor.*—Lucien is playing a role that covers him with contempt and doesn't know how to swallow it. He wants to combine the profits of his ministerial role and the sickly sensibility of the perfect man of honor. *Good.*" (*Lucien Leuwen,* ed. Martineau, 1945, II, 338.)

Stendhal seems to have thought so highly of this observation that, as was sometimes his habit with such notes, he incorporated it into the text several pages later, in the form of a reflection of Coffe's (which he discreetly refrains from communicating to Lucien): "See how he suffers from his absurdity. He thinks he can combine ministerial profit with the delicate sensibility of a man of honor. Is there anything sillier!"

Now, at the moment at which these events took place, Lucien was not altogether an innocent young man. He had served long enough in the Army to take the measure of its men, and, both in the employ of the Comte de Vaize and in his father's salon, had witnessed and served as a subaltern in some of the political intrigues of the time. When asked to undertake the electoral mission, he had accepted only when assured the action would be bloodless. He is thus well aware that his role is not, at least according to his own standards, an entirely honorable one. But when surprised, as he is at Blois, he reverts to a "natural" and undis-

simulated display of sincere feelings of anger and shame. His imperfectly
fitted mask slips, revealing ideals of honor and gentlemanly conduct
that are incongruous with his situation and with his role. It is this
incongruity that Stendhal labels "comic."

The narrative details of this incident are less important than the
sentimental reaction they elicit from Lucien, the evidence of his
sensibility. Stendhal in his notes stresses heavily the word *sensibility,*
qualifying it successively as "fine," "sickly," and "delicate." Let us not
be misled, however, by the apparently pejorative sense that Stendhal
gives to this word *sensibility* in a spirit of *sécheresse.* Lucien's sensibility
makes him vulnerable to mockery, but it also is his true strength and
virtue. And it is because this incident touches on Lucien's *feelings* that
it is significant. The factual historical information in Stendhal's novels
has no value for the modern historian, Léon Blum has observed; whatever truth his work has lies in what he *felt,* "in what could stir or hurt
his feelings." (*Stendhal et le Beylisme*, p. 12.) Indeed, Stendhal himself
asserted that he only wrote truthfully when his feelings were involved.
(*Vie de Henry Brulard*, ed. Martineau, 1949, I, p. 133.) In this episode,
the kind of humiliation Lucien endures is akin to feelings Stendhal
himself knew very well. When he mocks Lucien, he is to some extent
his own willing victim. But Lucien's story is not pure confession or self-
analysis. It is also the result of a problem Stendhal set himself in the
representation of contemporary reality. Stendhal's elaborated conception
of Lucien is meaningful only against the background of contemporary
society as he saw it. It is only by sharing Stendhal's view of that society
that we can understand his investing Lucien with a kind of "heroism"
that depends partly on his failure to succeed in it and on his lack of the
kind of hypocrisy Stendhal felt was necessary for such success.

A Problem in the Representation of Reality

Like all of Stendhal's heroes, Lucien Leuwen is disoriented and
unattached, a stranger in the fictional world in which he moves. His
sentimental isolation, however, is opposed to his bourgeois status, for
Lucien is a scion of the new aristocracy of the July Monarchy. "Since
July," his father tells him, "bankers have been at the head of the State.
The bourgeoisie has replaced the faubourg Saint-Germain, and bankers
are the nobility of the bourgeois class."

Thus, unlike Julien Sorel, the hero of this novel is confronted by no
important social barriers. This does not mean that in real life a banker's
son would find no doors closed to him in all France. Within the novel,
however, Lucien is rebuffed nowhere because of his origin. He is, in
fact, much sought after by provincial aristocratic hostesses and is a
highly privileged person. The *walls* of Verrières, which Mr. Turnell finds

so conspicuously symbolic in *Le Rouge,* have no counterpart here. Lucien has never had occasion to feel the savage isolation of "the unhappy man at war with all society." He has all a young man eager to be accepted by contemporary society could wish: wit, charm, beauty, intelligence, and the wealth and social position of his father.

Both Lucien's social origin and personal qualities vastly overqualify him for the bourgeoisie, as Stendhal understands the word when he expresses his horror of bourgeois pettiness and baseness and his distaste for "merchant grocers and the people with money." The loathed type of wealthy, powerful, rising bourgeois is better represented in this novel by Grandet, "the enriched ginger merchant who wants to get to be a duke," than by Lucien's cultivated, witty father, who is closer to the *haute bourgeosie* or the enlightened aristocracy of the *ancien régime* or even of the Empire.

The moral death of the aristocracy in the nineteenth century is a constant theme in the writings of Stendhal. In his opinion, the *émigré* nobility, sobered by the Revolution and uneasy despite the Restoration, lacked the courage to be witty and the energy to be passionate—a judgment that is manifest in the early pages of *Souvenirs d'égotisme* and in the second part of *Le Rouge,* when he had occasion to speak of the young noblemen of the time. "Good God!" he once exclaimed in the heat of his contempt. "How is it possible to be so insignificant! How can one depict such young men! These were questions I thought of in the winter of 1830, when I was studying these young men." (*Souvenirs d'égotisme,* ed. Martineau, 1941, p. 79; see also *Correspondance,* ed. Martineau, VII, 49.)

The problem of representing young Restoration aristocrats like Caylus and Croisenois, so despised by Mathilde de La Mole, came up again in the process of the creation of Lucien Leuwen, aristocrat of the July Monarchy bourgeoisie. The reader will recall that crucial moment when, from behind the half-opened shutters of her window, Mme de Chasteller saw Lucien fall from his horse. Commenting on the incident, Stendhal entered the following note on his manuscript: "No sudden passion, only pricked vanity. He knows that he sits a horse very well, and is irritated that this pretty woman should have seen him fall. The rich young Frenchman: (1) does not think of matters of love—his century indeed discourages him from being in love; (2) lacks the courage to love. Leuwen, the type of rich young Parisian.—No. that won't do—too stupid." (*Lucien Leuwen,* I, 299.) A firm decision, but as late as January 1835, when he was close to the end of the second part of the novel, Stendhal still betrayed uncertainty about Lucien's character. "What is Lucien's character like? Certainly not Julien's energy and originality. That is impossible in the world (of 1835 and 80,000 francs income). To suppose so is clearly unrealistic." (*Lucien Leuwen,* II, 347.)

In these irritated comments Stendhal reveals his distaste for the contemporary reality he feels he must portray. More than that, he see his
task impaling him on the horns of a dilemma. It would be "too stupid"
to make a hero out of an average rich young Parisian; but it would also
be "impossible" and "unrealistic" to endow any rich young man of 1835
with the qualities of a Julien Sorel. Stendhal has a fixed conception
(whether it is right or not is irrelevant) of the character of a particular
social or age group at a chosen historical moment: a rich young man
of the July Monarchy is dissuaded from love by his *century*. In Lucien's
social and historical situation, Julien Sorel's energy and originality are
as impossible as Mme de Rênal's character would have been "impossible
in the midst of the gay life that prevailed in France from 1715 to 1790."
(On the other hand, in Mathilde de La Mole, Stendhal did manage to
create a character who, he said, *was* impossible "in our century"—although Henri Martineau suggests that this remark was intended to
protect Marie de Neuville, one of the models for the character.) (*Le
Rouge et le noir,* ed. Garnier, p. 357; also p. 504.

Stendhal, of course, had no interest at all in creating a vulgarly "ideal"
type of hero or of indulging in the escapism of a daydream kind of novel.
In his estimation the always perfect and ravishingly handsome hero was
fit only for the taste of chambermaids, a taste he cannot be accused of
having pleased. He warned the reader of Lucien Leuwen to close the book,
if he were "bored, sad, consumptive, too noble or too rich." Although
the marginal notes reveal timidity before the public and a tactful reluctance to speak in undisguised language, Stendhal claimed dispensation
from the care of pleasing the general public, "which will consider these
pages coarse and insufficiently noble." ("Autre avertissement au lecteur,"
Lucien Leuwen, II, 313.)

It is, therefore, reasonably clear that Lucien's ambiguous status as a
hero can be partly explained by the conflict between Stendhal's wish
to make his central character a person who would be "possible" in the
upper bourgeoisie and in the time of Louis-Philippe and his conviction
that such a hero, if faithfully mirrored, would not correspond to his own
ideals of courage, originality and vigor. This conflict led him to create
a hero who, although a member and product of bourgeois society, is
not comfortable in it and is "maladjusted" and discontent in the role
assigned to him by the time and place of his birth. Although in principle
Stendhal sought to achieve "realism" in his novels, he toyed with the
idea that Lucien must be something of an anachronism. "He is not
made for his century," says M. Leuwen. No Manfred, René, or Chatter-
ton, the more subtly drawn Lucien is by virtue of his sensibility and kin-
ship with Stendhal a solitary romantic hero lost in a world to which he
does not belong. This does not really make Lucien "impossible." Lucien

feels foreign to his surroundings, but his character and behavior depend on them nonetheless. Heine maintained, we recall, that the truly "tragic poet" with his innocent belief in heroism had become an impossible anachronism, implying perhaps that "heroes" of the bourgeois present and future could be conceived only in a spirit of irony and with limited and confused sympathy. His thesis is exemplified by Stendhal's treatment of Lucien. Stendhal's narration of the action at Blois mocks Lucien's innocence and seems to turn him momentarily into a comic character. But Lucien's inability to play his part with consummate hypocrisy is funny only on one level; on another it is a betrayal of his heroic and tragic quality. Stendhal is a romantic ironist who laughs bitterly at what he respects most.

In *Dionysos, Apologie pour le théâtre,* P.-A. Touchard formulated the following difference between comedy and tragedy: "The relation between the image presented by the mirror and the spectator can be understood only within these two limiting cases: the spectator recognizes himself completely, and identifies himself with the image—or on the contrary he declines to establish this identity, denying any resemblance, any point in common. In the first case is born the tragic atmosphere; in the second, the comic. One implies participation, involvement, identification; the other, liberation, rupture, deliverance. (p. 31.) This distinction is not far from an epigram of Aldous Huxley's, "We participate in a tragedy; at a comedy we only look"—which is in turn reminiscent of Walpole's famous quip, "Life is a comedy to the man who thinks and a tragedy to the man who feels."

For those who are sensitive to what Jean-Pierre Richard calls the two essential Stendhalian climates of *sécheresse* and *tendresse, Lucien Leuwen* is simultaneously a comedy and a tragedy. In a formula Stendhal himself used in one of the prefaces he wrote for this novel, he seems to imply that he wrote a comic work with a tragic hero: *"Except for the hero's passion,* a novel must be a mirror." ("Première préface," *Lucien Leuwen* I, xxxiii. My italics.) Lucien is not entirely tragic, however. Although the participation of the reader (Stendhal) and his identification with his hero are intense, in some situations, among them the scene at Blois, the reader is also very much a spectator, and his participation is diluted, weakened or relieved by his apparent withdrawal and his refusal to "establish identity." There is a double process: maintenance of the tension of participation and temptation to be delivered of it. The result might be described, not as spontaneous and uncontrolled laughter, but as a wry, ironic smile. At such moments, Stendhal's style is richest and reaches its most appealing heights, mingling the passion, sympathy, and violence of the romantic writer with the cool, remote intelligence of the enlightened analyst.

The Duplicity of the Stendhalian Hero

Lucien Leuwen is not a story of simple and open conflict between an individualistic hero and society. Lucien undertook his electoral mission unenthusiastically, as part of a job he did not want but had accepted because it fitted the role his father wanted him to play in society. This role is illustrative of the uneasy marriage of Lucien's sentiments and his conduct, a duality that is an aspect of what we might call his "duplicity" (since *hypocrisy* may be too harsh a word). This duplicity is inseparable from the question of the Stendhalian hero's engagement in society and from the quality of his heroism.

Lucien, I have said, does not disengage himself so absolutely from society as some of the more extreme romantic heroes, Schiller's Karl Moor, for example, or Byron's Manfred or Balzac's Vautrin. He is constantly making half-hearted efforts to engage himself and to do what is expected of him. With no need to rise in society, Lucien's only strong personal ambition is the pursuit of happiness. It is neither necessary nor possible for him to behave with bourgeois prudence or to display the driving courage of a Julien Sorel. His search for a career is motivated only by his awareness that society expects him to "succeed." To please his father and in response to the challenge offered him by his cousin Ernest, Lucien undertakes, though with lukewarm enthusiasm, the task of integrating himself into a society from which he is profoundly alienated. Ernest, the successful academic bourgeois, deplores Lucien's lack of gravity, his failure to assume an air of importance and substance. "Be serious," he advises his cousin, "assume the role of a grave and earnest man." But for Lucien the role Ernest wants him to play is rather that of *un homme triste,* and, worse, he fears that once he has mastered the role, it will become a reality. Nevertheless, he accepts one part after another, in the army, in the offices of the ministry of the interior, during the electoral campaign, and in the courtship of Mme Grandet. All these roles he accepts out of a sense of duty, because they are what is expected of him.

The idea of action undertaken not for pleasure or intrinsic value, but as a response to duty, had been exposed earlier in *Le Rouge.* There the major steps toward the seduction of Mme de Rênal and Mathilde de La Mole are described as acts of courage, dutifully performed but accompanied by no thrill of pleasure. Julien's enterprises, indeed, seem much more than Lucien's the calculated gestures of a role, because the hero of *Le Rouge* is socially more insecure and more susceptible to ridicule and the fear of humiliation. Julien plots the conquest of his employer's wife so that he may not be mocked for failure to do what others might expect of him and—even more important—so that he may not despise himself. The role does later turn into reality, perhaps even according to Stendhal's elaborate formula for the development of love; nevertheless, even at the moment when Julien invades Mme de Rênal's bedroom, the idea of *duty* (Stendhal himself underlined the word) never ceases to be present in his mind. "Did I play my part well?" is the essential question he asks himself after the victory.

This "inauthenticity," as we might call it, is only one of the many aspects of Stendhalian duplicity: masks, roles, poses, diplomacy, discretion, timidity, charlatanry, and hypocrisy, as well as the corollary attributes of sincerity and *le naturel*. All these aspects are of importance in relation to the problem of the Stendhalian hero's situation in contemporary society. They also are an expression of the author's own personal insecurity and timidity. In the marginal notes of *Lucien Leuwen* one often finds the treatment of a problem in the text compared with something similar in the life of Dominique. For that matter, Stendhal's fondness for pseudonyms, anagrams, and code names (like Clara and Zotgui), and his frequent denial of personal responsibility for the statements of obviously sympathetic characters, add another dimension to the question of duplicity in his work. Moreover, we should remember that although Stendhal respected sincerity and naturalness, he was also contemptuous of naïve and blundering frankness, courageously forthright though it might be.

Stendhal felt that the exercise of hypocrisy and other modes of duplicity was a function of life in the bourgeois nineteenth century. Stendhal said once that the hypocritical Don Juan, in all his authentic vigor, was possible only in the Italy of the Renaissance. Nonetheless he called the nineteenth century "a hypocritical century" and declared the necessity of charlatanism in the degenerate time of the Restoration. "The more public opinion becomes queen in France, the more hypocrisy and *cant* there will be; that is one of the disadvantages of liberty." (*Mélanges de littérature,* II, 283.) It is evident that a contemporary hero incapable of some kind of duplicity would be defenseless, according to Stendhal. Disagreeable though the connotations of the word may be, duplicity is a means Stendhal allows the man of sensibility for coming to terms (or perhaps evading having to come to terms) with a world in which he feels apart and different.

This is also much the same conclusion reached by Victor Brombert, who, in a delicate and illuminating study of the "obliqueness" of Stendhal's style and of the oblique way in which he reveals his heroes, finds a relationship between Stendhal's own fear of the reader and Lucien's father's concern for public opinion:

> Stendhal's fear of the reader is expressed in the character of Lucien's father by his constant concern for the impression Lucien makes on social

opinion. He never ceases to repeat to his son that he must learn to play a role and carefully hide his own true self. However secretly charmed he may be by Lucien's naïveté and by his "extravagances," he is afraid of unveiling his true feelings, but fears even more that Lucien will seem ridiculous in the eyes of others. Doubly vulnerable through Lucien, he instills in him the need for wearing a mask. Is not hypocrisy the only way of keeping one's independence in a hostile world? (*Stendhal et la voie oblique*, pp. 78-79.)

Lucien Leuwen does not have the kind of courage that has made other men shake their fist at the universe and defy their adversaries. He fits a series of masks to his face and flees into exile at the end. Already at Blois, he has a sense of being trapped by his own life. "I've done things wrongly all my life," he keeps repeating to Coffe, "I'm in a mudhole and there's no way out." But even Julien Sorel, with all his aggressiveness and calculation, cannot bring himself to define his situation honestly and lucidly until after he has been condemned to death. Then, at last, like the present-day hero of Camus's *L'Etranger*, who is also "liberated" by being condemned to death, he asserts openly his final and absolute opposition to a world in which he does not belong.

Julien is in a special situation, different from that of either Stendhal or Lucien. He is constantly on the defensive, in fear of the reprisals that revelation of his true sentiments might provoke. He learned the use of hypocrisy as a weapon of defense early in his childhood, to combat the ridicule, abuse, and brutal blows of his father and his elder brothers. Julien's rise from his peasant origins was at each step an assault upon a new bastion of society. In his subordinate position, at the Rênals' in Verrières, in the seminary at Besançon, and in the Hôtel de La Mole, he was at all times susceptible to hidden and sometimes nonexistent affronts; he imagined that those around him, jealous of their superior position, were constantly plotting to humiliate him and keep him in his place. Julien's hypocrisy is therefore doubly inspired: it is an attack, calculated to further his aggressive movement toward worldly success; but it is also a protective mechanism, the product of fear and insecurity.

Yet, sometimes the mask slips and uncovers the "natural" Julien beneath it. He is "himself" when he complains to the Abbé Pirard of his boredom at the dinner table in the Hôtel de La Mole and when he speaks with Altamira at the Duc de Retz's ball. On both occasions (and this by Stendhal's careful design, as he charts the course of Mathilde's passion), he is overheard by Mathilde. Both times, Julien's value rises in her esteem. To Mathilde, who, like Stendhal, despises the men of her time and class and judges Julien by standards she has derived from history, his secret character, proud, passionate and uncompromising, is a revelation of his true superiority.

Julien keeps his true thoughts and feelings secret from his father and brothers. Among them he is, as Dr. Sansfin says to the young Lamiel, "surrounded by coarse creatures to whom one must always lie in order not to be the victim of the brutal force they have at their command." He must make use of hypocrisy and charlatanism to succeed among the calculating bourgeois and timid aristocrats of the Restoration. His "real" qualities, those Stendhal himself admires, win the love of Mathilde, who, the author declares, is "impossible" in the nineteenth century. But, ironically, Julien does not dare to be sincere with her. Although she is won by his courage, his pride and his passion—qualities that must remain hidden to the world—Mathilde would be intolerant of his timidity, his fears and his anxiety. He is capable of pleasing Mathilde *naturally* when he does not know she is observing him, but alone with her, he must counterfeit a temperament that is not his own in order to please her special taste for being dominated and humiliated by her lover.

Julien is only really liberated from the practice of hypocrisy when he has nothing more to gain and nothing more to lose. In the courtroom at Besançon, before a jury of "indignant bourgeois," who he thinks will surely condemn him, he attacks their *caste* and denounces the suppression of the poor. In his cell he reaches the conclusion—Stendhal's own—that in his time almost everyone is and must be a hypocrite. What he had earlier taken for a particular he now recognizes as a universal. Even Napoleon, he decides, was a charlatan. " 'I have loved truth. . . . Where is it? . . . Everywhere there is hypocrisy or at least charlatanism, even among the most virtuous, even among the greatest.' His lips curled with disgust. . . . 'No! Man cannot put his trust in man.' "

The shadings of Lucien Leuwen's character are subtler and more delicate. Julien Sorel had been conditioned to be aware of his duplicity and had consciously (though unhappily) embraced hypocrisy as the only means suited both to his ends and to his situation. Lucien's comfortably secure place in society, on the contrary, did not require a posture of defense. Launched upon his career, Lucien is surprised and disgusted to discover that his new roles put him into ambiguous situations to which his childhood and adolescence had not accustomed him. It is important to recognize that he is not *naturally* a hypocrite (any more than Julien Sorel is and that duplicity is not such an ingrained habit that it has become an essential part of his character. Comparing Lucien with her circle of friends in Nancy, Mme de Chasteller realizes that, like herself, he is tender, sincere, and ardent. This is Stendhal's own judgment: "She knows Leuwen and perceives *that he is not a hypocrite.*" (Note at the head of the first volume of the manuscript; see *Lucien Leuwen*, II, 318.)

Stendhal is very careful to limit Lucien's exercise of hypocrisy in love. The young hero's courtship of Mme Grandet is a calculated act, but undertaken reluctantly and abandoned when Lucien is at the very threshold of victory. He toys with the affections of Mme d'Hocquincourt, but is determined not to let her become his mistress. "He does everything needed for her to adore him," Stendhal writes in a marginal note. "He forces himself to play this comedy, but swears never to possess her. One day, tempted after a very emotional scene, he runs away. Lucien plays at *rouerie;* it is his only pastime."

There is admittedly a complication introduced by the charlatanism Lucien practices when he pretends to a piety and to political beliefs that are abhorrent to him. He does this to obtain admission to the society of Mme de Chasteller. But this is not part of a Don Juanish seduction. It is love and not merely the desire for physical conquest that motivates his hypocrisy. He knows that Wertheresque love may be impotent if Don Juanish techniques are not employed to insure its success. Yet, Lucien can not play the part of a Don Juan. He lacks the talent. He is embarrassed and awkward in Mme de Chasteller's presence and incapable of abusing the advantages he has secured by his entrance into Nancy society under false pretenses.

Stendhal himself, we know, had complicated feelings about the great European myth of Don Juan. He was obsessed by the concept of the Don Juan type of character and found a troubling correlation between Don Juan's success in love and his cynical, polished hypocrisy. Stendhal admired Don Juan as an embodiment of some traits of his personal image of the Renaissance man, bold, vigorous, and cunning; but he also despised him for his insincerity and was jealous of his success. In Stendhal (and in Lucien Leuwen) the sensibility and the virtue of Werther are dominant traits. Don Juan's libertine competence and success were impossible for Dominique and his hero, whose delicacy and timidity reward them simultaneously with a feeling of superiority and with frustration and regret. Like Valéry's Narcissus, Stendhal might well have said of his *inépuisable moi:* "J'y trouve un tel trésor d'impuissance et d'orgueil."

Stendhal:
The Politics of Survival

by Irving Howe

While Henry James was working on *The Princess Casamassima* he remarked in a letter that the English upper class "seems to me to be in many ways very much the same rotten and *collapsible* one as the French aristocracy before the revolution—minus the cleverness and conversation. . . ." About the cleverness and conversation Stendhal might have had a caustic phrase, but he would certainly have accepted James' description of the English ruling class; as far back as 1819 he had written that he "hoped to have the joy of beholding a revolution in England." Stendhal was not, in any modern sense, a revolutionist or even a radical, yet he instinctively placed himself in alliance with the revolutions of his day: they gave him joy.

He stands in the sharpest contrast to those novelists of the nineteenth century who turn, somewhat later, to political themes. When Dostoevski, Conrad, and James take revolutionary politics as their subject, they write partly in order to arouse the educated public to the dangers stirring beneath the "vast smug surface" (as James called it) of society. They do this in various ways: Dostoevski by wrestling with political ideas, Conrad by forcing himself to confront the political milieu, James by divining certain problems of the political vocation. Involuntarily, they watch the coming-apart of the world to which they are emotionally bound. Antipathetic to radicalism, they lay bare the sources of its growing power. Alien to its style of life, they penetrate its central dilemmas in both experience and ideology. And even when their opinions spur them to vindictiveness or malice, they emerge as true witnesses.

Stendhal, however, is indifferent to their pieties. The Enlightenment that Dostoevski abhors is for him the era to which one can return with most pleasure; the God for whom Dostoevski yearns he treats as an hypothesis to be cheerfully dismissed; the stable and respectable morality toward which Conrad strives he spends a lifetime violating; the tone of massive solemnity James assumes in old age he mocks in his late writings even more than in his early. He is, in the best sense of the word, a dubious character.

And, one must quickly add, an enigmatic writer. No other modern novelist has so consistently approached political life in terms that so consistently evade political categories. Every page of his work is crowded with politics, but if you try to formulate his *position* you find that he has slipped past your fingers, as he slips past all his critics, and now stands at a disrespectful distance, thumbing his nose. Stendhal is not an ideologue in the manner of Dostoevski nor even a novelist of ideas; nonetheless, ideology and ideas swarm through his books. Living at the time he does Stendhal cannot avoid them, short of risking irrelevance; he juggles political notions with the reckless good fortune of the gifted amateur; but in the end he proves to be a profoundly nonpolitical man. It need only be added that in the time in which he lives, as in the whole modern era, the nonpolitical temper implies a political choice: and what is more, Stendhal, unlike many writers who follow him, knows this.

I

Though mentioned only casually in his novels, and then in accents of ambiguous humor, as a bogey disturbing the sleep of frightened monarchists, the French Revolution is the dominant force in Stendhal's novels. His adult life was spent in the backwash of the revolution, at a time when the monarchists tried, with a conspicuous lack of conviction, to restore what was forever gone and the republicans, exhausted by the fury of their own regime, lacked the strength to claim their historical privilege. The revolutionary leaders were dead, the revolutionary wave had passed, the revolutionary ethos had become corrupted; but the work of the revolution remained. Politically, the bourgeoisie could be made to suffer temporary defeat; socially, its rule was secure.

The modern hero, the man who forces society to accept him as its agent—the hero by will rather than birth—now appears for the first time: and he carries with him the disease of ambition, which flourishes among those who are most committed to the doctrine of equality and spreads all the deeper as the restored Bourbons try to suppress that doctrine. Before the revolution men had been concerned with privileges, not expectations; now they dream of success, that is, of a self-willed effort to lift oneself, through industry or chicanery, to a higher social level. Life becomes an experiment in strategy, an adventure in plan, ruse, and combat; the hero is not merely ambitious but sensitive to the point of paranoia, discovering and imagining a constant assault upon his dignity;

and Stendhal carries this outlook to its extreme limit, perhaps even to caricature, by applying it to affairs of love.

The great political problem of Stendhal's time is not really how to be rid of the Bourbon restoration of Louis-Philippe's bourgeois monarchy; both are certain to fall of their own rottenness, as the most acute minds of France, Stendhal included, quickly realize. Rather is the problem one of finding a viable order with which to replace these mediocre monarchs. The ideology of liberalism, which had inspired the boldest Frenchmen during the past half century, has now entered a state of permanent crisis from which it cannot escape, except by an act of self-transcendence. So long as the liberals had been powerless, struggling in common peril to destroy the *ancien régime,* liberalism could assume the appearance of unity: it could seem to be, and indeed be, a great energizing force by which men could at last come into the open air of freedom. But once in power, liberalism must crumble into the conflicting purposes it has concealed; behind the exalted motto of Liberty, Fraternity, Equality there cross a great many less exalted social interests. The successive stages of the French Revolution represent less a curve of temperament or blood-thirst than a clash of view on how far to extend the revolution. This quarrel repeats itself in all later versions of liberalism, the original innocence of the Encyclopedists being quite beyond recovery; a temporary façade of unity may be erected in moments of danger but it is only temporary and only a façade; liberalism, even as it continues to speak for humanity as a whole, is now at war with itself.

In his little book on Stendhal, Léon Blum suggests a similar idea. Stendhal, he writes, "is the man of confused moments, social inter-mixtures, periods of disorder . . . each time that, through natural historical developments, social classes find themselves mixed together at their surface but separated at their foundations, large groups of young people will be placed in the same equivocal position" as Stendhal's heroes. Stendhal, that is to say, is a writer of the moment when a great historical experience has reached its point of exhaustion.

Such a writer can no longer believe in the unity of society, neither the unity claimed by those in power, which is patently a fraud, nor the unity envisaged by those in opposition, which now seems distant and chimerical. In the novel he finds his most formidable means of criticism, for it is through the novel that the problem of society in conflict with the individual receives its fullest exploration. In all of Stendhal's novels the process of social division is shown to have gone very far, each character being highly conscious that his allegiance belongs less to society as such than to some embattled segment of it.

Nor can Stendhal place much hope in the unity of the people, certainly nothing like the hope felt during the revolution, for he sees the people—or as we would now say, the masses—in their phase of lassitude and despair. He does not harbor that mean contempt for the masses which will be expressed by Flaubert; he is not hostile, and when they stir to action, in the 1830 revolution, he becomes lyrical in his praise of their capacities ("The lowest rabble," he writes to Sutton Sharpe, "was heroic, and after the battle was full of the noblest generosity"); but the *mystique* of the plebes, the emotion of democracy seldom reached him in uncontrollable abundance. Like intellectuals of a later age Stendhal feels that the hope placed in the people has proved to be unwarranted; he hardly recognizes that this disappointment is itself a sign of how much the people, exhausted though they may now be, have changed the shape of history in the preceding decades.

Stendhal's cult of energy follows logically from his gradual loss of belief in the unity of society or the redemptive power of the people, yet it would be quite impossible without the immediate memory of the revolution. It is an energy he attributes to the exceptional man, the hero who surmounts history rather than the people who bear it. His political Bonapartism and his aesthetic notion of "the happy few" are closely related to the cult of energy as well as to each other, all three involving an opposition to aristocracy *and* democracy, privilege *and* equality. Taken in political terms and perhaps not only in political terms, the cult of energy implies some motivating sense of desperation, a need to assert, rather too emphatically, the values of social and intellectual fluidity.

Stendhal, I have said, is not a systematic thinker, but in his appreciation of Napoleon he shows far greater insight than many historians. The common notion that he was a mere idolator of Napoleon is absurd; he attacks Napoleon for dickering with the Jesuits, and even more for becoming a despot. "In France," he writes, "the despotism of Napoleon was most poisonous; he feared the works and the memory of the republic, over which the people stood guard; he hated the old enthusiasm of the Jacobins." But Stendhal would have immediately rejected the view that Napoleon is the first of the modern totalitarian rulers, for he sensed that Napoleon had meaning in terms of the past rather than the future, as a glorious historical memory rather than a possible national revival. *Le Rouge et le noir* constantly stresses the contrast between the loathesomeness of the society through which Julien Sorel must rise and the heroic spontaneity of the lost Napoleonic age. *La Chartreuse de Parme* opens with a quick reference to Napoleon's triumph in Italy—and critics have wondered what place this passage, as well as the long description of Fabrice at Waterloo, has in the novel. Both seem to me indispensable, for the book has as a central purpose to demonstrate the difficulty and tedium of trying to survive now that Napoleon is gone. The Waterloo episode, particularly Fabrice's famous inability to decide whether he has been in battle, is marvellous not merely for its direct graphic power but also as a way of showing that the young hero can no longer connect with—can no longer find a place or a meaning in—the Napoleonic experience. Fabrice's journey is a flight backward, into the radiant past; it does not succeed; its not succeeding is a condition for all that follows in the novel.

Stendhal realized that Napoleon took his meaning from the revolution: he betrayed its libertarian ethos and consolidated its property relations. But while criticizing Napoleon for becoming a despot, he also realized that under Napoleon there was still a chance for the ambitious young man, for the young man from the provinces whose father is a stuffy monarchist unwilling to allow his son a sufficient allowance for comfort in Paris. Napoleon perpetuates the bourgeois principle of social mobility: corporals do become marshals; and in the era of reaction that roughly parallels Stendhal's mature life, the loss of this principle seems very costly indeed. At the same time Stendhal betrays no hope whatever that Bonapartism can be revived; he senses that for France at least the age of bourgeois glory is at an end. "The shape of our civilization," he complains in 1831, "precludes great movements, or anything resembling passion." As a statement of the immediate condition this is entirely right, as a prediction it is remarkably wrong.

Stendhal ends with only the dimmest political hope or perspective. The idea of society, the memory of Napoleon, faith in the masses, the claims of liberalism—none will quite do. Nor does he know anything of the hopes that for a time will buoy later writers: the vision of socialism, the idea of a pure aesthetic. "Born too late or too early," says Arnold Hauser, "Stendhal stands between the times, just as he stands between the classes."

Not above the classes, as his admirers sometimes like to suppose, but apart from them. And that may be why he finds it so desirable to identify himself with the Encyclopedists, who were hardly obliged to think of social classes at all. Stendhal's admiration for the Encyclopedists implies an effort to construct a *pure* liberalism, a liberalism not yet tarnished by history, a liberalism of concept to set off against the liberalism of practise, which he rightly finds both timid and absurd. (It is surely no accident that among the political movements of his day he feels closest to the Carbonari who, because they are still fighting to unify their nation, can with some justice retain the heroic tone of a unified and classless liberalism.) That Stendhal finally arrives at an intellectual impasse may follow from his occasional faint awareness that the political idea of liberalism, once put into practice, can hardly avoid social squalor and disintegration. His feeling for the Encyclopedists is consequently a romantic—a nostalgic—feeling, despite the fact that they were far from being romantics and he, as a literary craftsman, is an opponent of romanticism.

Stendhal's relationship to romanticism is extremely complicated and is made still more complicated by the ambiguity of the movement and the sheer contrariness of his own mind. Insofar as romanticism involves a celebration of the individual ego breaking past the previous limits of history, Stendhal is a romantic. Its rebellion against the "materialism" of early capitalist society is also congenial to him, though he does not seem to be aware that the assumptions behind this rebellion are themselves grounded in the rise of capitalism. But insofar as romanticism involves the idealizing of one or another pre-capitalist society, Stendhal demurs; and when it degenerates into a wilful inflation of language and emotion, he stands firm by the Roman style of the republic and Napoleon.

If what I have been saying has any truth, it follows that Stendhal occupies a central position in Western intellectual history (not thought): he is one of the first creative writers to look upon politics and society from the exclusive standpoint of the intelligentsia, one of the first to measure history by its effects on the intellectuals as a special, marginal and imperilled group. The dream of "the happy few"—which will soon turn into the nightmare of the artist's alienation—remains the one indestructible buttress of his life. In many respects he is a déclassé; in the most honorable sense of the word he is a dilettante; and in the absence of any large sustaining faith—for it is significant that in all his novels liberalism, gasping in defeat, is feared because of its past rather than its power—he begins to speak, somewhat like Byron though with greater seriousness, for those in the modern world who feel themselves estranged and "homeless." The letters of his final years are crowded with sentences such as one might expect to find in the notebooks of twentieth-century intellectuals. "Ideas," he writes, "are the bugaboos of people in power." And "people in power hate people whose words get printed." His last, unfinished novel *Lamiel,* far from being the customary gesture of reconciliation by which writers are expected to usher themselves out of the world, is the wildest and most preposterous, indeed the most anarchistic, of his books. In this fragment Stendhal recreates his typical situation in extreme terms: a hero is forced by a sluggish society to break its bounds of decorum and law, only the hero proves to be a heroine who discovers in a few quick pages the venality of official politics, the banality of official love, the pervasiveness of boredom and the possible pleasures of playing the female castrator. Each of Stendhal's novels takes him further away from respectable society; his opinions mellow but his work toughens; his basic feeling is that for people like himself there is no longer any place: people, that is, who value ideas and conversation.

To the extent that they deal with politics, Stendhal's novels ask one question over and over again: how can we—we Europeans of cultivated tastes—survive in this era of cant and reaction? It is a question not entirely irrelevant to our time, and Stendhal's answer, insofar as he has one, may be summarized in a single word: ruse. Not hypocrisy; not what is often and ignorantly meant by machiavellianism; but ruse, the strategy of having one's cake and eating it, being both a rebel and a *bon vivant,* deceiving society to undermine it and wooing society to enjoy it. Because of this complex and, at times, ambivalent point of view, Stendhal proves more satisfactory than most writers on that difficult political problem, the relation of ends to means: if nothing else, he abstains from moralizing. His books have been called devil's manuals for machiavellian rulers, but they are nothing of the sort: they are really devil's manuals for men in revolt at a time when there is no possibility of revolt. Stendhal had only a limited sense of society but he had a superb sense of history and an especially superb sense of his particular moment; he measured with the greatest realism the extent of European reaction during his time; and what some critics call his "silly mystifications," those strategems by which he tried to outwit Metternich's police, may have been, at least in motive, not quite so silly. He knew that in this age the great problem for men of intelligence was simply to survive, and to survive without becoming fanatics or flunkeys. Only now, from the distance of a century, can we fully credit the seriousness behind the silliness.

What complicates Stendhal's politics still further, and his novels as well, is that he recognizes no precise boundary between political and private categories, he allows each to dissolve into the other but not to destroy one another. Unable to solve the crisis of liberalism, he evades it by abstracting from the liberal position a code, a style of life, a vision of joyousness—it is one of the most glorious evasions in literary history, though his belief in the possibility of such an evasion marks Stendhal as a man of the pre-totalitarian age. Liberalism is elevated from a politics into a personal strategy, a way of outwitting the dullards who control things; rationalism is flipped onto its back and made to proclaim a recognition of its own limits, of the presence in human life of phenomena that hardly conform to its orderly procedures. Against the stabilized hypocrisy of society Stendhal exalts the insubordinate freedom of the person, what he calls *espagnolisme,* the vitality of instinct and emotion which creates a valid order of its own, brushing aside both morality and convention. To trick society you must employ ruse, but the energy that makes ruse possible comes from *espagnolisme.* Stendhal thinks of it primarily as a private endowment, but in all his novels it plays a political role: it motivates the rebellion of the favored characters and still more important, it defeats their rebellion, upsets their plans, renders their ruse unsuccessful. *Espagnolisme* in Stendhal's novels represents the triumph of emotion over ideology, of humane impulse over calculated cleverness. Stendhal's heroes are always advised to calculate and he himself seems always to concur in this advice; yet his greatest joy is in seeing calculations undone, even those of which he approves, the calculations of his insurgent heroes.

It is characteristic of Stendhal that even his praise of spontaneity should be highly calculated—though, by way of further bedevilment, one must add that his machiavellian ruses are often disarmingly playful and innocent. No writer who admires elegance as much as Stendhal does, can be long content with spontaneity as a principle of existence. His very admiration for elegance, however, reveals his political predicament, for elegance is a quality likely to be most admired in a static society: neither Danton nor Napoleon was elegant. Stendhal is one of the first modern writers to raise elegance to a political virtue and yet remain—it is the mixture of the two that one finds so impressive—quite free from the usual kinds of snobbism. Stendhal does not suppose that elegance and cultivation are confined to any social class and he is quite certain that they are largely absent from the class in which they are supposed to bulk largest; but he fears that these qualities must, in the nature of things, be limited to a marginal elite, "the happy few"—and this anticipation of the artist's loneliness in a mass society becomes all the sharper as Stendhal learns to accept his situation as a great writer barely recognized in his time. His books are full of ambiguous and frequently funny references to America: he greatly admires the democratic statesmen, particularly Jefferson, yet feels he could not live here: imagine, a country without culture or conversation! His criticism of America, often similar to Tocqueville's, deserves to be taken seriously, but it should not be assumed that Stendhal was serious each time he made it. He admires the liberal idea but shrinks from democratic fraternity; the warmth he feels for the people is genuine but he would just as soon feel it from a distance; all of his liberal impulses are modified and complicated by the extent to which he retains deep attachments to the French past. His liberalism, in short, is that of a man who is the product of an old society. When Lucien Leuwen says, "I need the pleasures provided by an ancient civilization," he speaks for Stendhal.

The very patterns of Stendhal's prose seem emblematic of his political situation. In all of his novels there frequently occurs a sentence structure that Stendhal has made his own: it begins with a limited statement and after an intervening colon or semi-colon proceeds to a second statement that is not so much a development from the first as an oblique or ironic comment on it. Ordinarily the colon is a bridge, here it is a chasm. Stendhal's construction controverts his claim to spontaneity, it is perfectly adapted to his passion for "the sublime unexpected," which also means, to his position as a cultivated and skeptical liberal. The assertions of Rousseauian liberalism have here been transformed into a complex but still subversive wit.

Stendhal is a unique intellectual figure and a unique novelist. His vision of the good life is essentially Nietzsche's—minus the philosopher's neurotic swagger; both hope for an intellectual "superman"—though Stendhal is free of the confusions that attach themselves to Nietzsche's use of the phrase; their ideas as to style, though not their styles, are very similar; and the interplay of Dionysian and Apollonian elements Nietzsche was later to call for is already achieved in Stendhal's work. Above all, the Nietzschian conception of the Good European—the man of superior cultivation, liberal tastes and disinterested humaneness—is anticipated in Stendhal. Summed up in a phrase, Stendhal's politics are the politics of the Good European.

II

Le Rouge et le noir is a novel about politics in an era which makes politics impossible. Though felt throughout the book as a directing energy, politics is seldom directly visible, except in the chapter where the nobles scheme to cauterize their country by entrusting it to English mercies. The society of *Le Rouge et le noir* is not totalitarian, it enforces conformity through pressures rather than terrors. It is a society of pall even more than of fear, though its fear of the immediate past, of that free play of politics it has dedicated itself to suppress, is more than acute. In the absence of freedom, the political impulse takes the shape of ambition or hatred or banditry: all three stir in Julien Sorel. The book suggests, among other things, the price that must be paid when politics is eliminated from the surface of social life, and as such might be read with belated profit by those literary people who fancy themselves above the "dirt" of politics.

Stendhal shows politics incarnated in non-political behavior, the struggle of the classes at a time when they lay dormant, crushed into a stupor of reconciliation. Nothing can appear directly in the world of this novel, nothing can be said openly: politics must break through in the guise of appetites, manners, and sex. Julien Sorel is a man conducting a secret war against society, and a war that confuses him so much, for he has no firm base in principle, that he spends half his time conducting it against his mistresses and himself; he represents the militant phase of Stendhal's policy of ruse, but a militancy that has lost its meaning with the defeat of the Jacobins. He is, as Stendhal says, "an unhappy man at war with all of society" but he cannot make proper distinctions among the various elements of society. He tells himself, "I will not follow the bourgeois, middle-of-the-road way of life, I seek rather some revolutionary exaltation," but this very exaltation, coming as it does in an age of social retreat, tempts him into crime. (Stendhal would have agreed with Oscar Wilde's remark that in the nineteenth century only the lower classes retain enough energy for crime.) Julien is the stranger in a hostile world but the stranger who no longer knows what he wants, who lacks, as Stendhal says, "the courage to be sincere." He is visited by libertarian emotions, he has moments of genuine compassion, but his major complaint against society is that it cramps him: he is bitter, above all, because it will not allow him to abandon, and perhaps betray, his own class.

The world as it presents itself to Julien Sorel is a battlefield: the battle has been fought and lost. Yet the image of warfare is crucial, for in no other nineteenth-century novel is there such a formulated awareness that society has broken into warring classes. Every character in the book identifies himself with a special interest. "Between the liberty of the press and our existence as gentlemen," says M. de La Mole, spokesman for the nobles, "there is war to the knife." M. Rênal, the rising bourgeois, cannot tolerate the thought that his rival has purchased two horses, and he finds relief only by hiring a tutor. That is the arithmetic of the bourgeois: two horses equals one tutor. And Julien himself, who thinks like a strange blend of Byron and Marx, begins his final speech to the jury almost—this seems to me a key to the novel—as if he were a *political* prisoner: "Gentlemen, I have not the honor to belong to your class. . . ." If Julien could be transported to the Russia of a half century later, he would be a terrorist; given the necessity for living in Restoration France, which he can neither accept nor resist, he is hero, madman, clown. At the end he submits to his death in the consciousness, again like a political martyr, that he has already become a symbol.

The suppressed politics of *Le Rouge et le noir* breaks out as hatred, class hatred; and while *Lucien Leuwen* is not nearly so fierce a book, there too the hardening of classes is a major theme. "In the provinces," writes Stendhal in that uncompleted novel, "there is no longer the slightest communication between hostile classes." But the theme of class relations does not receive so harmonious a rendering in *Lucien Leuwen* as in the two great novels. The first volume of *Lucien Leuwen* lists too heavily toward a Stendhalian romance, the second is overweighted with political detail, and the fusion of these two elements, actually the two sides of Stendhal's creative activity, is never quite achieved.

The novel returns, though at a lower pitch of intensity, to Stendhal's theme: "the quarrel that afflicts the Nineteenth Century [is] the resentment of rank against merit." But the social disintegration portrayed in *Le Rouge et le noir* has here gone much further: under Louis-Philippe's bourgeois monarchy neither royalists nor republicans are happy, government has passed into the hands of finance, the reactionaries have become grotesque and the radicals impotent. Money reigns; passion dies. Stenhal's contempt for this epoch is remarkably similar to that of Marx in his little book, *Class Struggles in France,* except that Marx writes with sarcasm and Stendhal in the tone of opéra-bouffe. Society has become a farce; nothing deserves to be taken seriously by men of intelligence. Stendhal is drawing further and further away from the society of his day, despite his expert verisimilitude in mirroring its surface; and the greater his distance the more he relies on comedy.

Those scenes in the second volume which detail the political corruption of the bourgeois monarchy, while vivid in themselves, lack the support from the rest of the novel that such scenes must have. Stendhal's sense of class relations operates primarily on the political level, while a novel like *Lucien Leuwen,* which ventures a tour of the social orders, needs a range of material that can be had only by plunging below the political level and into the recesses of the city. For this Stendhal, whether or not he had the gift, clearly lacked the patience; the social novel, in the sense that Balzac's may be so described, is not his forte; he prefers to hurry across the surface of society rather than break through it. Instinctively, Stendhal suspects Balzac's strategy of composition, just as he would have suspected, had he known it, Marx's sociology; for both Balzac and Marx, being committed to the nineteenth century in a way Stendhal is not, employ, as he cannot, the method of penetration in depth. Yet *Lucien Leuwen,* by reason of its structure, requires precisely this kind of penetration in depth—in any case: Stendhal will not make this mistake again.

III

La Chartreuse de Parme signifies Stendhal's most complete removal from the contemporary scene and his most complete triumph over it; the novel is the fullest expression of his alienation from the age—and of his refusal to be crippled by that alienation. Parma belongs neither to the nineteenth century nor, as some critics have argued, to the era of Machiavelli; it is an abstraction from time and place, a small-scale model of autocratic government; here politics, by a paradox that lies at the heart of Stendhal's greatness, takes on both the representative directness of a parable and the stylized extravagance of an opera.

Most novelists who turn to politics—I think especially of Conrad— tend to look upon it as an obstacle the world throws across the path of happiness. Stendhal too sees politics in this way, but his view and his manner of reaching it are far more complex. Politics keeps Count Mosca and the Duchess Sanseverina from the happiness within their immediate reach, it keeps Fabrice from running off with his dear little Clélia; politics is that force of the world which distracts men from their most decent instincts; but it is also something else which only Stendhal and Dostoevski among the nineteenth century novelists quite realize: it is an

outlet for the very passions it suppresses, it is not merely an obstacle to
the will but also a challenge, not merely the occasion for meanness but,
sometimes, for heroism.

The range of political behavior in Parma is narrow: there are no real
parties, ideas are suspect, the people are dumb, and the monarch, while
not an absolute ruler, has enough power so that his whim can shape the
daily lives of his ministers and his court. It is symptomatic of Stendhal's
growing disenchantment with the world of affairs—*La Chartreuse* occupies a place in his literary development somewhat similar to that of
The Tempest in Shakespeare's—that throughout the novel he treats
power in its aspect of pettiness, as a craven absurdity on the part of those
who employ it, a constant threat to intelligent men, and a certain corruption for weak ones. Power is something one must learn to evade or
soften, to escape from or make a truce with. Repeatedly the major
characters concern themselves with the problem that was to absorb
Stendhal throughout his later years: how to gull one's rulers. Stendhal's
attitude toward power is not that of the man at the top of the social
heap or at the bottom of it, but rather of the man on its margin.

The three central figures represent three possible attitudes toward, and
distances from, social power. Mosca manipulates it while privately
holding it to be a farce; Sanseverina tolerates it but is always ready to
oppose it with the full force of her personal desires; Fabrice bends to it
with the bow of the courtier and cleric but remains fundamentally
indifferent to its claims. Stendhal shares in all these attitudes, but in
none exclusively.

Mosca is a man who believes in the durability, if not the wisdom, of
the social world. In his youth he had fought with Napoleon's armies,
now "I dress up like an actor in a farce to win a great social position and
a few thousand francs a year." The key word is *farce,* which Mosca
repeatedly uses in speaking of the events at Parma—a clue, seldom taken
up, that Stendhal offers his readers. Mosca has had to accommodate
himself to the world but he does not accept its cant. He knows that
when he conducts the nightly search for assassins beneath the bed of
Ernest IV, not only is the monarch ridiculous but he too is ridiculous.
The burdens of power do not rest easily upon him: he finds it grueling
simply to keep his face pitched at the proper solemnity; and he knows
that the continual prudence his political position requires from him
must sap his energy both as public figure and private person. He is brave
but not heroic, intelligent but not creative. He has no illusion that he
is covering himself with glory or goodness, and like many men who are
not very cynical yet feel obliged to accept tasks they intensely dislike,
he affects a pose of cynicism by means of which he can anticipate,
overstate, and disarm the criticism that may be brought against him.
For he knows the ways of the world: when Fabrice suggests that he be

tried by "magistrates judging according to their conscience," Mosca replies with devastating mildness, "You would oblige me greatly . . . if you would give me the addresses of such magistrates; I shall write to them before I go to bed."

Mosca has high standards of personal honor and he knows that in his trade, as in his world, they cannot very well remain unbruised; but his great difficulty—it is this which almost ruins him—is that having lost the liberal élan of his youth he now thinks about the mechanics of government rather than the purpose of government. He is not power-drunk, he does not wish to hurt or humiliate anyone, he exerts himself to keep Ernest IV from outraging his office, but he acts from stray impulse rather than moral conviction. Mosca is a good man, but a good man without belief. He can never resist the temptation—it is the *professional's* temptation—of showing the monarch he despises how to carry out his despicable policies; he tells Ernest IV, for example, that the problem of the insurgent Carbonari can be met either by slaughtering ten thousand rebels or by making popular concessions. The advice is intelligent, we are quite sure which of these two courses Mosca prefers, and it seems likely that he has exaggerated the number of necessary victims in order to persuade Ernest IV toward leniency; but the trouble is that Mosca thinks purely in terms of "statecraft," banishing from his line of vision those more fundamental problems of value which would require him to start from a *judgment* of the Carbonari. Mosca's theory of governing, like Machiavelli's theory of government from which it derives, works well enough in periods of social equilibrium, when class relations are relatively stable, the masses are politically dormant and politics can therefore be narrowed to the art of maneuver and arrangement. Mosca does not realize, though Stendhal sometimes does, that all of his delicate calculations can be destroyed, on the one side, by the explosion of personal passions and, on the other, by the intervention of class movements. It is a mistake characteristic of those who like to think of administrative politics as a "science."

Numerous critics have said that in Mosca Stendhal was embodying a machiavellian vision of politics; Arnold Hauser, one of the best social critics of our time, writes that Stendhal's novels are "courses of instruction in political amoralism" and cites with approval Balzac's remark that *La Chartreuse* is the novel Machiavelli would have written had he lived in, and been banished from, the Italy of the nineteenth century. There is such an odd mixture of truth and error in these statements that it may be worth a brief digression to glance at Machiavelli himself, who is indeed, though not in the way usually supposed, an ancestor of Stendhal.

Like Stendhal, Machiavelli was a liberal at a time when liberalism was in rout. He believed that the best form of government was a republic, and in his *Discourses on Livy,* a far more important book than *The*

Prince, he formulated ideas about democratic government that remain valuable to this day. "In every republic," he writes, "there are two parties, that of the nobles and that of the people; and all the laws that are favorable to liberty result from the opposition of these parties to each other." Still more impressive: "Nothing renders a republic more firm and stable than to organize it in such a way that the excitement of the ill-humors that agitate a state may have a way prescribed by law for venting itself." At the same time Machiavelli, as a patriot, passionately desired the unification of Italy; otherwise, his beloved Florence would remain helpless before assaults from the north. He believed that Italy could be unified only under a prince, and his famous book is a guide, mainly serious but not without irony, for that prince. Machiavelli recognized that in politics there can be no easy correspondence between ends and means, and much of *The Prince* is occupied with saying: *If* you wish to achieve this end, you must use these means; but this does not mean that Machiavelli was "amoral," it merely indicates that he was honest enough to face the difficulty of adjusting political behavior to moral precepts. When he writes that "to use deceit in any action is detestable, nevertheless in conducting war it is praiseworthy and glorious," he irks us, first, because of the possibility that he is being ironic at our expense and second, because he is telling a kind of truth. Given war, deceit is necessary; given politics, which is often a mild form of war, intrigue is likely. Those who righteously condemn Machiavelli usually dislike him for preaching what they practice, and more, for describing what they practice.

Nonetheless, there *is* a difficulty in making out Machiavelli's thought, I mean in reconciling his two sides, the *Discourses on Livy* and *The Prince,* the republican and the hardboiled analyst. Partly, this is the difference between normative and descriptive treatments of politics, a difference made all the more acute by the fact that Machiavelli is one of the first political writers to set himself the task of describing what is rather than what should be. But the difference can be seen in another way: it symbolizes the problem of the liberal who, in a moment of social helplessness, retains his vision of the desirable society yet feels intransigence to be futile and therefore tries to adapt himself to the realities of power. Because of this effort, Machiavelli's political thought is not finally a unified system, as Stendhal's political insights do not quite add up to a unified version. Stendhal, and particularly that part of him reflected in Mosca, is also troubled by the difficulty of reconciling what he believes or would like to believe with what he must do or supposes he must do. (In *Le Rouge et le noir* Julien Sorel had already asked: "Who knows what one goes through on the way to a great deed?") It is this problem, more than any specific doctrine, that makes Machiavelli so "modern" a thinker and Stendhal so "modern" a novelist.

If, as has generally been done, we identify Machiavelli with *The Prince,*

La Chartreuse is far from being completely machiavellian in spirit. For it is essential to the novel that Mosca never has the last word on any important matter, that he is continually bested, as he knows and indeed wishes, by both Sanseverina and Fabrice. Mosca's advice to Fabrice is not too far from Machiavelli's to his prince: both provide a manual on how to rise in the world, if one must. When Mosca fails, it is precisely because he lives too closely by his own precepts, by his inured political habits. It is he who in behalf of Ernest IV omits the phrase "unjust proceedings" from the paper Sanseverina dictates to him, and it is this omission that allows Ernest IV to throw Fabrice into jail. Sanseverina rightly describes Mosca's behavior as that of a "miserable fawning . . . courtier"; she jabs him at his weakest point—the weakest point of all professional politicians and parliamentarians—when she says, "He always imagines that to resign is the greatest sacrifice a Prime Minister can make." On the other hand, Mosca's triumph, that is, his transcendence of his public self, comes when he breaks from the machiavellian system and allows his passion for Sanseverina to imperil his career and perhaps his life. It is then that he becomes a truly magnificent figure, a man capable of every precaution yet discarding all, a man for whom love is the means of recovering Fortune. In moving away from the Machiavelli of *The Prince,* Mosca approaches the other Machiavelli, the one who wrote that Fortune favors the young and impetuous: "like a woman she is a lover of the young because they are less respectful, more ferocious and with greater audacity command her."

Sanseverina, that superb woman for whom literary critics have been ready to sacrifice everything, also meddles in the politics of Parma, but there is never any question, in her mind or anyone else's, about the value she assigns to her meddling. She is interested in politics not as a means of regulating social tensions or of slaking thirsts for power, but as a form of action that brings into highest relief the contours of human character. She judges Ernest IV as a man rather than a monarch (it does him no good), she takes advantage of Archbishop Landriani's plebeian awe before titles, she is enchanted with Ferrante Palla's Robin Hood liberalism, she measures with admirable accuracy Fabrice's distance from the world. In all of her responses she immediately breaks through to the personal core: she is one of the least snobbish figures in all literature. Sanseverina is a romantic who personifies the Napoleonic principle in personal relations, or at least that principle as understood and elevated by Stendhal. The great passion of her life is her feeling for Fabrice, which is more than, though it certainly includes, an incestuous love, for it involves the desire to establish a kind of spiritual stake in another person and thereby to shape life again. Through the power of another being, she would return to the condition of youth, not to dominate Fabrice but to share in him. She admires generosity, impetuousness, gaiety, passion—and a certain ruthlessness in reaching for them. At the end of the book she accepts her fate, which is to marry Mosca and relinquish Fabrice. As Stendhal beautifully puts it, "she combined all the outward appearances of happiness."

Sanseverina dominating Mosca represents the victory of *espagnolisme* over calculated ruse, the power of desire to elbow aside the restraints of caution. In drawing her with an affection seldom matched in literature, Stendhal suggests that wherever passion is vital and full, morality must suffer some consequence. Sanseverina seems frequently to move beyond the margin of morality, though one is less inclined to suppose that she has achieved a Nietzschian transvaluation of values than that she is impervious, like some majestic natural force, to moral argument.

Fabrice stands still a step further, a long step, from the political world. Not that he lacks political opinions: Stendhal sees to it that he is properly provisioned. But Fabrice is not really concerned with politics, the world claims him far less than it does Julien Sorel. Unlike Julien, he is usually a passive figure, and passive despite his fighting at Waterloo and escaping from the tower. He begins to exert his will only when it is a question of winning Clélia—that is, of abandoning the world of Mosca and Sanseverina, the world of politics and affairs. Like *Le Rouge et le noir, La Chartreuse* ends with a strange ritual of sacrilege in which there is nonetheless a powerful if suppressed strain of religious feeling. Fabrice's sermons are violently false, they are *block* sermons, for he is not a religious man; but they do express a genuine emotional compulsion, an obscure but authentic need for purity and exaltation, a desire to preach. though he really has no message, for himself or his listeners, beyond the expression of that desire.

Psychologically, Fabrice suffers from an extreme case of self-alienation: he frequently seems divorced from his own activity, as if he were assuming a series of roles from which his inner self is quite detached. Socially, he is even more of an outcast than Julien Sorel, for while Julien is tormented by an inability to reach his place in the world, Fabrice doubts that one's place is worth having. Fabrice is a youth in whom there lies dormant a germ of moral aspiration which another age might stir to growth; that he finally becomes a cleric, making his life into a mockery of faith, is hardly an accident, for in however distorted a form he does possess the religious vocation. Though not dreamy, Fabrice is devoted to dreams—to escape, back into the self, deep into the cocoon of childhood and innocence. Perhaps his greatest scene, and certainly one of the greatest in the novel, is that in which he returns to the chestnut tree where he had played as a child and now acts out a ceremony of reinvigoration, thereby expressing his need to declare not merely his manliness, about which, like his creator, he is never entirely certain, but also the profound piety he feels toward his childhood and its still visible relics.

Taken together, Mosca, Sanseverina and Fabrice embody a remarkable interplay of values: worldliness, personal passion, and a kind of distracted innocence. They are people who have been stranded in a hostile world, people who are conscious that little is left for them to believe in except their desire to snatch some fragment of happiness for themselves and for each other. As Martin Turnell perceptively remarks, they form "an immensely civilized aristocratic elite and they stake everything on a single chance—happiness through personal relationships. . . . They are tragic figures precisely because 'they do not believe in anything.' For we cannot say that they 'believe in' personal relationships; they are passionately attached to them, but they are profoundly conscious of the absence of a *mystique* and of the precariousness of their way of life when it is pitted against despotism."

We are back, then, where we started: the debacle of liberalism and the problem of how intelligence can survive in an age of cant. Stendhal's characters do not make a long face about this, at least not for very long; they believe that if one cannot live heroically one can still live happily, provided one uses one's wits. Stendhal has not reached the feeling of Flaubert, that one cannot live heroically or happily, nor the feeling of Malraux, that happiness has become irrelevant but heroism, at whatever cost, mandatory.

Stendhal, it seems to me, was entirely conscious of the political dimension in his work. Surely it was only a man of the very highest political intelligence who could have conceived the idea of having the official leader of the Liberal party serve as the governor of the Citadel, reporting weekly to Ernest IV on his measures for keeping the liberals locked in their cages. No denunciation of the moral cowardice that has so often characterized modern liberalism has ever had the conclusive power of the image Stendhal constructed, as it were, in passing: General Fabio Conti, leader of the opposition, flunkey of the king, warden of his prison.

Still more brilliant is Stendhal's conception of Ferrante Palla, a character who deserves all the praise Balzac lavished upon him. To make the only effective liberal of Parma a somewhat mad poet and a highway robber as well, a Robin Hood completely cut off from the people yet staunch in their behalf—this is political wit of the highest order. When all the conventional liberals fail or sell out, the crazy artist remains in opposition. Wild, impetuous, extravagant, he throws up everything for love (love and liberalism are all the same in his eyes), writes great sonnets, and, alone in the world of Parma, is actually a happy man (perhaps, suggests Stendhal rather slyly, because he is a little mad.) Partly, he is what Stendhal would have liked to be, the man who remains in principled opposition no matter how absurd it makes him seem, had there not been the reality of a pot belly and the temptations of the opera and the salon to distract him. Comic though he seems, Palla is also a stirring figure, a call to resistance; he is the only man whose recklessness matches that of

Sanseverina, and it is symptomatic of Stendhal's meaning that it is the prime minister rather than the outlaw who wins the Duchess. In order to maintain his liberal intransigence, Palla must become a ridiculous, even a farcical figure, yet precisely his readiness to accept the costume of farce endows him with a redeeming dignity. In the world of Parma, heroism appears in the mask of self-parody.

It is this blend of seriousness and farce that makes *La Chartreuse* seem so enigmatic a novel, particularly the fact that the seriousness is not solemn and the farce not frivolous. Forever vivacious and subversive, Stendhal will not settle into one attitude long enough for our tired eyes to focus upon him steadily, he does not allow us the luxury of becoming dull; which leads us to suspect, of course, that he suffers from an unstable personality.

Stendhal is a difficult writer. There are some novelists who present only the difficulty of finding out what is happening in their books, and then it all becomes clear, even too clear. But in Stendhal the carpet is well-brushed, neat, and clean; the figure is sharply outlined, without mystery—only the meaning, the relationship of parts, proves elusive. I think this is largely due to Stendhal's mixture of tones. That a writer's characteristic accent should be ironic, does not disturb us; these days we insist upon it with a monumental lack of irony. Nor are we too disturbed when the characters, who have every right to be as clever as their creator, are habitually ironic about each other and themselves; though this does tend to complicate the tone of the novel rather more than we find comfortable—and it is consistency of tone rather than plot or characterization that allows us to fall into that comfortable drowse we call "getting used" to a book. But what makes for Stendhal's special quality, his mixture of dialectical speed and aloof coolness, is that he will frequently be ironic about the irony of his characters. Mosca pokes fun at Fabrice and with good reason, yet Stendhal, if by no more than a syntactical flip, makes sure that Mosca too does not get off scot-free. In a sense, Stendhal is very much the omniscient author who does not hesitate to show that the characters are of his manufacture; but once created they are treated by him with complete equality, as if they were old friends whose faults he knew perfectly well and whom he loved nonetheless. Irony here becomes a password admitting the favored characters into the charmed circle, the happy few.

The range of tone in *La Chartreuse* is, of course, wider still. In a few places, as if to strike a quiet contrast to the prevailing bustle and worldliness of the novel, Stendhal comes close to a touch of pastoral, a yearning for "the natural," of which all his characters, like Stendhal himself, are utterly incapable. Fabrice returns to his tree but must soon leave it; Mosca speaks wistfully of having at his disposal "Petrarch's old house on that fine slope in the middle of the forest, near the Po" to which they may retire as if to some sacred retreat of poetry and love. But such notes come at rare intervals; most of *La Chartreuse* is outright farce, even burlesque, particularly those parts in which Fabrice's outward conduct most closely approximates that of a Byronic hero. Fabrice breaking out of the tower, engaging in duels that bore him and pursuing women he does not want to love—this is the farce of the antiheroic novel, the inversion of romantic modes in order to assert, finally, romantic values. Sanseverina going through the idiotic motions of court intrigue, in fact, the whole treatment of love in terms of petty politics; Mosca living in fear because he has been so indiscreet as to refer to Ernest V as "that boy"; Rassi, that great clown of a scoundrel, telling Ernest IV precisely why he cannot do without him, for where else could he find so accomplished a scoundrel—all this is done in the colors of farce. At times the novel takes on the quality, half burlesque and half thriller, of a wild movie, what with signals flashing from tower to tower, heroes refusing to escape from prison because they love the jailer's daughter, duchesses poisoning monarchs and inciting crazy poets to open the dams.

The style in which all this is communicated has best been described by Nietzsche when he speaks of the author who "cannot help presenting the most serious events in a boisterous *allegrissimo,* perhaps not without a malicious artistic sense of the contrast he ventures to present—long, heavy, difficult, dangerous thoughts and a *tempo* of the gallop, and of the best, wantonest humor." The description fits exactly, though Nietzsche happened to be talking about Machiavelli; it establishes the true line of descent from the Italian to the Frenchman.

All the while, however, Stendhal is fundamentally serious in his meanings and intentions. The seriousness of the book is to be measured only if one fully apprehends the degree to which the action is farce; the tragedy of the book consists in the fact that these marvellously intelligent people must behave as if it should all be taken seriously and that if they do not, the consequences for them will be serious indeed. This is the political significance of their behavior, a behavior forced upon them by the politics of defeat. They live now as if they had read in advance Nietzsche's great maxim for rebels in an unrebellious age: "Objection, evasion, joyous distrust, and love of irony are signs of health; everything absolute belongs to pathology."

The Devaluation of Reality
in the *Chartreuse de Parme*

by Judd D. Hubert

In the *Chartreuse de Parme,* Stendhal has abandoned, or so it would seem, a militant position in literature, without, however, taking refuge in that heroic but unreal world, so foreign to the contemporary scene, which he had described in the *Abbesse de Castro.* In a sense, the *Chartreuse* provides a synthesis of two fundamental tendencies of Stendhal: his need for political action, for *engagement,* and his escape toward a purely imaginary Italy. Indeed, we may regard the adventures of Fabrice as a sort of Italian chronicle—as a transposition into modern time of the adventurous youth of Alessandro Farnese, who later on became pope under the name of Paul III.

These two conflicting tendencies play an important part in the novel. The first chapter describes, with a fair degree of objectivity, the sudden arrival of Napoleon's army in Milano. Fabrice himself is half French, even though he will never find out that his real father is none other than Lieutenant Robert, whom he will meet, under adverse circumstances, during the battle of Waterloo. Fabrice's participation in Napoleon's last campaign marks a wilfully derisive attempt on the part of the author to conciliate his own romantic Italianism with his historical predicament. The dismal failure of his young hero is by no means lacking in irony: Fabrice cannot convince himself that he has done his bit in a real battle; moreover, his own father unknowingly cheats him and makes a fool of him. Waterloo, where poor Fabrice behaves like a blunderer persecuted, in the manner of one of Molière's clowns, by coincidence, brings about a solution of continuity between a real but now legendary past and a future shorn of glory, where heroes, left to their own devices, must pursue a strictly egotistical form of happiness. It is perhaps for this reason that Fabrice tends to behave like a stranger wherever he happens to live. Exiled, for political reasons, from his own country, he must

"The Devaluation of Reality in the *Chartreuse de Parme*." From *Stendhal Club* (October 15, 1959). Reprinted by permission of the editors of *Stendhal Club*.

choose between the obscure existence of a "dandy" of limited means and a brilliant career in the Church, but without the slightest trace of a religious vocation. Neither solution can give a direction and a meaning to his life. Napoleon's defeat has reduced Fabrice and other young men of courage to a state of historical futility—to a situation which approximates in some respects our contemporary feeling of absurdity.

Obviously, the reader cannot take seriously or, rather, as historically meaningful, the carryings-on of Ranuce-Ernest IV and the endless intrigues of the court of Parma. The insignificant Prince, in his eagerness to reinstate the hierarchical splendors of the past, vainly imitates the external behavior of Louis XIV. He even requires his courtiers to powder their hair like so many participants in a fancy-dress ball. Quite understandably, intelligent people such as the Prime Minister, Count Mosca, and Gina, his mistress, consider politics, in this theatrical court, as an amusing and sometimes enthralling game, which has its accepted rules, just like whist. It so happens that the highest honor that the Prince can bestow on one of his subjects consists in inviting him to play cards at his table! Likeable characters, such as Mosca, Gina, and Fabrice owe much of their superiority, in the eyes of the reader, to the fact that they can play the game of politics without becoming in the least involved.

The frequent comparisons between the world of politics and that of the theater tend to reveal the futility of the times. The scheming Rassi, even at the height of his villainy as minister of justice, is compared to Punch, receiving or dishing out beatings. As a result, the reader can only laugh at his machiavelian plots and counterplots. Moreover, the redoubtable fortress of Parma owes some of its dreadfulness to stagecraft: in order to frighten the prisoners, the soldiers parade before them "a procession with a spy who plays the role of a poor devil marching to his death."

The invasion of the world of politics by the theater becomes even more ironical during the reign of Ranuce-Ernest V, whose greatest pleasure consists in performing scenes from the *commedia dell'arte* with Gina, whom he adores. Indeed, there is scarcely any difference between the political acts of the young Prince and the various parts he performs on stage. Everything becomes so theatrical that at one point Gina exclaims in the presence of Mosca: "I am dead tired. I have played theater for one hour on the stage, and for five hours in the study." In this particular instance, the duchess had had to perform in earnest, for how else could she have thwarted Rassi in his investigation of Ranuce-Ernest IV's assassination? She succeeds in diverting suspicion from herself and her accomplices by a childish performance: the reading of a La Fontaine fable —"Le Jardinier et son seigneur"!

Performances, pastimes, and games serve not only to make these palace intrigues ridiculous, but also to devaluate the present, to destroy the material world, thereby setting up an ideal form of happiness, timeless and yet perfectly human. Now, this happiness which, in all of Stendhal's novels, invariably coincides with perilous undertakings, assumes, in the *Chartreuse*, a childish quality. Father Blanès seeks happiness in spending most of his time in the bell tower of his church observing the stars through a makeshift, cardboard telescope, hardly better than a toy. He inscribes the results of these astrological observations on a playing card. Moreover, astrology, no less than politics and whist, has its rules: "Every prediction of the future is an infraction of the rule, and is dangerous because it can change the event, in which case the entire science collapses like a child's game."

As for Fabrice who, more often than not, indulges in childish pursuits, his first act upon being locked up in the Farnese tower is to laugh uproariously at the antics of a terrier bent on destroying the rats that infest his cell. And the hero will play the fascinating game of love in the most childish manner possible: Clélia describes their conversations by means of letters of the alphabet as a child's game, a "jeu d'enfant." Their games, thrilling and dangerous in spite or because of their very childishness, will somehow enable them to attain a sort of primal innocence or, as Madame Francine Albérès might put it, of *"naturel."* [1] Paradoxically, Fabrice's imprisonment in the high places of the Citadel has a liberating effect. As a result, he does not in the least wish to escape from his tower, which he regards as an earthly paradise, and return to his formal enslavement among the low places of this world. The hero's unexpected happiness in a perilous prison reminds us of those *précieux* lovers in seventeenth-century romances who adore the very chains that bind them. Stendhal, however, has transformed the old metaphor of the enchained lover by making imprisonment the cause rather than the result of passion. This reversal may perhaps stem from the fact that in the seventeenth century Eros was usually described as a cruel tyrant, whereas in the Romantic era society itself had taken over completely the evil functions of constraint, with love usually cast in the part of liberator. Whatever may be the case, we can construe the Farnese tower as well as the various events which take place within it as a vast metaphor with endless ramifications.

Long before his discovery of happiness in a cell, Fabrice had sought to escape from reality or, rather, from a distressing present. In his search for a real passion, he had become infatuated first with an actress, then with a famous prima donna, who, by the mere fact that they belonged to the fantastic world of the theater, enabled him to escape to an imaginary realm. And the strange pleasure he derives from his archeological diggings would seem to imply that any activity which allows him to escape from the bounds of his present predicaments must fascinate him: there is in-

[1] Cf. *Le Naturel chez Stendhal* (Paris, 1956).

deed no better way to kill time than to search the earth for the remains of bygone civilizations. His single combat with Giletti, which takes place in the midst of these excavations, strikes us as perhaps more ludicrous than heroic. Fabrice himself has the impression that he is actually taking part in a sort of spectacle—"un assaut public." After Giletti's death, the hero, in order to escape, must assume his victim's identity—the identity of a mediocre clown.

When Fabrice finally discovers his true vocation in the tower, he does not, for all that, abandon the world of the stage. Clélia, in warning him of an imminent danger, borrows one of Molière's best known tricks: she intones a recitative from an opera, improvising at the same time words suitable to the situation. Fabrice uses a similar device in order to inform Clélia of his return to the Citadel.

After the girl's unfortunate marriage, Fabrice finally brings her, so to speak, to his feet, by means of the passionate sermons which have already seduced the entire population of Parma. The hero has indeed made himself the star attraction of the principality, to the extent of reducing the foremost tenor of the times to sing before a nearly empty house. Can we blame the inhabitants of Parma for confusing profane with sacred love? After all, Fabrice's passion for Clélia which has made him so indifferent to the banalities of day-to-day existence and has brought him so close to the absolute, has also transformed his sermons into an irresistible spectacle, as seductive and secular as it is edifying and divine. And what could be more theatrical than the famous scene where Fabrice, sobbing in his pulpit and surrounded by a flock of people as profoundly moved as himself, finally assures his triumph over Clélia, seated, to her intense embarrassment, in a large and showy armchair, which sets her apart from the other spectators? Indeed, this performance almost dwarfs that other great scene where Gina had defied the redoubtable tyrant of Parma.

In order to ensure her own devoutly desired defeat, Clélia Conti had had to rely on bad faith: she had gone to church in order to listen to an eloquent and edifying priest, but not at all to Fabrice! A similar device enables her to conciliate her vow to the Virgin Mary never to lay eyes on her lover with her irresistible passion; and one may wonder whether the author is making fun of Jesuit casuistry. Indeed, the reader cannot help but regard the comedy which the heroine performs for her own edification as a crashing absurdity. Nonetheless, the strange game of hide-and-seek in which Fabrice becomes her unwilling playmate, allowed to approach his beloved only in the darkness, may have symbolic implications. It serves at the very least as a means to complicate the relationship and prevent their love from becoming commonplace. Moreover, it shrouds their love in mystery—an absurd and childish mystery—and maintains between Clélia and Fabrice a permanent barrier. Finally, this love, which had developed in the fortress of Parma under the most hazardous conditions which had consisted of rapid alternations of intimacy and evasions, must somehow remain faithful to its precarious and fabulous origins. Clélia, in consciously keeping her vow, actually succeeds in preserving the absolute character of their mutual love. In refusing to see Fabrice in broad daylight, that is without any separating partitions or obstacles, she is apparently striving to return to that state of precarious innocence where her duty to save a young man as innocent as herself somehow justified her love. She may even have realized that without some sort of barrier love and happiness must become impossible, for barriers, in the *Chartreuse de Parme,* are more often than not passageways to another world, far removed from the present.

Passageways occur quite frequently in the course of the novel. They allow the hero to escape from the present, for what else can a hero do during a debased transitional period, lost between the epic days of the French Revolution and that new era which should start toward 1880 or perhaps 1935? These chronological passageways take the form of omens and presages. Fabrice, whose behavior strikes the reader as perfectly spontaneous and unpredictable, is paradoxically obsessed with forebodings of the future. Far from frightening him, they enable him at certain privileged moments to transcend the limitations of his present existence and thus endow his adventures with all the magic of a dimly perceived or imagined future.

Most of the omens concern the hero's imprisonment in the Citadel, where he will unexpectedly discover what he had vainly sought elsewhere: love and dangerous happiness. He might almost apply to himself these lines from Rotrou's *Le Véritable saint Genest:*

> Ainsi souvent le Ciel conduit tout à tel point
> Que ce qu'on craint arrive, et qu'il n'afflige point,
> Et que ce qu'on redoute est enfin ce qu'on aime.
> (Act I, scene v.)

Some of these omens take the form of premonitory events. For instance, Fabrice, recovering from a wound suffered during the retreat after Waterloo, communicates by means of sign language with Aniken and her sisters, who do not understand French. Moreover, the hero shows reluctance at leaving them in order to escape to France: "Where could I be better off than here?" he was saying to himself. The first time he sees Clélia, then aged twelve, he reflects that this young maiden would make a charming prison companion. Now, each of these events prefigures Fabrice's imprisonment in the Citadel; and Stendhal accumulates these presages in order to increase the importance of the hero's enforced sojourn in the Tower and give it, so to speak, a heightened existence. What seems to matter most in the novel is the gradual destruction of all obstacles capable of preventing Fabrice from attaining a great spiritual experience. And only in the Tower will he reach a state of transcendence, where his life will at last be freed from time's constraint. Both spatially and temporally he will dominate the horizon. Thus omens, in Fabrice's pursuit of happiness, have a function somewhat similar to that of involuntary memory in Proust's endeavor to recapture the past, in spite of the fact that omens and memory must necessarily operate in opposite directions. Fabrice's incarceration within partitions too frail to hold him coincides paradoxically with the expansion of his spiritual being. Within the Tower he has attained, in every sense of the word, the very heights of human existence.

This Tower is not only the "high place" in Fabrice's search but also in that of Clélia who, even before Fabrice's arrival, had much preferred the solitude of the Citadel to the intrigues of the world below. The Farnese Tower, however, differs in one significant respect from the rest of the fortress, for it exists also in a timeless universe. A Prince of Parma toward the middle of the eighteenth century had had it built to serve as a comfortable prison for his son and heir, who had failed to repel the advances of a youthful stepmother. Strange as this may seem, this vindictive ruler had forced his subjects, all of whom had witnessed with their very eyes the erection of the new structure, to make believe that the Tower was no less ancient than the rest of the castle. Thus, from the very beginning, Fabrice's lofty prison had been connected with a chronological ambiguity, marvelously suited to his double evasion. And thus Ranuce-Ernest's angry ancestor had unknowingly built an earthly paradise, a hallowed spot consecrated to the god of love. Fabrice, luckier than Kafka's hero, not only had found his way into the castle, but he had discovered its only secret.

A Theoretical Outline of "Beylism"

by Léon Blum

The life of Stendhal testifies that his System,[1] applied to his own needs, procured him but imperfect results. Such is the usual case with theoreticians and moralists: their lives explain their theories, often inspire them, but rarely confirm them. Nonetheless Stendhal never stopped believing in the practical effectiveness of his System, and this penchant which seems fundamental to him was reinforced by the all-powerful influence exercised on his mind by the reasoners of the eighteenth century and the *idéologues* of the Empire. Montesquieu, de Tracy, and Helvétius figure, along with Shakespeare, among his youthful idols. He maintained that Helvétius was "the greatest philosopher that France has had," and when, around 1820, he recalled this opinion, he professed to believe it still.[2] He considered as one of the cardinal events of his life his encounter with Condillac's *Logic,* about which his mathematics teacher at *l'École Centrale,* M. Dupuy, used to say to him: "Study it well, my boy; it's the basis of everything." As for Destutt de Tracy, whose book he knew by heart, he was so choked with admiration the first time he found himself in his presence that he could not speak. Faith in philosophical theories, with most people, is rarely more than an illusion or a brief infatuation of youth. Stendhal held on to this neophyte's enthusiasm all his life. Mérimée once noted that the very word *logic* was enough to fill up his mouth. "We must, in all things, be guided by *Lo-Gic,* he would say, leaving an interval between the first syllable and the rest of the word."

"A Theoretical Outline of 'Beylism.'" Translated by Richard L. Greeman. From *Stendhal et le Beylisme* by Léon Blum (Paris: Albin Michel, 1947), pp. 120-146. Reprinted by permission of Les Editions Albin Michel. This study first appeared in the *Revue de Paris* (Spring 1914). The essay reprinted here constitutes a major part of the chapter "Dessin théorique du Beylisme."

[1] The term refers to Stendhal's faith in a "practical method" for happiness, which he himself called *Beylisme.* [Ed. note.]

[2] "The only thing wrong with Helvétius is that he did not live in some forgotten corner of the Alps and did not cast his books down on Paris, without going there himself."

Like Helvétius and like Condillac, he was an empiricist, a sensualist, and a rationalist; like them, he made the senses the basis of all knowledge; like them, he believed that ideas come out of controlled and generalized sensations; like them, while limiting the role of reason to the logical classification of experience, he believed in its total power over Nature. He thus reduced the universe to a sort of mechanistic unity which could englobe states of consciousness as well as exterior phenomena and which submits the problems of the heart to the usual rules of experimental method. If we wanted to bring in proof of this logical, in short, scientific tendency in Stendhal, we would be obliged to quote half his works. This tendency is outstanding even in his manias, of which the most persistent is probably that for definitions and catalogues: What is laughter? What is vanity? Who are the ten greatest geniuses of mankind? In the extreme, it is expressed by the conviction that the exact knowledge of the facts, the rigorous application of logical procedures can lead to everything, even to happiness, can take the place of anything, even genius; that the writer's gift, for example, consists in a certain number of definable or assimilable recipes, and that art is just one of the aspects of universal science. He wrote to his sister Pauline that only education, that is to say an exact method in the service of the Will, produces great men, and that consequently all that one needs to become a great genius is to wish it. To Edouard Mounier he wrote that he no longer dared to dream of literary glory, not being "learned enough." These texts go back to his youth, but Stendhal never wavered in the systematic faith which they reveal and in which his grandfather, Gagnon, the doctor and Encyclopedist, was most likely his initiator.

Thus the immediate characteristic of "Beylism" is the belief in the general applicability of the System, the implicit affirmation that it governs emotive states and the moral universe like the other phenomena of Nature, and, consequently, that the conquest of happiness operates according to the same laws as the search for truth. But this first principle, although incontestable, cannot be conceived or applied by the common herd. In order to acquire an impartial knowledge of oneself, in order resolutely to adapt one's conduct to the peculiar exigencies of one's nature, one must give proof of rarer gifts: independence of mind and strength of will. Thus the second characteristic of "Beylism" is that it relates exclusively to an elite. Stendhal writes and thinks only for "the happy few," for the small number of original personalities who dare to violate "the great principle of the epoch: be like everyone else." The sheeplike mass who are the slaves of the great law of social propriety, the flabby souls who make no distinction between happiness and tranquillity or stability, have nothing to do but turn away as quickly as possible from a teaching that is not made for them, and every page of Stendhal reiterates this warning to the unworthy reader. Despite all the differences, "Beylism" is based on a vision analogous to Nietzsche's. Certain ideas are the meat of masters and others the pasturage of slaves. The masters are those who dare to be themselves, who neither bow down nor conform, who, against all wear and tear and all compromise, preserve the impulsive vigor of their original instincts.

But Nietzsche, who places his superman sometimes in heroic action, sometimes in the monastic life of the thinker, was able to conceive of his victory in an ideal sense. Stendhal, on the contrary, confronts his elite with daily reality; he plunges them into social life, into that routine of exchanges, tedious obligations, and minor relations that the world imposes on us; that is to say, instead of imagining, like Nietzsche, a triumphant elite, he starts from a plagued and almost persecuted elite. The world does not permit of differences; originality offends it as much as rebellion, and, if it cannot really crush originality, it punishes it. In any case, the conditions of life in society are not exactly propitious to the flowering of original personalities. Young men brought up by society know how to dress themselves with tact, to relate anecdotes with finesse, to enter a café gracefully, but any idea that is not handed down to them, that is to say hackneyed, seems to them an impropriety, and any strong feeling, a lack of taste. The small number of generous souls to whom "Beylism" addresses itself must thus develop themselves, in all likelihood, outside of those elegant circles where we must suppose them placed through some fortuitous circumstance, and thus where their singularity must be doubly offensive, being that of inferiors and intruders. Even Lucien Leuwen, though the son of a banker, is disconcerting to the society of the *Chaussée d'Antin*. Similarly Octave, who is the only son of the Count de Malivert, surprises the society of the *faubourg Saint-Germain*. Since their virtue is not cut along the common measure, it is not acceptable, and is turned to ridicule. All the more so for a Julien Sorel, son of a woodcutter, who is rather the typical case! It must follow logically that preliminary efforts, according to the System, must move toward formulating some sort of defensive tactics. Before embarking upon the "quest for happiness," the elite will have to defend itself against the world, that is to say, insure its personality against the wear and tear of interaction with others, protect its sensibilities against injury from contacts, and preserve its pride against the humiliation of showing pain.

To this end, the first rule is to practice a systematic mistrust and to create a *tabula rasa* through universal doubt. It is necessary to challenge all authorities, believe only in that which one could have verified by oneself, presuppose that the friend one is listening to has some interest in deceiving, that the author one reads is a flunky paid to spread lies. The member of this elite who lives in society is beset by hostile intrigues and false conceptions; he must parry the former, and cast aside the latter by means of a permanent skepticism which he must be careful not to display: "One must be mistrustful, most men deserve it, but be very careful not to reveal one's mistrust." A fatal error, the first into which generous spirits are likely to fall, is to judge others according to ourselves and to attribute to their acts the motives which determine our own. The System can protect us against faulty judgment, the source of inevitable deceptions. Each individual must be looked upon as a distinct reality, and explained by the totality of the facts we can relate to him. The fact, the cold and naked fact, is the only basis for a knowledge of the world. "Give me lots and lots of facts," the young Stendhal had written to his sister Pauline. And like the experimentation practiced by the scientist, the observations we make on men should be free from all emotional or moral prejudices. We must look at things with a clear eye, shunning all misleading appearances; "error is in all things the obstacle to happiness." But in this battle one must be careful not to allow to the world the same advantage one has taken over it. The very veils we withdraw from others must remain tightly closed around our own inner secret. The very protective necessities which command caution also prescribe dissembling. When you write frankly and openly, the police are lying in wait; when you act or when you think, public opinion is on the lookout. Thus you must deceive the world as you would throw spies off the track; to this purpose you fill your private papers with pseudonyms, words with special meanings, and intentional contradictions; you conceal your actions under an apparent submission to the laws of society, and your emotions under the impassive air of someone "a thousand miles from the immediate emotion." We have already stated it: for the member of the elite, oppressed or threatened by a hostile world, hypocrisy is the only means of maintaining independence. Let us hide our originality and our differences from society; yield to it the concessions it demands; then, our peace once assured by this dissimulation, let us live secretly, according to our own inclinations and our own law.

Stendhal's astonishing letter to Pauline, dated November 25, 1807, is the document which expounds this policy with the harshest frankness.[3] One would be tempted to compare this little handbook of machiavellism to the famous letter of the Marquise de Merteuil, in Laclos' *Liaisons dangereuses,* if one were not able to feel, from the first words, that this wisdom had been paid for by much suffering. Stendhal advises his sister to marry a rich man, without love, for the main reason that society condemns the improprieties of unmarried girls but tolerates all the liberties taken by young wives. What is all this for, in the end?: to gain some freedom and some elbow-room in one's "quest for happiness." Let Pauline acquire her independence by paying to society what it demands, after

[3] See also the letter of August 25, 1805, published for the first time by M. Paupe from the Chéramy manuscripts.

which she may create her happiness in her own way. Romantic souls imagine that they will find an open door and freedom everywhere, but it is books, "these damned books," that feed their perilous illusions. If they do not know how to liberate themselves through guile and cunning, they open themselves to cruelty, to scorn, and even worse, to false pity: "Two years ago, when someone gave me advice similar to that which I want you to follow, I said to myself 'A cold heart!' and I was careful not to believe a word; but many misfortunes finally opened my eyes. I decided to look around me, to check for myself the things people told me, and only to base my opinion on those which were proved."

The character of count Mosca, in *La Chartreuse de Parme,* is little more than the putting into practice of these rules of conduct. Their value, according to Stendhal, must be held to be general, and whoever observes them rigorously will preserve both his freedom of action and the integrity of his personality. But it goes without saying that the details of application will depend on individual natures. In spite of common traits, the elite is composed of an infinite number of distinct types; it is up to every individual to determine precisely his own weak points, the learnings and the weaknesses which expose him most dangerously to the world, and then, once recognized, he must correct them, harden himself. For Stendhal, for example, the weak point is vanity, the fear of ridicule, the perpetual feeling of being seen. This anxiety of his is so consistent that he preserves it, as M. Faguet has observed, even toward his readers; hence, his incessant dialogue with his "Dear reader" and the continual warnings: "I am jumping forward twenty pages here. . . . All of this development is terribly boring, etc., etc." But introspection, practiced with the very vigor of a clinical examination, has permitted a sure diagnosis. Stendhal knows the disease; he has determined the cause, which is not overweening pride or native insociability, but a hypertrophied sensibility. Mozart, a child prodigy, invited to give a concert for the young Archduchesses, asked them before sitting down at the harpsichord: "Do you love me?" Stendhal knows very well that even with indifferent strangers his whole personality is asking: what do you think of me? do you like me? . . . and that he will painfully search out the answers in all their glances. He has followed the disastrous effects of this predisposition; he has confirmed that it has exposed him to thousands of hurts, and that, to make matters worse, it paralyzes his resources because it "drives away almost all the natural quality." Effort and self-control must thus be used to combat it: "I must drive all vanity from my heart, it is an open door to misfortune." The method which has allowed the localization and explanation of the disease shall furnish the possible remedy: turn upon vanity, convince it that it misunderstands its own interest, that this concern for the opinion of others grants too much importance to the common herd, to those fools one despises and that it is necessary to rise

above them under pain of "impertinence toward oneself." When one
has seen to the bottom of one's vice or weakness, a statement which
touches to the quick, an appropriate argument directed at the part of the
soul in question, can suffice for a cure. If the effort fails, since it is important above all "not to show oneself inferior" there is still the
"System" to be turned to, in order to dissimulate one's misfortune and
one's suffering. It is thus that Stendhal will dissimulate to the very end
his susceptibility and his emotionalism which had proved incurable: "I
have learned to hide all this under an irony which is imperceptible"—
he means "impenetrable"—"to the vulger herd."

Introspection and inward experimentation thus furnish the means to
limit the effects of the outside world on our sensibilities and also those of
our own natural weaknesses. Through the application of the same devices,
the will, upon reflection, is able effectively to work out exercises to counter
melancholy, for example, or boredom. But the method is not only a critical or defensive one; it also assumes a positive and expansive character.
It allows us to direct all our actions toward their real goal, which is
happiness. Along with Helvétius, La Rochefoucauld, or Bentham,
Stendhal maintains that our self-interest, that is to say, our own particular notion of happiness, is the sole motive of our resolutions, and that
instrumentality to happiness is the sole reason for deciding between
courses of action. In his eyes happiness is not a fantastical notion or an
ideal conception, but rather a tangible object which is ours to attain. Our
instincts lead us to it: it suffices to enlighten them through the use of
reason, and to reinforce them through the will. The System will teach
us that kind of impartial clear-sightedness which will allow us to recognize
the contrary forces in ourselves and to set up a battle-plan; it will persuade
us that the vital force of our personality should serve the real necessities
of our own happiness, and not be turned to the profit of the usual
hackneyed common conceptions. When we have become fully aware of
the essential demands of our personality, when we have concentrated all
our active will to this end, when we have resolutely rejected the false
principles of accepted morality or of religion, the false promises of
society, then happiness can be logically obtained, through necessary
stages, like a mathematical proof. In this proceeding, we will come up
against the eternal enemy: society, but we will know how to combat it,
that is to say, to deceive it. As soon as the appropriate tactics have rid
us of its hold, happiness will depend on nothing other than our own
lucidity and courage: it is necessary to see clearly, and to dare.

In this generally accurate, though somewhat systematized analysis, for
which the *Correspondance* or the diaries of Stendhal have furnished all
the elements, it is the heir of the eighteenth century whom we have
discovered, the student, not of Voltaire, whom Stendhal knew early but

never liked, but of the logicians and Encyclopedists. Stendhal takes from them the conception of a life subjected to critical attention and to system, of which all the logically connected actions leading up to a concrete and tangible goal are governed by a purely human idea. But the thinkers and the novelists of the eighteenth century were extremely consistent with themselves when they formulated this mathematics of action. The final ends of human action being, according to them, purely material interests or purely sensual pleasure, their system was exactly in tune with their ethic and one could imagine that a well-defined code, a rigorous system of practical guides, could be set down for the use of the ambitious, the voluptuary, or the libertine. The deep-seated originality of "Beylism" is to have directed this strategy toward an entirely new object: happiness. It is to have proposed to passionate souls a logic that was conceived only for sterile hearts and positive ambitions. A mechanics of happiness and not of pleasure: this formula contains a profound innovation. Stendhal takes off from Condillac and Helvétius, philosophers who explain all knowledge by the senses and reduce all reality to matter; but he crowns them with a conception of happiness into which sensual and material elements no longer enter. Happiness, as Stendhal understands it, goes far beyond a mere titillation of the senses; it brings into play the profound vital forces of the soul; it implies a leap, a risk, a gift of self in which the whole personality is involved. It is independent of action and has nothing in common with good fortune or success. No external contrivance can procure it, because it is not the satisfaction of a desire. It is a blooming-forth, a moment of total forgetfulness and perfect consciousness, a spiritual ecstasy where all the mediocrity of reality is destroyed. The most intense states of love, the joy that works of art may give can furnish some idea of it; whatever is not this is nothing, and barely deserves the name of pleasure. "Beylism" is not made for those second-rate "bons vivants" who search out pleasure in a mere flattery of the senses, but for the exigent spirits who crave the combined satisfaction of the intellect, the imagination, and the will. In an article published soon after Stendhal's death,[4] a forgotten critic, Auguste Bussière, had already pointed out with striking clear-sightedness this significant characteristic of the doctrine: for Stendhal, he said, the great pleasures come from the heart.

Very early, in the time of his youthful admiration for Helvétius, he had already forseen the flaw of his System: "Helvétius drew with great truth for cold hearts and with even greater falsity for ardent souls." Now the ardor of the passions is the indispensable condition of happiness and marks the real distinction between men. Later, going over the memories of his beginnings in Paris and trying to find out what happy influence had preserved him from the pettiness of the milieu and "the bad taste of

---

[4] This article appeared in the *Revue des Deux Mondes*, January 15, 1843.

liking Delille," we hear him answer himself: "It was this personal doctrine founded on true, deep, and self-conscious pleasure, extending to happiness, which Shakespeare and Corneille gave me." As for the roads that had led him to that notion of happiness, by this point we have already gone over them more than once. The imagination, swollen with reading, had conceived of life as a beautiful book, had seduced the unsuspecting soul with enchanted promises, and adorned reality with all the fantastical invention of poets. This romantic habit was reinforced by "Espagnolism," that is to say, by that lofty feeling for one's inner dignity that scorns petty rewards and wishes naught for the soul but the highest objects. Abstention and renunciation are preferable to struggling for vulgar satisfactions. "I love the brave," Zarathustra would say, "but often there is more bravery in abstaining and proceeding, so as to reserve oneself for a more worthy enemy." Finally, in this at once poetic and scornful conception of happiness, there is also resentment and rancor. Stendhal would doubtless have attached a higher price to that petty change with which ordinary men content themselves, to "those slighter pleasures that make life amiable," or at least that make it bearable, if fate had been more liberal in giving him his share. During his love-starved youth and his solitary manhood, he taught himself to put aside all that of which the spite of the world had defrauded him. The grapes were too sour: he disdained from on high those mediocre satisfactions as they danced away before his eyes. Later, much later, when he had become the gray-templed man of wit whose sayings were copied by others, he developed a more gentle indulgence for the lesser pleasures of this world: an "endless" conversation, the art of story-telling, the company of unprudish women, and a mild punch served around midnight. The naturally open and sociable part of his personality could attach itself quite painlessly to these almost mundane pleasures. Aside from these autumnal infractions, the edifice remained intact, just as his first imaginative flights and the concentrated efforts of his pride had erected it. Only happiness can make life pay, and only those intense emotions for which one would pay with his life create happiness.

Here again, it was in the eighteenth century that this passionate ethic originated. This part of the code, however, connects Stendhal, not with the logicians and the materialists, but with the man who was their most avowed enemy: Rousseau. There were no ardent souls in France before "the immortal Jean-Jacques" and the Revolution. Jean-Jacques was our professor of passion, of raptured enthusiasm, and Stendhal is merely picking up his lesson. Thus Stendhal blends, in his work and in his System, the two opposing currents of the century: that which Romanticism had cut off, and that which Romanticism had drawn out and developed. Between these two tendencies—the mechanism borrowed from Helvétius and Romantic individualism after the manner of Rousseau—there is nonetheless a manifest contradiction. The scientific precision of observation and logical rigor in one's conduct may open avenues toward pleasure or success, but not toward happiness understood in this way. To be sure, "Beylism" furnishes an effectual method for tempering the soul against the world, for the protection of the sensibilities or self-esteem; we can even find in it what Stendhal himself would have refused to see—a practical handbook for success, a course in the ways of arriving. But what logical progression could lead us to a happiness which is a gift, a form of Grace, something like an ecstasy of tenderness or of dream? What link between the concerted proceedings of the intelligence or of the will, and this poetic and almost mystical transport of the heart? It is possible to provoke and to cultivate pleasure, to go through the different stages, to learn to handle it like a sensitive instrument; but no effort of will can create happiness, and no operation of the mind can dissect and analyze it. Emotion and passion constitute the most spontaneous reactions in a human being, and the ones that are the hardest to understand, and, far from being able to determine or to follow these mysterious workings, a logical system would make them forever impossible in a spirit entirely given over to it. The two tendencies that Stendhal attempts to combine are placed, in reality, at the most opposite poles of thought and of action, and when one verbally sets forth the simple formulas: "system of happiness," or "mechanics of happiness," the contradiction descends even into the words.

This contradiction, however, lies at the very heart of "Beylism"; better still, it is the essence of it, and, by bringing it to light, we feel we are touching upon and pointing out the very secret of Stendhal. One feels persisting in him this juvenile mixture of forces that life ordinarily separates before they are put into action: the early presumptions of the intellect which pretends to bring all under its sway; the youthful ambitions of the heart that wishes to experience all. By a miracle all his own, the co-existence of these refractory elements lives on in Stendhal through the bubbling turmoil of the years of apprenticeship. The demands of System did not dry up passion; nor did passion allay or discourage intellectual faith. Through the effect of a double influence and of a double revolt, it is possible to follow to the very end in his works the combination of a heart and a mind that contradict each other; of an intellect that believes in the necessity of order and the effectiveness of logic, that subjects everything to rational explanation and empirical verification; and of a sensibility that thirsts for, and values, only disinterested exaltation, free movement, and ineffable emotion. That this fundamental opposition compromises the solidity of the system is very possible; but it is the artist, not the philosopher, that we are looking for in Stendhal, and a work of art can conciliate opposites much better than dialectics. What is unique and undefinable in his charm comes from this happy fault. Like those young faces of which it might be said that life has not yet specialized their attractiveness, one finds in him hints of many things, promises of still others; he excites in the reader at the same time forces of curiosity and of sympathy that no other author has been able to concentrate. He awakens, excites, flatters, caresses everything, and—the secret of his charm—without ever satisfying. The contradiction which remains carries perfect satisfaction over into a "beyond," and his works are thus crowned by the poetic prestige of the unfinished and the elusive.

This same antinomy should furnish the key to Stendhal's characters, if it is true, as we have tried to show, that their creator constantly incarnated himself in his creatures. Thus can be explained the fact that their behavior conforms to the needs of a boundless sensibility, that the inward thrusts of passion bring forth, during all the intense moments of their story, an unbroken surface of reason, and that one perceives in their conduct neither design without indiscretion nor enthusiasm without design. It should also furnish the key to his opinions, if it is true, as we believe, that his opinions in everything were drawn exclusively from his personal experience. And thus can be explained that he should have counterposed on all important subjects two different opinions, one of which translates the conviction of the intellect where the other expresses the conflicting needs of the heart. The intellect, empiricist and positivist, professes the philosophy of utility and the religion of the fact. The character of Olivier in *Armance* is particularly significant in this respect, and, under the species of Olivier and of Lucien Leuwen, Stendhal seems, at moments, even to come close to Saint-Simonism. The heart, on the other hand, is repelled by the material satisfactions by which most men are contented and fooled—those petty interests which turn one away from the real life. In its distaste for anything profitable, for those large, well-cultivated tracts of land, for the kind of positive activity exemplified by the Swiss or Yankee personality, it turns back, with a nuance of regret, to the old courtly society as described by Duclos and Lauzun, whose graceful, free and easy carelessness is a form of elegance. In politics, all his thought-out convictions lead Stendhal to democracy. He held at once to the lessons of Montesquieu and of Rousseau. He was strong on the two Houses, and one remembers that Julien Sorel, in the seminary, exposed himself to the worst reprisals in order to read *Le Constitutionnel,* the liberal sheet of the times. But, while the reason recognizes democracy for the best of governments and protests against all social distinctions between men, the heart and the nerves demand those perfectly harmonious feelings that only the contact of an elite can procure. "I had, and still have the most aristocratic tastes. I would do anything for the happiness of the people, but I should prefer spending fifteen days out of each month in prison to living among shopkeepers." The same contradiction is found in his aesthetics: he held, as we have seen, that the devices of the artist constituted a definite and certain "technique," that is to say, a science; he considered the work of art as a determined phenomenon that the activity of natural laws, historic conditions, and physical temperaments controls, and this was the great innovation of his *Histoire de la peinture en Italie;* but, at the same time, creative inspiration and the ecstasy of contemplation of the Beautiful seemed to him the realization of a mystery, a pure emanation of the inner life, a sort of ineffable revelation which swells from the most secret regions of the heart. Even for the imitation of the coldest objects, the painter must have a "soul." Beauty is that which speaks to the soul, that which throws it into revery, that which transports it into "those noble distances" where it believes the happiness that reality keeps from it is to be found; and, if the notion of beauty varies through history, it is because all the generations of men have not agreed on the notion of happiness. Stendhal maintained in turn, or both at the same time, that the work of art is an almost pre-determined product, and the expression, that is to say, the spiritual life, is all of art.

The same contradiction holds in his manner of writing: purely logical when it is a question of explaining feelings or beings, purely poetic when it is a question of expressing them. This is why, when one calls Stendhal an analyst, when the analytical spirit has been seen as his *faculté maîtresse* in the sense that Taine attached to the term, the judgment is not incorrect; rather it is partial, incomplete, and only accounts for one aspect of his genius. Doubtless the material of his books was entirely furnished by introspection or inner experimentation, and he conceived this double work in the manner of the scientist who isolates the phenomenon in question, attempts to obtain it in the pure state, and then studies the variations of it under different reactions. He wished to see the heart just as it is, putting aside all the causes of error or illusion. Since he believed in the mechanical continuity of states of consciousness, since he held that the feelings just as well as the other phenomena of nature have each a sufficient reason, he schooled himself to place them in their proper order. Hence his characters' actions and emotions are always justified by their motive, and, as Paul Bourget has shown, he passes on to his characters themselves the task of justifying their conduct. Stendhal's heroes are soliloquizers. Let us note in passing that, if they carry on this perpetual discussion with themselves, it is not because they are affected by the "mania of self-dissection," it is not that Stendhal has made them "quibblers, scrutinizing their most intimate secrets, and reflecting upon themselves with the lucidity of a Maine de Biran or a Jouffroy." By a genial vision, which is the glory of his heroes and which places Stendhalian analysis high above the ordinary psychologies, Stendhal, in fact, conceived of critical self-curiosity and perspicacity as a necessary adjunct of personal scruples, of the feeling of honor. If his characters examine them-

selves, it is not to know themselves, but for self-control, to assure themselves, at each critical turning-point of their lives, that they are doing
nothing unworthy of their own self-esteem. The problems they put to their
consciences are moving, since their dignity and even their happiness are
in the balance, and if they dissect themselves, it is not out of a pedantic
attention or a morbid mania, but rather a kind of vital necessity. But,
even in this work, Stendhal leaves voluntary gaps, which Zola has pointed
up with rare perspicacity: those "analytical leaps," those "danses du
personnage" which correspond to a sudden intuition, to the rapid jolt of
the unforeseen. And above all—here is the essential point—he never
maintained that in ordering the elements of a chapter or the motives of an
action along the lines of deduction, a novelist would have exhausted all
of his task.

The working out of a psychological novel involves a preliminary work,
to which the name of analysis is appropriate, which consists in rounding
up a certain number of facts and ideas through observation and reflection,
in determining the relations between them—in a word, in establishing
between the motives and the feelings of the characters the same kinds of
apparent logical connections that a playwright tries to create between
the events he is dealing with. This preparatory operation does not demand, strictly speaking, any properly literary talent, and does not
presuppose any other faculties than those that the philosopher, the doctor,
the politician, and even the businessman employ regularly in the practice
of their profession. Where talent and art come in is in the putting to use,
in the animation of the psychological raw materials thus assembled; and
the real sign of talent, the very condition of art, is that the preliminary
operation be absorbed in its result. It is no longer a question of explaining an emotion, but of communicating its quality and force; not of
cataloguing the motives behind an act, but of bringing out its human
signification or dramatic accent; not of listing the elements making up a
character, but in making the very life and specific individuality felt.
Analysis falls short of this task because to analyze means necessarily to
generalize, to bring out the common principles of distinct realities. Only
evocative synthesis, of which poetry is the most perfect mode, can bring
us into communication with the pure emotion, with the real being, with
the essential in life. Art begins with this synthesis, and Stendhal, at the
same time that he is an analyst and a logician, is an artist.

Hence, he only held himself to the analytical method in stories composed for demonstrative purpose, like the one he placed at the end of the
book, *De l'Amour*. Since his goal was to prove a theory by an example, to
follow the development of a feeling along a predetermined route, he
follows it in fact, step by step, with an explanation and a justification of
the itinerary, the whole thing worked out in advance with prodigious
care, and the effect being that of a prodigious aridity. This exception

set aside, one feels him, once he has finished his preparation, to be searching out the wholly significant act which reveals the depth of a character, the shade of feeling that reveals the uniqueness of a being, the pointed fact or inspired word which brings to light the virgin states of the soul. Far from relying on the agency of causes and forces to express emotions, he confides to us his vexation that common language is incapable of translating them, and that it is impossible to pour the essence of life into the too rigid mold of words. In order to establish contact between his character and life, then between his character and the reader, he proceeds by shocks and jolts, by rapid and repeated suggestions. No commentary, no explanation, but on the contrary unforeseen grasps, sudden dashes which search out and find the intangible regions of feeling. Taine, who was the master of modern analysis, felt better than anyone else the purely emotive character of this manner. He even added that this virtue produces obscurity. "The reader," he said, "should be able to discover without their being explained to him, the relations and repercussions of such delicate, such strong feelings in characters so original and so great." Elsewhere he says, and admirably, relating Stendhal to Goethe, Byron, and Musset: "Each word is like a blow to the heart. The abruptness, the destructiveness, the mobility of the passions, all their turmoil, all the madness, all the oddness, all the profundities of human emotions, I feel them at once, not after study, by reflection, as when I read others, but right off, and in spite of myself." It is thanks to this search for substantial life, by this appeal to the passionate sympathy of the reader, to the feelings called forth in him, that Julien Sorel and Fabrice del Dongo have been cherished or hated like real people. Only the emotion of art can create such miracles. Moreover, did not Stendhal himself, conscious of his double nature, often feel that the invincible surges of his feelings were outweighing the perfect ordering of his logic? When he made himself re-read the Napoleonic Code each morning, was this anything other than the defense of Condillac's pupil against the sentimental excesses *à la Rousseau* into which he felt himself spontaneously drawn? "I make every possible effort to be dry. I want to impose silence on my heart which believes it has much to say. I am forever trembling to have set down nothing more than a sigh when I think I have written a truth." Thus the logician was mistrustful of the poet, and the poet, likewise, in his moments of pure abandon, was mistrustful of logic and analysis. "Such tender feelings are spoiled if set forth in detail." That is the unfinished sentence on which the *Vie de Henry Brulard* ends, and on which one can only dream.

Truth in Masquerade

by Jean Starobinski

When a man puts on a mask or takes on a pseudonym, we feel challenged. That man eludes us. We, in turn, want to *know,* we decide to unmask him. From whom is he trying to conceal himself? What Power does he fear? What manner of Glance shames him? Once again we ask: what kind of face had he that he felt the need to dissemble it? And other questions follow immediately from the preceding ones: What does this new face in which he masquerades mean, what significance does he give to his masked demeanor, what is he now trying to simulate having dissimulated that which wanted to disappear?

Doubtless political precautions play some part in Stendhal's pseudonymity. For one thing, Fouché or the Terreur Blanche explain and justify César Bombet.[1] Customs officials, concierges (and jealous husbands) would have had good reason to open his letters or decipher the cryptic writing of his diary. There is indeed matter for concern. For this somewhat over-loquacious libertarian the danger is quite real, as proved by the registers of the Austrian police and the papal chancellery. But danger is only a pretext, almost an excuse. Stendhal's concern is disproportionate to the actual menace. Even far from any danger Stendhal still plays at wearing masks. And not only those masks that abet his disappearance and favor incognito. Stendhal's pseudonymity is not an escape into anonymity. It is an art of appearing, it is a deliberate altering of human relations. For Stendhal attempts to flee the system of nominal values only to dominate it and better to manipulate it.

One discerns here an act of protest. To take a pseudonym is, first of

"Truth in Masquerade." Translated by B. A. B. Archer. From *L'Œil vivant* by Jean Starobinski (Paris: Librairie Gallimard, 1961). All rights reserved. Reprinted by permission of Librairie Gallimard. The essay originally appeared in *Les Temps Modernes* (October 1951). The pages reprinted here are only a part of the essay "Stendhal pseudonyme."

[1] Joseph Fouché was Minister of the Police during the Empire. The Terreur Blanche refers to the persecutions and political repression durring the first years of the Restoration. César Bombet was one of Stendhal's many pseudonyms. [Ed. note.]

all, either out of shame or resentment, a repudiation of the name trans-
mitted by one's father. A name, like the effigy whose heart (or "heart
region") is pierced, contains in substance the life one wishes to anni-
hilate. If a name is truly an identity, if through it the essence of a human being can be reached and brutalized, the refusal of a patronym is
a substitute for patricide. It is the least cruel form of murder in effigy.
Humiliated by his father, Stendhal avenged himself by calling him
(notably in his letters to his sister Pauline) "the bastard." The insult is
clearly aimed at the legitimacy of the name. In his filial hatred, Stendhal
concocts the most extraordinary hypotheses for disclaiming any relationship with the Beyle family. One can see the development of a veritable
system of filial interpretation: he feels himself far too unlike Chérubin
Beyle to be his legitimate son; he is probably the secret heir to a more
impressive lineage. The "myth of birth" (which plays its part in the
Chartreuse) is a deep-rooted reverie of the young Henri Beyle. It is
Stendhal himself who would be the bastard, but the defamatory accusation is hurled at the father.

Our name awaits us. It was there before we knew it, like our body. The
common illusion consists in believing that our destiny and our reality are
inscribed in it. Thus one confers upon a name the dignity of an essence.
Stendhal in some ways plays along with this illusion. If he rejects the
patronym Beyle, it is because he sees in it a predestination from which
he intends to escape. That predestination binds him to France, to
Grenoble, to the middle class, to the paternal universe of parsimony and
sordid calculation. And because he envisages the risk of being tied to
his name, he tries to offer himself greater possibilities by taking a new
name. He would not have found pseudonymity necessary had he felt free
in spite of his name, had he known how to accept his bourgeois and
Grenoblois identity as a purely official convention that in no way prevented him from seeking all possible destinies.

In assuming a new name, he not only grants himself a new face, but
a new destiny, a new social rank, new nationalities. (He is the last of the
Cosmopolites of the eighteenth century, but also the first of the "good
Europeans" of the nineteenth.) Some of the pseudonyms are German:
Stendhal, for example, is the name of a Prussian town. On the other
hand, since happiness can flourish only in Italy, the imagination of young
Henri Beyle constructs a whole Italian genealogy for the maternal side of
the family. His mother, of whom he was enamored, cannot possibly
belong in Grenoble. His image of her is thus repatriated in the warm
and voluptuous contryside of Lombardy. And so, with each trip outside of France, Stendhal has the impression of rejoining his true world;
he enjoys living outside his country just as he enjoys living outside his
name. His passion for traveling, his pleasure in flight coincide perfectly
with his pseudonymity.

It is useless to enumerate Stendhal's pseudonyms; there are more than a hundred. Alongside this list one might draw up another of the pseudonyms Stendhal bestowed upon his friends, some of which—for the game is contagious—they adopted for their own use. This is the tangible sign of the "understanding" that sets them apart from the rest of the world. They know henceforth that they belong to an exclusive group. The *Happy Few* are a small society who cultivate the rational knowledge of the human heart. But these rationalists like to surround themselves with the prestige of concealment, even to the point of assuming in jest certain esoteric manners. Secretiveness, or the simulacrum of secretiveness, becomes part of their system, and their complicity is confirmed by pseudonymity. In every clandestine society, initiates receive a new name; Stendhal and his friends all but adopted an initiatory language.

Stendhal's pseudonyms are amazing in their diversity. Some of them are episodic and disappear immediately upon use. Others persist throughout Stendhal's lifetime: along with the stable pseudonyms are unstable ones. Some of the pseudonyms are intended to charm: Dominique, Salviati, are names of love, components of a more elegant and more amorous nature. The entire effect of these seductive identities resides in the tenderness of the name which magically invokes a trusting intimacy. In other cases, for greater eminence, he takes some princely name. But there are also pseudonyms for sheer amusement; names that are grotesquely middle-class to the point even of caricature—Cotonnet, Bombet, Chamier, Baron de Cutendre, William Crocodile. Some of these pseudonyms are for exhibition—funny, glorious, tender. Others are pseudonyms of escape, to render him invisible to or protect him from bothersome individuals.

Such prodigality in the use of pseudonyms makes one wonder what is a name. In obliging us to pose such a question, the masked egotist walks off with the first victory; he manipulates us and leaves us uncertain. We discover, in fact, that a man is never completely within his name, or completely behind his name, just as he is never completely within his face, or back of it. We can not persevere very long in either the realistic illusion or the nominative illusion. A name alternately appears as something full and something empty, in some cases fraught with great density of existence, in others reduced to a superficial and meaningless verbal convention. An entire life is concentrated in it as it is reduced to a symbol. But this symbol is only a symbol; we can learn nothing from it. We no longer know before whom we stand. This is what the egotist anticipated. "I am not where you expected to find me."

Pseudonymity is thus not only a rupture with parental and social origins, it is a rupture with others. Our identity, which binds us to our name, delivers us at the same time as hostages to other consciences. It offers us up defenseless to the judgment of others. The egotist, however, is out to retrieve himself. He destroys the name that makes him vulnerable in that part of himself which reflects the gaze of others. In so loosing the bond that delivers him, unarmed, to outsiders, he hopes to escape all injury to his pride.

If it is true that our name contains the uniqueness of our life while at the same time transmitting its symbolic description to other consciences, then the egotist's striving will be to preserve this uniqueness while simultaneously destroying or undermining the reciprocity of consciences. He certainly cannot prevent the world from using his name, but he can arrange for his name to cease designating him. He dreams somewhat ingeniously of being in the situation of seeing without being seen (a desire clearly expressed in certain pages of Stendhal's intimate writings).

A name is situated symbolically at the confluence of existence "for oneself" and existence "for others." It is an intimate truth and a public thing. In accepting my name I accept that there be a common denominator between my inner being and my social being. It is at this level that the pseudonym proposes to effect a radical disjunction. It purports to separate two worlds at the very point at which, through the intermediary of language, their union was made possible. Through this act, the egotist revolts against his membership in society. He refuses to be offered up to others, and at the same time he is given to himself. For him, the freedom to act is conceivable only under insubordination. That is why he has recourse to the pseudonym which unties his hands. The first requirement of egotistical individualism is the dissociation of personal existence from its manifestation to the world. *Noli me tangere* could be his motto. But there he reveals his basic weakness. What is he afraid of? In permitting too clear an identity to appear he is afraid of being too clearly understood, of being wide open, which means for him being annulled, ceasing to mean anything in the eyes of others. If he had enough confidence in himself, he would not seek in this way to establish his value on the mystery of his conduct. The egotist, who suffers from being misunderstood, suffers even more from being understood. Through fear of his person being reached by others, he will devote himself systematically to the separation of his person and his personation.

In the equation $I = I$, the name (in the eyes of others) acts as the equal sign. Confined to our name, our identity becomes alienated; it comes to us through and from others. But the egotist revolts against this identity that is imposed from the outside. Why should he not be the sole master of this oneness that makes him identical with himself? In giving himself a pseudonym he affirms his basic autonomy. Is he, however, progressing validly toward the possession of himself? He gives himself a verbal identity as exterior and contingent as that attributed to him by others, the only difference being that in place of others he confers it upon himself. A pseudonym eliminates perjury and allows the invocation of a plurality of *I*'s as a splendid alibi.

Noblesse oblige, it is said. That which obliges is the name, the title. The egotist is irritated above all when feeling that his name, in constituting an obligation toward himself, established a necessary relationship with others. Only he is responsible whom one calls by his name and whom one summons to answer. But if my name no longer designates me, I am no longer obliged to respond, unless it be to him who still possesses the right and power to name me. "To me alone," says the rebel. Nothing prevents him from playing out the game still further by refusing to hold himself responsible to himself. From that point on he no longer carries his name, he is carried away by an imaginary name. Thus he can indulge in a feeling of dizzying propulsion in which the energy of movement seems to come entirely from the mask, rather than from the "real" being who dissembles behind the mask. The mask and the pseudonym generate a perfect dynamics of irresponsibility.

The pseudonymity of Stendhal has this quality of movement and, among other ends, aims at effecting a change on the social ladder. From Henri Beyle to Baron Frédéric de Stendhal is quite an advancement. The essence of Stendhal's pleasure does not lie in the fake nobility that he assumes, but in the movement itself. For movement is the law of pseudonymous existence, it is the *sine qua non* of its success. As a matter of fact, Stendhal just as willingly assumes ridiculous names which in no way enhance him. What is important is never to tarry in the invention, is to renew constantly the surprise that non-plusses others. The mask must be a procession of masks, and pseudonymity a systematic "polynymity." Otherwise the egotist is recaptured by others, the misunderstanding he sought to flee will only be aggravated and to his disadvantage. He must always be a few lengths ahead of the others. He must even dissemble whatever is systematic about his secret behavior. For to allow the perception of a system is to render oneself explicable and thus lose any benefit from the secret. A ridiculous undertaking indeed if he gives the impression of following a *system* of escape! He who is too ostensibly in search of mystery risks spoiling all his effects and never becoming an enigma to others. His imposture defines him once and for all. A certain manner of candid living, given to confession and perpetual avowals, is sometimes more effective than the use of a mask. Stendhal knew this very well. His confidences, with their qualifications and infinite contradictions, make him more mysterious than his strategy of impersonation.

Stendhal's indefatigable and elusive pseudonymity is totally different from the simpler pseudonymity of those who once and for all assume an advantageous name that will more readily consecrate their glory. Most of the writers and artists who take an unchanging and definitive pseudonym do not seek to disconcert the consciousness of others, but rather to install themselves in it with greater prestige. The name they choose, and which confers upon them a more impressive life, character, and destiny, is only intended to attract celebrity. Their purpose is merely to place on their side all the phonetic possibilities that seem indispensable to success. This temptation exists in Stendhal but counts for very little. Certainly he is enamored of glory; he wants to make a name for himself. But he also wants that name to remain on the outside and grant him the freedom to inhabit a thousand other names.

In the case of Stendhal, the theme of confinement must be underlined. A name, a body, a social status, all are prisons. But their doors are not so well locked that the dream of escape is impossible. Of course, one takes leave of one's name more easily than of one's body, and a pseudonym is a substitute for the desired metamorphosis. (This impatience with having to tolerate one's body can be found in almost every writer who has had recourse to a pseudonym. However different, Voltaire and Kierkegaard share a certain anxious attention to their bodies and their ailments. In this sense pseudonymity represents a manifestation of hypochondria.)

In order to express this imprisonment, the metaphor of the cell naturally appears. One sees chains, thick walls, high well-guarded towers. These images stubbornly recur in Stendhal's works. The heroes who are imprisoned and who escape—Julien at the seminary, Fabrice in the Farnese tower, Hélène Campireale in the convent, Lamiel at the Hautemares—seem each time to recreate an archetypal situation. The theme of *amour-passion* is curiously involved. Imprisonment corresponds to the birth of the highest form of love, which derives its power from its impossibility. Desire, then, implies distance and insurmountable separation. Octave, confined within the fatality of his impotence, loves Armance all the more ardently in that he can not abolish the impediment that keeps him from her. Octave, however, is loved in return, just as all the imprisoned heroes are loved in return in spite of the locks, or perhaps because of them. Extreme unhappiness thus meets extreme happiness. It is in this that one clearly sees the power of compensation that pervades Stendhal's fiction. If society avenges itself on the exceptional individual by imprisoning him, from his very high tower he can avenge himself on society by transforming his solitude into a contemptuous and hopeless happiness. The motif of high places, stressed by Proust as a fundamental theme in Stendhal, merges with the theme of confinement. These glorious prisoners need but one long look to dominate the world. In these heroes, who are visited by love in prison, one must recognize (among other things) the figurative transposition of Stendhal's secret desire—to be loved in spite of his ugliness, in spite of the prison that his body and age are for him; to love and be loved from afar through the power of a glance. Destruction does not threaten this love, either because it can never be consummated in possession and marriage and is consequently never exposed to destruction, or because even if consummated it always remains furtive and clandestine, thus lightening in an extraordinary way the importance of the body.

We have then to do with a man unhappy with what he is and discontent with his body ("Why am I myself?"), and who is torn between two conflicting desires: to affirm himself by an act of power which will impose on others his absolute singularity, or to metamorphose ceaselessly, to become other than himself, to split in two so as to become both an accomplished actor and an invisible spectator through some form of efficacious travesty. These two tendencies, which Stendhal's behavior manages to keep from becoming totally contradictory, are expressed in two affirmations that must be juxtaposed without any circumspection: "The only thing of value in this world is the self." However, in *Souvenirs d'égotisme,* one finds: "Will I be believed? I would wear a mask with pleasure, I would change my name with delight. The thousand and one nights I adore fill more than a quarter of my brain. Often I think of Angelica's ring. My supreme pleasure would be to change into a tall blond German and wander about Paris." [2] The desire to be oneself; the pleasure in conjuring up impossible sorceries to cease being oneself—this is the premise we must examine.

Scattered through the *Journal* and other autobiographical writings of Stendhal are a thousand references to the use of a mask and to the pleasure of "the feeling of living in many versions." "Look at life as though it were a masked ball" [3] is the advice Stendhal gives himself in his diary of 1814. The essential thing about this profession of faith is not the accusation directed against the comedy of society nor the excuse it provides for any disguise, but rather the intense complicity between pleasure and travesty. The significance of Stendhal's hypocrisy, even more than the pragmatic success of the scheme, is its elegance of means, the aesthetic achievement of "gamesmanship." Hypocrisy, in the masked ball, becomes the rule of the game. The struggle for power or fortune becomes part of the festivity, and through an ultimate return to gratuitousness, the hypocrite has no further ambition than the perfection of his own game. He need only indulge in the pleasure of being so completely outside himself.

In an almost pristine form, there exists in Stendhal's writings the admission of a profound relationship between the "principle of pleasure" and the desire for metamorphosis. It can be found in a curious piece that he wrote at the end of his life entitled *Les Privilèges du 10 avril 1840.* In it, he formulates his permanent reveries—at an age at which

[2] *Souvenirs d'égotisme* in *Œuvres intimes,* ed. Pléiade. (Paris: Librairie Gallimard, 1955), pp. 1449-1450.
[3] *Journal, in Œuvres intimes, ed. cit.,* p. 1041.

most people are concerned with their last will and testament—under the format of a contract with God. The text begins with the line "God has given me the following licence." Let us look at one of the articles.

> Article 3.—The *mentula*, like an index finger for rigidity and flexibility, this at will. Size, two inches longer than original, same thickness. But pleasure through the *mentula* only twice a week. Twenty times a year, the licencee may become whatever individual he wishes, provided that individual exists. One hundred times a year, he shall know for 24 hours the language of his choice.[4]

The desire for erotic power, the desire for metamorphosis, and the desire for command of a new language are strangely juxtaposed. According to good logic, such utterly different wishes should not appear side by side. But good logic is here mistaken and it is the imagination that is right. It freely improvises and, under diverse aspects, translates a unique affective inspiration. The desire for erotic power and the dream of metamorphosis, which appear simultaneously, express a twofold aspect of a single wish for power. What is involved in each case is the submission of sexual life and the body to conscious will. This body that he must accept as a contingent fact, Stendhal dreams of retrieving from contingency and of offering to himself freely according to the caprice of a totally voluntary act. As to the sexual mechanism, so wholly dependent on the involuntary system, so independent from the exercise of will, it too will be able to respond to some deliberate command. One sees in this the imperialism of will taking as object not the exterior universe or the cosmos, but the body itself, which becomes an obedient tool. In the text cited above, we discern two meanings in the desire to have control over his body in order to possess *another* body. For sexual possession and metamorphosis are, in fact, two ways of "entering into the body of another." Desire here provides a choice between two kinds of attainment. It imagines in turn the infallible triumph of an extroverted sexuality, and the narcissistic satisfaction of inhabiting a body that remains his own while becoming another.

In this refusal of the body in its reality and limitations, there is nothing to bespeak disincarnation. Stendhal exalts physical existence by imagining it liberated from any servitude. Having a body becomes wonderful as soon as one receives it from oneself. This chimera is very similar to the mythical dream of a portion of immortality. While inhabiting an opaque body over which we have no mastery we live in a manner of dubious cohabitation with death. For it is precisely through that element in our body which eludes our will that death reaches us. To become lord and master of our body would mean to avert the threat. All at once, every enslavement of the human condition disappears; one passes into the ranks of the gods.

[4] *Privilèges, ed. cit.,* p. 1559 ff.

Les Privilèges is a text dating from Stendhal's later years, and manifests a Faustian desire for rejuvenation within the completely pagan perspective of new beginnings that defy death. Metamorphosis, for Stendhal, is an opening onto the future. It is an acceleration of existence, but one that turns its back on death. (Notice that for Kafka metamorphosis is the exact opposite. It is the aggravation of the physical condition, the slowing down of existence. Energy stops and becomes paralyzed; the future is cut off and shrinks concentrically until it is reabsorbed in the unique manifestation of destruction.)

One finds in ancient mythology two opposing forms of metamorphosis. For Zeus, it is an instrument of aggression and amorous conquest. For Proteus, it provides the means of escape and inaccessibility. For Stendhal, conquest and escape are linked and figure as complementary attitudes. The desire to appear and disappear are to him both part of the same "complex." They are two ways of being significant in the eyes of others, and of not being annihilated by the gaze of others. Ashamed of his ugliness, Stendhal knows that he can not be loved and desired as he is. He dreams of being seen in an image other than his real one. By shrouding himself in mystery, and trying to remain enigmatic, he invents a maze of appearances in which the glance of others will henceforth loose its way. He will be sought beyond his body in a trompe-l'œil perspective. The mask, when perfect, tempts one to imagine a world behind the mask. Pure mirage, but one toward which the victim rushes, only to deliver himself to his seducer.

Stendhal knows still other ways of diverting the gaze of others from his ugliness, for example, by forcing others to look at themselves. By posing in society as "connaisseur of the human heart," he has occasion to unsettle his interlocutors, who experience with little equanimity the piercing look that scrutinizes and interrogates them. Through a reversal that constrains others to feel gazed upon, he ceases to be the person looked at. He then expects to fascinate more easily those whom he previously disconcerted by their own mystery. He reaches them through their narcissism.

Stendhal, according to his contemporaries, was a past master at grimaces. One need only recall the appearance, in the Ancelot's salon, of Monsieur César Bombet, merchant in nightcaps. The hours he spends before his mirror—arranging his dress or his toupee, dying his hair, manicuring his nails—are real sessions of makeup. They reveal a man preparing for the outside world like an actor for his audience. If Stendhal takes infinite pains over his elegance, it is because he understands that his ugliness can only be annulled by his carriage, through which his body ceases to be a thing and becomes a symbol. And when, instead of seeking elegance, he opts for some kind of grotesque derision, it is also to make one overlook his ugliness through comedy and buffoonery. He who provokes laughter has already been accepted. One is no longer aware of his unsightly nose, but notices rather whatever amusement he can provide by means of his nose. By thus exploiting his physiognomy (as his uncle Gagnon advised him) he attracts attention, but not to his ugliness. Hidden behind the mobility of his grimaces, his ugliness becomes almost unreal and clears the way for the pleasure of pleasing.

Let us continue our perusal of those remarkable *Privilèges du 10 avril 1840*. We shall find some examples of metamorphoses imagined by Stendhal, and will be surprised to discover that, after having wished for exquisite worldly elegance, he manifests the desire to be transformed into an animal. This is to provide him with the pleasure of elementary vitality.

Article 5.—Beautiful hair, beautiful skin, fine hands that are never rough, fragrant and delicate odor. The first of February and the first of June each year, the clothes of the licencee shall become as they were the third time they were worn.

Article 6.—Miracles in the eyes of all who do not know him: the licencee shall have the face of General Debell, who died in Santo Domingo, without any imperfection. He shall play perfect whist, écarté, billiards, chess, but shall never win more than 100 francs. He shall shoot, ride, and fence to perfection.

Article 7.—Four times a year, he shall turn into whatever animal he wishes; and thereafter, turn back into a man. Four times a year, he shall change into whatever man he wishes; in addition, he shall be able to dissemble his life in that of an animal, which animal shall, in the event of death or impediment on the part of the first man into whom he was changed, be able to reinstate him in the natural form of the licencee. Thus the licencee shall, four times a year, and for an unlimited period each time, inhabit two bodies at once.

This double transformation, to perfection and animal, corresponds rather well to the tendencies in Stendhal's amorous life. In effect, his experiences in love were either far above or far below his station. One finds practically no middle-class ladies among his mistresses—they are duchesses or slatterns. Love has no attraction for him unless he feels called upon to transform himself. His first passions were for actresses with whom he fell in love while reciting lines from Molière and Racine. He loved them because they led him into the world of metamorphosis and because, more than any others, they gave him the pleasure he sought— pleasure that can flourish only in an atmosphere of theatricality. He assumed, after having made their conquest, that he would love them more and longer than other women. For with them he expected to continue the exercise of metamorphosis, even to the minutest details of daily living. Such living is the only kind not threatened by boredom, which takes over as soon as the power of metamorphosis wanes. It happens that

Stendhal is bored from the outset by middle-class women since he has
no need to transform himself in order to seduce them. As to the lady of
high society, the creature idealized "à la Correggio," what matters is
that she remain constantly inaccessible. For to conquer her is to have lost
the need to surpass oneself. When metamorphosis becomes useless, love is
also paralyzed, frozen in the ice of boredom. Distance and obstacles are
thus essential to Stendhalian lovers, not only to give value to the conquest, but above all to necessitate a transformation of the individual,
which itself constitutes satisfaction. Love for a woman already won
can only endure by becoming clandestine or illicit—by obligating Fabrice
and Julien to repeat constantly a masked exploit.

The passage quoted above invites another comment. Stendhal dreams of
inhabiting two bodies at the same time. The metamorphosis he desires
is not a depersonalization, but a multiplication of the self, a veritable
"superpersonalization." Not only does he wish to become another, but to
become many others.

Stendhal adopts a pseudonymous existence both as a means and an end.
He enjoys it for its own sake, but also in view of the effect it produces
and the advantage it nets his pride. This is to say that all through his
many metamorphoses Stendhal is concerned with preserving his vigilant
conscience that secretly collects the spoils of his masked demeanor.
Though altering his appearance he is nonetheless determined to maintain
permanent clairvoyance; he ceaselessly surveys—from the vantage point of
a chief of staff—all the movements of the battle, in which only the
simulacrum of his thoughts is involved. One's powers of observation must
never falter or misinterpret, if one is watching for the desired effect. And
so an invulnerable interior is erected, since it has become pure observation
of the self and of others, and cannot be reached in turn by the gaze of
witnesses. Having made of his face and body an instrument of which he
freely disposes, he is no longer their captive. He no longer accepts them
as a fatality. The mask (and the pseudonym) thus appears as the attainment of liberty. This liberty makes use of a body from which it has
finally disengaged itself and which can be maneuvered at will. Here we
have a true mechanism of release, one from which this man, who was
always ashamed of his body's clumsiness, knew how to profit. One need
only think of the use of the mask as an accessory to the dance, whether
primitive rites or modern dancing, to see that the effect of release is a
permanent feature of masquerade. Irony, so cherished by Stendhal,
achieves the same disengagement and the same release. But irony is nothing other than the spiritual quintessence of the mask.

Behind the game that conceals appearances, Stendhal plans to keep
his lucidity intact; a lucidity that harbors his true permanence and his
inalterable identity. He conserves the functions necessary for seeing him-

self act. A highly alert self must be ever-present in order to savor this experience of successful activity, which is one form of the pleasure. This taste for metamorphosis in Stendhal is directly allied to the taste for action and energy. Doubtless there is in the first place an impediment to spontaneous action; doubtless the recourse to metamorphosis manifests the need to utilize devious means to rejoin the world. Whatever the case, metamorphosis for Stendhal is always basically voluntary and dynamic, as proved by *Les Privilèges du 10 avril 1840*. This distinguishes Stendhal from seekers of passive metamorphoses. I doubt that Stendhal would have enjoyed the narcotics that transform existence into something fabulous at the cost of submitting to passivity. The mid-nineteenth-century taste for hashish and opium corresponds to a sensibility that differs greatly from Stendhal's voluntarism. Metamorphosis can be experienced actively or passively—to be metamorphosed, or to metamorphose oneself. Stendhal chose to metamorphose himself actively. He is in such need of others that he can not abandon himself to a daydream in which he no longer confronts his rivals and adversaries.

We know that Stendhal's worldly ambitions were meagerly fulfilled. The fall of the Empire marked the end of his social success. His chances for advancement in the reactionary world of the restoration were slim. In spite of the subtlest of tactics, Stendhal ran into insurmountable limitations and barriers. Can one really quit one's body? Mephistopheles does not appear on the scene every day to strike a bargain. The world of the imagination is then free to provide all the triumphs if reality resists too stubbornly. But that would mean stopping the game, renouncing once and for all his claim to society. Stendhal does not consent to this. One avenue remains open for conquering the world, while at the same time allowing him to conjure his metamorphoses. It is literature, a devious route that Stendhal first thought of using to achieve success. It must be noted that Stendhal banked on social success before banking on literary success. At the time he decided to write, his primary aim was to gain prestige, not to create a masterpiece. In seeking literary fame he was out to rebound into high society. As a young man Stendhal's velleities for the theatre were specifically directed toward the kind of theatrical success that promises quick celebrity. His plagiarisms were a financial speculation, at the same time providing the pleasure of cheap metamorphosis. After purloining someone's book, Stendhal *ipso facto* is obliged to go into hiding to deny his theft—superb occasion to dissemble. This situation that he deliberately provokes permits him to justify his love of the mask. Travesty thus becomes indispensable. But success is not that easily attained. At a loss for another alternative, Stendhal finally decides to hand over his private dreams to the general public. It is his last trump and he is reluctant to play it too fast. Endowed with a little more artfulness and greater savoir-faire, Stendhal might not have resisted the temptation to become a successful hack writer, contemptuous of his audience yet flattering at the same time. Perhaps it was out of awkwardness and an inability to dissociate completely from himself—the same awkwardness that paralyzed him in the face of others and doomed to failure his political ambitions—that Stendhal remained attached to his dreams of happiness, to his desires, his intimate preferences. Stendhal's good fortune as a writer lies in his incapability of leaving himself. In the reveries of metamorphosis in which he becomes Julien, Fabrice, Lucien, Lamiel, he changes face, body, social status, even sex, but it is always to tell his own life story while introducing greater fortune and greater misfortune. Unlike Balzac, he does not pursue the secret lives of others. He begins his own life anew in another body, the way one starts a card game with a fresh deal. Stendhal's metamorphosis does not attempt to concretize the basic alienation expressed by Rimbaud's "Je est un autre." It aims not at a change of being, but at a change of contingency. That is how he can remain himself while giving himself the destinies of Fabrice or Julien, who recompense him for his failures. This is how he consoles himself for not having been appointed prefect. The vexation of living under "the most knavish of kings" finds its compensation.

Compensation for Stendhal consists not only in imagining his characters happy in love, but merely in imagining them alive. They live under his eyes, they are others and himself, they live for him by proxy but without compromising him. He keeps his distance from his invented brothers but guides them from afar. After a while he sees them emancipate, take surprising decisions almost against his own will as creator. They are truly alive since they act freely, and yet never cease acting for Stendhal's benefit. He thus obtains the desired pleasure. He lives outside himself, he really inhabits "two bodies at the same time" since his imaginary figures have active bodies and autonomous destinies. In addition, we notice that these characters themselves do not forget to masquerade in their turn. The desire for metamorphosis that suscitated them perpetuates itself in them. One could enumerate the successive costumes of Fabrice del Dongo: barometer salesman, hussard, rustic, laborer, priest, English eccentric, valet. . . . Thus freed from his body and his ennui, Stendhal henceforth belongs to his characters who lead him where they will. His inner development has completely infiltrated into the unforseeable development of these "others" who are nevertheless himself. He thus gives himself the illusion of living out his destiny outside himself, seeing all without being seen, as though watching from a darkened box the spectacle of ultimately attained happiness and power.

Knowledge and Tenderness
In Stendhal

by Jean-Pierre Richard

Throughout all his lives, whether real or imaginary, and at all levels of his experience, Stendhal presents a dual image: there is the lucid and logical mind, desirous of attaining truth even by the most arid paths of analysis; but there is also the chimerical dreamer, the passionate lover, swept away at the slightest pretext by romantic melancholy and by visions of bliss. It is, as a matter of fact, "in this rare combination of passion and perspicacity" [1] that his principal charm, his foremost claim to originality, have usually been found to reside. But as a rule, one is content with abandoning Stendhal to this duality, bothering little to proffer a concrete description of the attitudes between which he is torn, or a formula that might make possible a fusion of these two rival tendencies. In this essay I have attempted to show, on the contrary, how these opposite movements co-exist, and what transitions, compromises, or evolutions there might have been from the one to the other. In all the spheres explored by Stendhalian experience, I have tried to detect the presence and the interpenetration of these two essential climates of *dryness* and *tenderness,* the attraction of the two polar principles of determinateness and indistinctness, between which his works and his very life seem irrevocably split.[2]

Everything begins with sensation. In a human being no innate idea, no internal sense, no moral conscience precede the impact of sensation. The Stendhalian hero faces the universe as unequipped and unprejudiced as the first man on the morning of Creation. Stendhal inherits from his eighteenth-century forebears the image of a hero naked and pure whom

"Knowledge and Tenderness in Stendhal." Translated by Paul J. Archambault. From *Littérature et Sensation* by Jean-Pierre Richard (Paris: Éditions du Seuil, 1954). All rights reserved. Reprinted by permission of Éditions du Seuil. The pages reprinted here constitute the first part of the essay "Connaissance et tendresse chez Stendhal."

[1] Maurice Blanchot, *Faux-pas* (Paris: Gallimard, 1943).

[2] Unless otherwise indicated, page numbers for quoted texts refer to the *Œuvres complètes de Stendhal,* ed. Henri Martineau, Divan.

experience alone will gradually teach. Julien at the seminary, Fabrice at Waterloo, are both *ingénus,* worthy sons of Voltaire's Huron or of Montesquieu's Persian, formed by their own sensations, and led by them to the knowledge of things and to the awareness of themselves. However —and this is what makes them radically different from their elders—they are not content to wait passively for experience to come; they go out to meet it, and if need be even provoke it. A product of the Napoleonic era and a disciple of Maine de Biran, Stendhal was schooled in the virtues of activity and effort. Life looms before his heroes like a vast jungle of the senses, through which they will have to hack the most savory path they can. For them, happiness is not something to be awaited, as in the epicureanism of old; it is something to be pursued, to be forced. Sensation is a prey, at once the gift of chance and the reward of courage. The *chasse au bonheur* might then culminate in the triumph of one or two perfect moments, whose emotional content is enough to sum up and justify a lifetime.

Stendhal had known such moments. Very few of them, to be sure; but enough so that around them, as though around a few isolated peaks, the whole landscape of his life was ordered and arranged. Sunday the 24th of Thermidor, the day when, "after having taken for the first time some extract of little centaury and orange blossoms," Stendhal hits upon "thoughts which mark the beginning of my notebooks of strongmindedness"; the Sunday at Claix when he writes his first good verses; the fireworks at Frascati's, with Adèle's head reclining on his shoulder; reading *La Nouvelle Héloïse* above the church at Rolle; hearing for the first time, in a small Italian town, the *Matrimonio Segreto* sung by an adorably toothless actress: every lover of Stendhal knows and treasures these precious moments when chance managed to fulfill the needs of the soul to exact measure. Stendhal's own devotion to these moments is unflagging, and to the last he strives to preserve the trace of them within himself.

But it was precisely one of the great Stendhalian paradoxes, that a being so passionately dedicated to the pursuit of happiness should, in the end, confess how nearly powerless he was to describe for himself the various nuances of that happiness, and even to keep in focus his mental image of it. One can live or relive happiness, one cannot recount it; the very violence of its rapture prevents it from being examined or known. "There is one part of the sky we cannot see," writes Stendhal, "because it is too near the sun." [3] All the more reason for our being unable to gaze at the sun itself. In a word, happiness, "the perfect happiness that a sensitive soul experiences with insatiable delight to the point of annihilation and madness," [4] is a blinding ecstasy. When the blissful moment is

[3] *Vie de Henry Brulard,* II, 319.
[4] *Vie de Henry Brulard,* I, 182.

past, when the sensitive soul returns from its trance to itself, it finds that it can only imperfectly recall that state of ecstasy in which it had immersed itself.

Such confusion, however, cannot satisfy Stendhal. To gratify his soul, the quest for happiness must not exclude the knowledge of happiness. Thus he will attempt to recall those seemingly lost moments, and to reclaim from indistinctness those overly powerful joys, those overly vague sensations. Stendhal's experience begins with passion, but his most lucid venture lies in circumscribing this passion, in knowing it fully, and in establishing between these burning moments of his life a continuity of feeling that poses no threat to his consciousness. To achieve this, he must no longer *feel*, but *perceive*. Stendhal will have recourse not to Rousseau, that great master of feeling souls, but to the masters of intellect—the *Idéologues*.

> So long as I have not marked the limits of a truth, and have not summarized it, it is only half discovered. . . . It is like trying to imagine a line without knowing its direction. By setting its limits, I shall be guarding against misapplied truth, a great source of error. *'Tis true.*[5]

Such is the first step toward reconquest. Truth, to be possessed, must be defined; in other words, its boundaries must be drawn. For lack of a perimeter that delimits it, truth gets lost or diluted. In short, to know is to circumscribe.[6] It is by liberating sensations, ideas, or feelings from the confusion of direct experience, that consciousness truly raises them to the level of existence. Nothing but that which is clear exists for consciousness; nothing is clear that is not distinct, and nothing is distinct that is not confined and confirmed by a line. Thus the universe will be fragmented; out of its previously amorphous mass independent entities will begin to take shape and these entities will exist side by side, juxaposed, restricted to themselves and enclosed. In a universe of sheer effusion and abundance, analysis seeks to establish a new rule, the rule of the *quant à soi*.

But how can this program be made to work? How can one circumscribe pure effusion, or encircle a blinding light? Is it not in the very nature of happiness to defy the eye, to elude analysis? Of course, Stendhal would reply, but we can resort to other means: define it *indirectly,* by describing sensations that border upon it, or those from which it is totally absent. "It seems," he writes in *Henry Brulard,* "that I can only paint this exquisite, pure, fresh, divine happiness through the enumeration of the

---

[5] *Filosofia Nova*, II, 56.
[6] See also Destutt de Tracy: "He would therefore not know, in the proper sense of the word *know*, which always connotes the ideas of *circumscription* and of specialty." (*Eléments d'idéologie*, IV, 71.)

pain and boredom which are totally absent from it." [7] Thus the inside of
a mask describes in its own way the face on which it was molded. In this
case emptiness suggests plentitude, and shadow summons light. Painters,
says Stendhal elsewhere, do precisely that. "The painter has no sun
on his palette," but he can create an illusion of brightness, either by
exaggerating the dark sections—the *chiaroscuro* technique—or by using
general tonality, by spreading a uniform, diffused light over the entire
canvas. [8] Stendhal himself makes sparing use of literary chiaroscuro; it is,
"indeed, a sad way of describing joy," to translate it in terms of suffering
or boredom. In *Henry Brulard,* for example, faced with "the difficulty,
the deep regret of depicting inadequately and thereby spoiling a blissful
remembrance," [9] he would rather forego the attempt and be silent. The
Chartreuse succeeds, however, where *Henry Brulard* had failed; and this
success seems due to Stendhal's adoption and transposition of this device
of *general tonality,* borrowed from the greatest painters. Over the greater
part of his novel he casts an atmosphere of happiness, a veil of delicate
and poetic gaiety that readily conveys the highest joys, making them
almost immediately accessible. The ecstasy of happiness seems the most
familiar of experiences in the *Chartreuse,* so that, while preserving all its
charm, happiness ceases to be stunning or dizzying.

There are many other forms of vertigo, however. Once the truth has
been trapped and tamed, it must still be prevented from slipping away, or
from getting caught in the inner current which constantly proposes new
truths to the mind. "As in Ideology, one must know at every moment how
to keep one's intelligence from running away; similarly in art, one must
hold in check a soul ever willing to enjoy, but never to examine." [10]
This divine impatience sums up all of Stendhal: the raptures of his mind
differ little from the surgings of his desire. He is always impatient to go
faster, to go beyond and consume an acquired truth and dash off after a
new one. He writes: "My soul is a fire that consumes itself when it is not
ablaze. I need three or four cubic feet of new ideas every day." [11] In the
intense heat of such fire, no thought ever has time to crystallize, to settle
within him. His ideas are barely sketched, when new ones are already
crowding them out and taking their place. His thoughts never go beyond
the nascent stage: they are doomed to adolescence. He gives none of them
the time to develop, to ripen, to become commonplace. The life of the
mind too is "made up of forenoons."

[7] *Vie de Henry Brulard,* I, 185.
[8] "If, to render a simple *chiaroscuro,* he must darken the shaded areas, he will, to
render colors that he cannot brighten, resort to *general tonality,* since his own light
is not bright enough. This light is golden with Veronese, silver-like with Guido, ash-
grey with Pezarese, etc." (*Histoire de la peinture en Italie,* I, 61.)
[9] *Vie de Henry Brulard,* I, 185.
[10] *Vies de Rossini,* I, 180.
[11] *Correspondance,* II, 137. *Civ. Vecchia,* I, II, 1834.

Stendhal found it necessary, however, to control this flood of ideas. In a world of boundless or voluble realities, analysis seeks to re-establish an order, an immobility. That is why its primary tool is language. Thus Stendhal, in the wake of the *Idéologues,* places his faith in words. He considers them parapets: they are means of immobilizing and molding the shapeless. On the 24th of January, 1806, for example, he dreams of the perfection he will undoubtedly have attained ten years hence, when he will have become full master of his style; when, as he puts it, "I shall have acquired the habit of seeing the boundaries of every truth, or, as a means to that end, of not letting my imagination carry me away; and of attaching a consistent and specific meaning to each of the words that convey a nuance of character." [12] This "consistency" will be assured by a prolonged study that "consists in knowing and determining the meaning of words." [13] "Before drawing a character," for example, it will be necessary "to determine that character fully . . . , that is, the word that identifies him. Thus, before creating a *conceited man,* give a perfect, half-page description of *conceit,* setting it completely apart from actions that designate pride." [14] A word can delimit truth only on condition it has itself been previously delimited. Analysis will be concerned with categorizing language so as better to sort out the emotions involved. Thus the abstract takes precedence over the concrete; and the young Stendhal, before venturing out into the world, sets out to create a vocabulary for himself.[15] Once this task is completed, he need fear no confusion; no fuzziness can slip between the conception and the expression; reality will come to fill the empty categories of language to their exact capacity; and knowledge of the world will be reduced to an exercise in style. The end result and the crowning point of the ideological structure is indeed *grammar.*

As precise as this new rhetoric would have liked to be in its definitions and in its rules, it still had to standardize and condense its findings through absolutely immutable symbols: measurements and numbers. A meaning can vary, but a formula remains the same. If Stendhal's love of

[12] *Journal,* II, 323.

[13] *Ibid.*

[14] *Molière, Shakespeare,* p. 251.

[15] One feeling for each word, but conversely, only one word for each feeling. This must be the central principle governing the creation of a model vocabulary. Stendhal is quite logical, then, in despising the false wealth of *synonyms:* "Nothing makes the learning of a language more discouraging than this vicious proliferation of synonyms. I describe as 'vicious' any proliferation of synonyms having exactly the same meaning. Pedants call this 'richness of language.' A well-ordained vocabulary will relieve us of this baneful abundance. . . ." And if one considers as synonymous the equivalent words in the several dialects or in the various foreign tongues, one might imagine a kind of totalitarian simplification that would create a universal language by abolishing all the equivalent terms save one. "In this way young people will find it less difficult to learn Italian, and one by one the dialects will disappear." (*Mélanges de littérature,* III, 130).

mathematics was great, it is because he very soon recognized its immobilizing potential, its power of precision, which raise it far above all other creations of the human mind in the scale of rigid thinking. He loved it not at all for its power of deduction and continuity or for its relentless movement, but quite to the contrary, for the fixity that its formulas and its theorems force upon realities that are by nature unstable. Mathematically defined, a line can no longer bend, split in half, or deceive. One can rely on the eternal certitude it provides. Mathematics is, therefore, the royal way of the mind; its exercise cannot lead one astray, nor cause one shame. That is why the mathematicians in Stendhal's novels most often attach equal importance to moral discipline and to mental rigor. In turn, they are not graced with that flexibility of mind and manners that makes for great worldly success; their intransigence might even appear harsh at times, and inelegant. But Stendhal never ceases loving and admiring them, never gives up trying to pass for one of them. He calls for "a series of equations for Apollo's profile." [16] Or else he considers "careful, intelligent, painstaking design, modeled on the Ancients as David understands them, an exact science similar in nature to arithmetic, geometry, or trigonometry." [17] He has a weakness for numbered notations, for little outlines that illustrate the life of the heart, for curves and graphs that summarize the changing faces of passion. In short, mathematics shines in the Beylian heaven like a pure, unparalleled model.

Back on earth, the Stendhalian character will resort to *law,* the juridical science, to satisfy his need for precision. For law regulates human relations. Stendhal's fondness for the *Code Civil* is well known. But can one believe that his appreciation was a purely stylistic one? Is it not more likely that Stendhal valued the *Code* simply because the *Code codified?* Law too is an immobilizing machine, a defining mechanism. It settles once for all; no margin exists around it; it can be interpreted, but it cannot be twisted; one is either within the law or outside it; it is not the spirit, but the *letter* that decides. Stendhal's novels offer very curious examples of this constraining power of the legal formula, whether written or sworn. Clélia pledges herself to darkness, without appeal. And count Mosca's great mistake is to have omitted writing, at the prince's dictation, the words *procédure injuste,* which would have obligated the monarch and saved Fabrice. For the accepted formula is binding, even if one has the power to go beyond it.

Just as mathematics defines what is true, law strives to promote what is just; but this effort is sometimes vain. For if geometry can never engender error, law too often agrees to serve and consecrate injustice—as when a decree appears not *before,* but *after* an arbitrary action. Con-

---

[16] *Marginalia,* I, 335.
[17] *Mélanges d'art,* p. 42.

trary to mathematics, which is always a priori, law is content in such cases to legitimize a past criminal act, to confirm an established fact, to sanction an action that it had neither the wisdom nor the power to forbid. It becomes a mere instrument in the hands of the mighty, and, for the great majority of men, a machine of power and oppression. Thus Rassi, in the *Chartreuse,* clothes the lowest knaveries of his masters in juridical garb; his procedural guile can transform the most fantastic aberrations into norms of behavior. Law, having become an instrument of bondage, now serves as a hindrance to the liberty of the individual; it traces the boundaries beyond which any venture will draw disapproval. Trapped, in short, within this network of rules and prohibitions, men relapse into abject and precarious misery. They become nothing but potential prisoners. It is approximately symbolic that the Farnese tower casts its shadow on the duchy of Parma.

There remains one solution, of course: revolt, or evasion. That is, refuse to obey, or scale the fence. Thus Fabrice slides down his rope, and Julien defies his judges. Both of them know the thrill of severing relations and proclaiming for all to hear, that henceforth they shall derive the law from themselves. At the core of Stendhal's liberalism, the temptation of anarchy will therefore balance off the temptation of legality. Stendhal dreams of great eras of the past when every energetic soul took his destiny in his own hands. As a rule, however, this aristocracy of rebels led to the worst chaos. And Stendhal early discovered that the only authentic form of rebellion in the modern world was hypocrisy. Accordingly, Julien and Fabrice strive to disguise their actions, to create their own prisons so as to escape social confinement. They play the game of legality, but a legality whose arbitrary character they have already recognized. For a juridical restriction, far from being discovered by logical reasoning like a mathematical structure, rather expresses a state of fact, or masks a social barrier. Why then not attempt to cross this barrier? To survey all the forces that law sanctions, to test them and exploit them to one's own advantage, to combine mathematical precision with juridical cynicism, such will be the art of the accomplished politician.

Politics too begins with analysis: it is an exercise in lucidity. "Vagueness kills politics." [18] Precision, realism, dryness, these must be the essential virtues of the ambitious man. In this respect, there is no difference between practical and speculative activity:

> To be a good philosopher, one must be dry, lucid, without illusion. A successful banker has part of the character required to make philosophical discoveries: that is, a *clear vision* of what is, which is somewhat different from talking eloquently about glowing fancies.[19]

[18] *Mélanges intimes,* I, 368.
[19] *Mélanges de littérature,* II, 283.

Thus Lucien Leuwen's father tries his hand at finance, politics, and high society with equal success. He handles millions with no less skill than he does men. In both areas, the same methods assure him of equal success. Unlike Balzac, who believes that every form of activity has a specific character of its own and that each requires a particular technique, Stendhal relies upon the universal and proved value of analysis. The human heart does not change.[20] Once he has learned to understand the mechanism of those few great passions that spur men to action, the apprentice *idéologue* may consider himself the master of all possible situations. He deciphers the enigmas of behavior; he probes the secrets of the heart; whether banker, lover, or prime minister, he is blessed with an equal clairvoyance that assures him of victory every time. For "once the motivations for human actions have been discovered," what can be simpler than to provoke another person into the desired action? It suffices to pull the right lever, to provoke the right motivation. The "logical" seduction of Mélanie and, on a higher plane, Julien's taming of Mathilde, are marvelous illustrations of this technique of *directing* others, a few scandalous examples of which Stendhal might have found in Laclos. "I read her soul like an open book. Every day I learn to read more clearly in it. I know the passions." [21] At its best, analysis endows anyone who masters its secrets with an almost magical power: his universe becomes totally transparent.

Such, at least, is the wish of the apprentice *idéologue*. More often than not, however, his wish is ineffectual, and before too long reality has dampened his hopes. Contrary to his expectations, lived experience continues to be a pit of mystery and darkness. Despite all the efforts of analysis, the "other" remains unpredictable: first of all, because the other can guess and predict what I am about to do. Opposite intuitions cancel each other out. "Would that I were the only one to have read Helvétius!" dreamed Stendhal. But even if one is the only one to know the great book, can one be certain of one's predictions? No, Stendhal concedes, for our present state of knowledge does not allow us such a degree of certitude. Human behavior grows out of an interplay of forces whose *direction* we can easily determine, but whose intensity we are not yet able to calculate.

Thanks to the theoretical facts at our disposal, we manage easily enough to differentiate these forces; but our knowledge is too vague for us to measure

---

[20] "The march of the human spirit," as Destutt de Tracy was fond of saying, "is always the same in all branches of human knowledge. . . and the certitude of its judgments is always of the same nature, and always has similar causes." (*Traité d'idéologie*, I, 175.)

[21] *Journal*, II, 56.

their intensity with precision. Consequently we are unable to know the resultant force: human behavior.[22]

An element of uncertainty creeps into the wheelwork of the mechanism. It explains, among several other reasons, why the *roué* does not succeed in seducing his victim, and why his plans miscarry, just like those of the too-crafty politician. In one and the other instance, the intrusion of an emotional unknown wrecks analytical divination.

A providential wreck it is, incidentally, that re-endows love with its element of chance and transforms politics into a dangerous, therefore amusing, exercise. Omnipotence is boring: it always wins in advance. But when there is a possibility of losing, then all interest is revived. Mosca and the duchess know Ranuce-Ernest through and through. The mechanics of his personality holds no mystery for them. They are merely ignorant of what element will prevail in a given situation. When the duchess asks him to treat the queen with greater deference, she does not know whether offended pride will prove stronger than the desire to please. And Fabrice's life, later on, will hang on a similar dilemma: is it better to sacrifice Fabrice or keep Mosca? Satisfy vengeance or ambition? The forces balance off; and the outcome remains in doubt. Ranuce-Ernest chooses not to choose, prolonging the anguish, and the novel, until the day when the duchess decides in his place, and in opposition to him. This episode however, would not be as spellbinding for all its participants, were it not for the suspense uninterruptedly sustained, for the uncertainty of the stakes involved, and for the constant fear, rather successfully symbolized by the coach in permanent harness.

This does not mean, however, that one should resign oneself to obscurity. When logic is unable to measure intensity of feeling, it concentrates on the discovery of its subtlest movements. Sharpness of knowledge depends indeed, for Stendhal, on the number and the precision of details that it encompasses.

In perception or in knowledge, a detail corresponds to the ultimate entity distinguishable to analysis. It is the atom of perceptible reality, the hard and indivisible particle on which vision stumbles, then rests. Thus it tends to shrink ever closer to the absolute limit of the point, and the contour that girds it represents the last possible fragmentation, a sort of *ne plus ultra* of analytical geometry. Time and again Stendhal

[22]*Mélanges de littérature,* II, 174. See also Destutt de Tracy (*Eléments d'idéologie,* I, 169). "We have no adequate instruments to measure directly the degree of intensity of man's feelings and inclinations, or whether these are good or depraved. . . . That is why research in these sciences is more difficult, and its results less rigid." Feelings can, then, be determined only by their *effects:* "An accurate measurement of effects helps to appraise their causes." This is a posteriori knowledge, which, of course, dooms any kind of prediction to failure.

repeats, echoing the *Idéologues* and particularly Destutt de Tracy,[23] that the only truth is detailed truth. Detail is that which, by localizing and stamping a sensation, transforms it into perception. It is that which gives shape and authenticity to characters and landscapes: the profile of a sail on the horizon, the face of a young girl seen from the top of a steeple, a fishbone lost in a bishop's plate. Finally, as an essential complement to egotism, detail is that which makes memory seem vital, and description realistic. In his reconstruction of reality, therefore, the novelist must strive to rediscover or invent the trifling circumstance. That is why Stendhal, in reference to Mérimée's *Vénus d'Ille*, praises "the very neat and even sharp configurations," and "the remarkable attention to little things (the sign of a good novelist), and the daring to stress these little things." [24] Elsewhere, however, he seems to think that Mérimée's daring is eclipsed by his excessive passion for brevity:

"He made her get off the horse, on some pretext." This is what Clara would say. Dominique says: "He made her get off the horse, pretending that the horse was losing one of its shoes, and that he wanted to nail it back in." Shorten the *elaboration* of this detail, but put it in place of "on some pretext." [25]

The great sin against the novel, then, is not to write: "The marquise went out at four," but to omit the circumstances of her going out. Banality is the fruit of an impoverished and too-rapid vision, and the very concision of the narrative only serves to conceal its vagueness.

In Stendhal's view, the unpardonable sin is to drown out a contour, to dissolve the truth. Concision is only half bad. But what about over-amplification? Over-amplification, to be sure, does not attempt to destroy truths, but it distorts them badly. One might compare it to a painted design on the surface of a balloon, the outlines of which grow larger and more shapeless as the distension increases, until they eventually disappear. Similarly, the enlargement of a whole suppresses its details much more than it underscores them. Such is inflated style, that is, "exaggerating the large strokes, and forgetting the small ones." [26] An unpardonable omission, especially if it is the outgrowth of a desire for literary *effect*. Thus, for example, Mme de Staël forces herself to inflate her feelings:

---

[23] According to Tracy, *sensation*, the primary and undifferentiated element, becomes *judgment* when it is described in more explicit detail. *Perception* is nothing more than this sensation in greater detail and, as it were, unfolded before the mind. "We can summarize the history of any animate being in two words: he *senses*, he *judges;* that is, what he had at first sensed as a confused mass, he *then senses it in detail.*" (*Logique*, p. 327.)

[24] *Marginalia*, II, 316.

[25] *Ibid.*, p. 96.

[26] *Fil. Nov.*, I, 103.

She wanted to be very sensitive. In her heart of hearts, she made it a matter of glory, a point of honor, an ecstatic dream, to be very sensitive. Later, she added to this exaggeration. Since she also sought tenderness, she fell into verbiage.[27]

Such is the woeful punishment for an unbridled tendency to sentimental outpourings. Distended and diluted, the feeling eventually disintegrates in the effort to amplify it;[28] and for want of restraint, the soul discovers it is a shattered void.

More dangerous still are those authors whose conscious aim it is to render a contour shapeless or a determination unclear, by projecting ideas or feelings into an infinity of possibilities. Exaggeration destroys detail, but it leaves form intact. *Vagueness* attempts to destroy all form in a vaporous vibration. Feeling is now defined by its yearning for infinity, by its horror of all limitations. Thus Chateaubriand, lowering all the barriers, lets the passions dissolve into the notorious *vague,* where they lose all their power of expansion. Stendhal considers this the lowest form of hypocrisy. To his mind, ecstasies and evanescences only camouflage true feeling. Religion, ideal love, these are only convenient veils for what one dares not confess. Stendhal will tear off all these veils. He wishes to send back to the literary surplus stores all those uniforms that had for thirty years kept the *ingénu* hero in wraps, body and soul. (The romantics will, on the contrary, draw generously from these same warehouses.) Under the fluttering chemises of a Fragonard or a Boucher, one could still make out the body's charming candor. But David drapes the mystery of the human anatomy with a Roman peplum, Ingres with an imperial velvet, Gros with a military tunic. The century buttons its clothes. Stendhal sets out, on the contrary, to undress his heroes, to search for "the true delineation of nakedness, the delineation of the passions, far different from *Valentine's* bright drapery." [29] Out of horror for the loose, floating garments that drape and deceive, he throws into sharp relief the lines of muscles and sinews.[30] Romantic lithography is fond of having

---

[27] *Aux âmes sensibles,* 53, N.R.F.

[28] On the other hand: "What a feeling gains in intensity, it loses in extension. —F. A. Chateaubriand" (*Fil. Nov.,* I, 10.)

[29] *Marg.* II, 216.

[30] He writes in his *Journal:* "I, whom drawing has accustomed to seek the nude beneath the cloth and to imagine it clearly." A number of passages in his essays on aesthetics demonstrate how this analysis of the body which is anatomy satisfies his craving for precision; and also how this anatomical knowledge, pushed too far, entails a certain aridity of vision. For example, Stendhal praises Guido "for bringing out with mathematical precision the most fleeting lines of each muscle." (*Écoles italiennes de peinture,* III, 202.) But elsewhere (*Peinture en Italie,* I, 182), he admits that even as subtle as *this,* such muscular expression is at best very rudimentary, since "tender passions find no visible expression in mucular movement." *Rêverie,* then, will attempt to envelop the contours, draping the bodies once more in their veils of modesty.

transparent scarves and veils undulating in the moonlight. The *diaphanous,* that vague, erotic quality of the body, is the current fashion. Stendhal, on the other hand, considers himself satisfied only when he has succeeded in describing and in animating that supremely naked of creatures: man reduced to his anatomy.

Landscapes, too, have their muscles. Painters display them on canvas like great harmonious bodies; and Stendhal scrutinizes them with the cold eye of the anatomist. In every exterior spectacle, he first notices the lines of force around which the whole coalesces, the visible boundaries that separate masses. Nothing pleases him more than the panoramic view of an entire countryside as clearly delineated as a topographical map. Nowadays he would be a fanatic for aerial landscapes. Thus from the heights of the Sainte-Baume he experiences an entirely cerebral joy in seeing "Marseilles, the islands, the sea, like a well-drawn map." [31] He needs a clear sky, with a purity uncluttered by clouds or mists, where the contour of each examined detail is profiled against the precision of the adjoining detail, where the motifs stand out in arabesques. He challenges "the indeterminate skyline of the forests" (a good example of Chateaubriand's shameful flabbiness), by observing that "in France the contour drawn by the forest against the sky is composed of a series of small points. In England, this same contour is composed of large rounded masses." [32] A great number of texts, just as curious as this one, bear witness to this fondness of Stendhal's for a nature whose forms are modeled on a series of superimposed pieces and geometrical shapes.

A mountain, for example, seen from below, is a choice sample for analytical vision; the eye arranges its slopes and ravines in an architecture of superimposed planes. The little town of Verrières, at the beginning of *Le Rouge,* "spreads out on a hillside whose smallest furrows are darkened by clusters of healthy chestnut trees." [33] Stendhal is also very fond of Alpine countrysides "where the air is so pure and the view so clear that no more than a quarter-mile seems to separate you at any time from the peaks of snow, whose slightest crags and bends are plain for the eye to see. You might even see the chamois romping over them." [34] The primary function of light, in this instance, is to harden contours; morning washes the shapes clean of the confusion into which night had plunged them. Thus, in these famous lines from the *Chartreuse:*

The morning breeze was beginning to temper the oppressive heat that had prevailed during the day. With its feeble white glow, the dawn was already silhouetting the Alpine peaks that rise east and north of Lake Como.

[31] *Journal,* III, 56.
[32] *Mémoires d'un touriste,* Lorient, 7 July, II, 133.
[33] *Le Rouge et le noir,* I, 3.
[34] *Marg.,* II, 363.

Their masses, white with snow even in the month of June, *contrast*
sharply with the bright blue of an ever-serene sky. . . . The dawn, as it grew
brighter, *pointed up* the valleys between by whitening the soft mist that
rose out of the gorges' depths.[35]

A splendid illustration of the mind's gradual effort to shed its veils and
emerge into light. The spectator is rewarded with the most perfect joy,
as each detail, visual or aural, leaves its indelible mark on him:

Fabrice could distinguish the sound of each oar-stroke. This simple detail
sent him into ecstatic raptures.[36]

A curiously passive ecstasy it remains nonetheless. For these landscapes,
so thoroughly cleansed of all uncertainty, lack a vital, human complexion.
They do not compel the eye to examine, or the imagination to pursue.
Instead of caressing their surface, the eye has stripped them, made them
sterile, deprived them of any true relief. The world stretches out like a
vast panorama: horizontally it unfolds like a military map; vertically it
stands up like a stage set. It would be false, by the way, to think that
the objects are not *distant* from one another. Quite to the contrary:
clarity of vision being of value only if it appears like a victory over
indistinctness, the spectator projects the contemplated object into distance, so as better to enjoy retrieving it from distance. Like the far-
sighted, he wants to see from a distance the way one normally sees from
close up. But in the course of this purely intellectual game, distance
becomes artificial: it is a provisional indetermination, which the "operation" of sight victoriously reduces. In short, relief exists only to be flat-
tened immediately; space enters only to confirm its own defeat, to
declare that it no longer withholds any unexplored or exciting secrets,
that it merely served as the limpid medium for a perfectly successful
experience. The eye has traversed space without exploring it; experienced
its hollowness, but not its depth. We shall later see Stendhal coming to
grips with these important problems of optical illusion and of perspective. In considering them, he will be led into paths far different from
those into which his passion for distinctness has drawn him for the
moment. At present his geometry remains two-dimensional. Add a third
dimension—intensity of feeling, depth of space, contagion of love—and
this plane universe will need to find a direction in which to grow. It will
then be time to abandon a mechanical for a dynamic vision of things, to
discover in the world and in the mind a whole vital interplay of relations, and, by a conversion somewhat similar to that described by Proust
at the end of *Le Temps retrouvé,* to erect a psychology in space. For
the time being, however, the dryness of Stendhal's vision protects him

---

[35] *La Chartreuse de Parme*, ch. VIII, I, 271.
[36] *Ibid.*, p. 292.

from oscillating lines and ungirded forms. The "ideological" landscape admits no smudges, no shadows, no mystery.

Will it be just as easy to sketch an *interior* landscape with India ink? Sentiments, indeed, live in clusters; they mingle, interpenetrate, and overlap. The whole French tradition of psychology has tended toward the exploration of an ever-growing complexity, while at the same time it has tried to unravel this complexity in the light of an ever more limpid means of expression. Stendhal was admirably equipped to participate in this tradition: first, through his knowledge of ideology, which carried the passion for subdivision to the point of obsession; but especially through his instinctive taste for clarity. To know what he is experiencing, he must untangle the emotional knot of this experience, isolate every nuance of feeling, assign it a name and a place, in short place it in one of the pigeon-holes that language analysis has prepared for it. And if he wishes to avoid schematization, that is, preserve both the complexity and the clarity of feelings, he will have to present as temporally dissociated that which immediate experience had offered him *as a whole.* He will have to spread in time the various strands that composed the emotional knot. Each feeling will be discernible as it succeeds the other; each will become detached from the other; and, as the prism refracts dull, gray light into a brilliant rainbow of colors, the disintegration endows each element with an added brightness and vitality.

Feelings thus acquire an individual existence, a life, a death, and a character all their own. Each of them as Stendhal puts it, "occupies the soul," fills it to overflowing. "From then on he had but one thought. . . ." "He could think of only one thing. . . ." How many times in Stendhal's novels do similar turns of phrase underscore the absorption of a character by a feeling, his complete insensitivity to anything other than that feeling, his obliviousness to everything that might divert or distract him from it? "Thoughts" settle in the foreground of consciousness, as hallucinatory and imperious as movie closeups. They block every exit, bar every flight. No mental reservation comes, as with Proust for example, to balance or retard their attack. Their contours fit the shape of consciousness perfectly. There are no shadows in Stendhalian souls, no fringes around them, nor even any lace work. Pure and perfect, emotions spring from the depths in one stream, one mass. The Stendhalian hero's candor and elegance of gesture are due, without question, to this internal brutality, and to the fact that, like an arrow flying toward its target, he is at every moment concerned with only one project, obsessed with only one thought, propelled by only one irresistible impulse. Nothing clings to him, holds him back, or slackens his offensive. He can soar without ballast.

This holds true even for those moments of interior struggle, those clashes between Julien and Mathilde for example, when the soul of the hero seems torn and motionless. Even then the hesitation is merely made up of an extraordinarily rapid succession of contrary movements. The desire to love, the desire to resist love, follow each other at such speed that they might appear to co-exist. But, on closer observation, one notices that they never intermingle, and that each of them controls the soul in turn with total supremacy, but in a span of time too brief for the hero to swing into action. The dramatic tension, in this instance, is the result of a restrained movement, a static vibration. We have only to remember, in contrast, those moments when passion has had time to settle in and cleave to the soul: for example, the thirst for vengeance that spurs Julien on to murder at the end of *Le Rouge*. Is it necessary to invoke catalepsy or hypnosis to explain his frantic ride on horseback, his stuttering tongue, his mechanical and distraught somnambulist gestures? We should rather see in this obsession an extreme case, a pathological and all-too-perfect example of the tyranny that feelings can wield over the soul, transforming their victim into a momentary madman. For, though he may live in broad daylight, the Stendhalian hero has his own share of demons. He too is possessed.

And these demons are ever changing. Feelings hold sway but do not linger, and their departure is as abrupt as their presence was imposing. They leave no trace behind them; more often than not, in fact, the subsequent feeling contradicts or negates rather than prolongs the preceding one. Stendhal is a master of hiatus; and that is a characteristically logical consequence of analytic division. For, to attain pure emotion, analysis has had to sever all the connections around it, prevent all adulteration, break all the internal joints. In short, it is the discontinuity of feelings that guarantees their integrity. To keep their purity intact, they must grow by abrupt changes and in zigzag directions, without finding within the subject that they inhabit any internal medium that might soften their collision with one another. The soul, in this case, is not a viscous liquid, but a vacuum where they can only crash into one another, then vanish:

> One thing to note carefully: the soul merely has *states*, never *qualities*, in its inventory. Where is the joy of a weeping man? It is nowhere, it was a state.[37]

The whole life of the heart is subject to this rule of the preterit. Nothing can link these states with one another; they hold the soul prisoner to a choppy, successive present.

This psychological discontinuity is strained and heightened by still another interior exigency: Stendhal believes that *shock* is necessary to keep the soul awake. "Sensibility," he writes, in keeping with the *Idéo-*

logues, "whatever the manner, whatever the organ in which it functions, lives only by mutations and contrasts." [38] For such is the hypnotic power of habit, whose symptoms and damaging effects Maine de Biran had only recently described. In short, man lives only when shaken up. Thus we can explain the extraordinary violence of emotions in the Stendhalian world, and the brutality of their appearance: a world where ideas "come upon you like a cramp," [39] where the hand grips the rapier as swiftly as suspicion grips the heart, where at each instant the heroes are overwhelmed by the discovery of what they feel or the revelation of what they have become. Lucien Leuwen sees himself loving, then ceasing to love, then loving again, with the very same astonishment, as if he were someone else: "Since yesterday I am no longer master of myself; I am obedient to ideas that flash upon me without warning, and I cannot foresee anything a minute ahead of time." [40] Without admitting it to himself, however, he relishes the freshness of this world where unpredictability reigns. To be natural, then, is to surrender to change, shock, surprise, and forgetfulness; to refuse always to resemble or ever to foresee oneself. The Stendhalian hero is not endowed with a *character:* he is not straining constantly toward his definition or his essence; rather he lives day by day, following the mood of the moment and the luck of his encounters. Free and malleable, he glides, like the novel that relates his adventures, over an eternal present.

This present remains vital because its very pace is erratic. Nothing is more monotonous than a unified sequence of adventures, as so many bad picaresque novels can attest. But with Stendhal, adventure retains its full flavor because the soul welcomes it differently every time. The *tempo* of interior life accelerates or slackens according to whether the atmosphere at a particular moment is tense or relaxed. There is in Stendhal a psychological velocity, whose function it is to measure that essential dimension for which linear psychology would be unable to account: intensity (or depth) of feeling, and its relative importance. The notion of *internal rhythm* thus comes to topple the assumptions of two-dimensional psychology: the "states" arise and vanish with greater or lesser speed, depending on whether the passion is building up or relaxing. As a movie camera might convey a character's confusion by multiplying the speed or the incoherence of the images that his eye can grasp, so too the novel might accelerate frantically the psychological sequences in moments of violent crisis. The well-known analysis of Mosca's jealousy illustrates to perfection this technique of internal acceleration. Mosca watches imaginary gestures dancing before his eyes; he *sees* kisses that do not exist; meanwhile, the various thoughts that the situation conjures up in his

[38] *Fil. Nov.,* I, 369.
[39] *Chartreuse,* I, 253.
[40] *Lucien Leuwen,* I, 348.

tortured brain file past his mind at a frantic pace. Other than the emotions that manifest it, his jealousy resides in this very vertigo. For, as the youthful Stendhal of *Filosofia Nova* had already noticed:

> As far as style is concerned, form is an integral part. *As for emotions, their rhythm reveals them.* The rhythm that enters into a work must therefore be proportionate to the emotions contained therein. Only men of genius can see this.[41]

Rhythm, therefore, must be considered the dynamic substitute for this third dimension that Stendhal still refuses to take into account. The speed at which these psychological states unfold allows him to transcend them and join them together in a synthesis which is, in fact, a feeling. Formal unity serves as a prelude to substantial unity.

It even appears that Stendhal established secret correspondences between the internal rhythm of the psychological states and the external rhythm of the events narrated. In *Le Rouge,* during fits of passion, windows shatter, coaches run wild, events pile up, everything happens at once. Between these frantic moments, however, joy creates long spans of tranquility and silence, when nothing happens save the little commonplace events, with their happy intimacy. The structure of the book, which follows the internal rhythm of Stendhalian improvisation, is based on the involuntary alternation of gallops and halts, of tense and relaxed breathing, of life concentrated and life unfolded. Julien, that tireless horseman, also knows the good hostels. He is well practiced in the art of halting. He pauses a moment on the mountain that he has just finished climbing, and abandons himself to a dream of simple life: "The traveller who has just ascended a steep mountain sits at the top and finds in rest a perfect joy."—But he soon adds, "Would he be happy if he were forced to rest forever?" [42] He must then leap up again, to pursue the goal ambition assigns him. It is this internal resilience, this elasticity of soul, that make of him a true Stendhalian hero.

Accentuate the contour, force the determination, exaggerate the discontinuity, and the *comic* is obtained. Laughter (a shaking of the body), arises at the sight of a shaken man. In comic instances, movements and moments are no longer linked at all to one another. Separated by increasing intervals, they assume a chaotic and ridiculous existence. Discontinuity now becomes incoherence.

The comic comprises degrees. If the distended intervals grow to a point where the entrance of each new element elicits surprise, while remaining slow enough so the surprise is not shocking, then a *smile*

---

[41] *Fil. Nov.* II, 38.
[42] *Le Rouge et le noir,* ch. 23, I, 273.

plays on the reader's lips. The sentiment that provokes a smile is one that betrays but does not disturb one's expectation. So it is for the "giddy young girl," for whom every novelty is a delightful caress, "whose every sensation," as Stendhal puts it, "is an added pleasure and elicits an agreeable surprise, giving rise to the *Sous-Rire.*" [43] Go a step further, increase the intervals even more: this time abruptness will provoke laughter. One laughs at the lie that reality gives to habit, at the sudden crack in the solidity of things, at the sudden break in continuity. One laughs at Lucien Leuwen thrown from his horse into the mud of Nancy in the presence of his beloved or at Rassi cringing grotesquely when kicked by his prince. In short, comedy—just like tragedy—relies on the emotional impact of the unexpected:

> Might not the *unexpected* be the *sine qua non,* without which there is neither laughter nor tears? If so, one could avoid laughter or tears, by bringing about that factor which provokes laughter or tears in someone by the minutest degrees possible for that person.[44]

Stendhal will discover these invisible charms when he initiates his heroes into the ways of tenderness. Through their vagueness and modulation painting and music will teach him all the instabilities of progressive truth. But it is on stage that Stendhal wishes to achieve a comic effect, and theatrical truth is not progressive. Far from joining together, theater juxtaposes and separates. Like sculpture, it is fond of frozen and exaggerated truth:

> Nothing places in a more ridiculous light the kind of exaggeration indispensable to the theatre, than the eternal *immobility* of sculpture.[45]

Theater progresses, therefore, by successive immobilities; each theatrical instance drapes itself in a sculptural or grotesque dignity. It is a world where men are statues, and feelings are of stone.

The whole difference between the comic and the tragic reposes, then, on the degree of stress with which, in this motionless parade, gestures and feelings will be underlined and encircled. Since the discontinuity remains the same in both cases, the deciding factor here is boldness of contour, with its corresponding power of isolation. When acted on stage, an emotion, however stone-like it is supposed to be, is often echoed by the spectator's genuine feeling. Between stage and audience, there can arise the kind of sympathy that is at the root of all *tragedy.* A feeling, when shared, is already half-liberated. The comic, on the other hand, in-

[43] *Molière,* VII.
[44] *Fil. Nov.,* I, 250.
[45] *Mél. d'art,* p. 131.

exorably makes both character and spectator prisoners of themselves. The former it fills with an obsessive concern for himself and his little designs, the incurable short-sightedness of evil passion, and not with that generosity of attitude that makes of every tragic hero a noble suppliant. To the latter it gives a "vision of his own superiority," stirring within him a thrill of self-adulation, little conducive to coming out of oneself. Comical relations thrive, then, on the distant confrontation of two solitudes, one of which judges the other. The footlights accentuate the distances in a way that precludes any temptation to sympathize or pity, that is, any tendency toward the tragic.

> The comic fails when the characters that make us laugh do not appear sufficiently arid and sadden the *tender* portion of the soul. The sight of sorrow would make the spectator neglect the awareness of his own superiority.[46]

There is no comedy without dryness. Laughter severs human contact.

The isolating power of comedy will reveal itself even more clearly in this absurd and excessive art form known as caricature. Henceforth all that counts is the contour, the shell. The inside no longer exists, and man is reduced to his own vain show . . . or his own distortion. Rênal, Valenod, Rassi, Sansfin have no real existence; like hard and hollow puppets, they are nothing but their gestures, their mimicry. There is no living thought in them; their outward shell covers a great silent void. Similarly, the *habitués* of the *Hôtel de La Mole* are little more than living dead; absurdly anachronistic, they seem to have been emptied of their substance by history, and only their most superficial parts—their etiquette —survive them. They represent without question the most polished expression of Stendhal's comic vision, if indeed this vision is fated to project only bodies emptied of souls, and "truths" emptied of meaning, in short, if it is to include merely deceptive appearances, intended simply to rebuff every form of genuine contact and of human sympathy.

Such is the extreme that Stendhal attains in his effort to distinguish and to limit the truth. After having broken the continuity of things, the mind enclosed them within contours which it intended to be more and more rigid. So long as the cult of detail saved it from schematization, its vision remained sane, if somewhat arid. Now the comic temptation has induced Stendhal to destroy the detail, and to empty the truth of all content, to the benefit of an overstressed contour. In this more and more formal universe, the line ceases to be a means and becomes an end; the mechanism for determining becomes more important than the thing being determined. At the extreme, which is the comic, the act of determination kills the object determined. Stendhal, to be sure, had learned from the

[46] *Peinture en Italie*, II, 172.

eighteenth century the art of living on one's surface, and of letting a smile veil the vast emptiness of the heart. But the point we have now seen him reach must necessarily represent an untenable extreme. It will be imperative for him to repopulate the truth, to give it back its vital content, its interior fulness. We shall now see him succumb to the inverse temptation, as he descends into obscure regions where, presumably, deeper joys await him.

Stendhal or the
Romantic of Reality

by Simone de Beauvoir

Stendhal loved women sensually from childhood; he projected upon them his adolescent aspirations: he liked to fancy himself saving a fair unknown from danger and winning her love. Arriving in Paris, what he wants most ardently is "a charming woman; we shall adore each other, she will know my soul." Grown old, he writes in the dust the initials of the women he has loved best. "I think that reverie has been what I have most enjoyed," he confides. And images of women are what feed his dreams; their memory gives lively interest to landscapes. "The line of the cliffs as seen when approaching Arbois, I think, and coming from Dôle by the highway, was for me a tangible and evident image of Métilde's soul." Music, painting, architecture—everything he prized—he cherished with the feeling of an unhappy lover. If he is strolling in Rome, as each page turns, a woman arises; in the regrets, the desires, the sorrows, the joys they stirred up in him he understood the inclination of his own heart; he would have them as his judges: he frequents their salons, he tries to appear brilliant in their eyes; to them he has owed his greatest joys, his greatest pains, they have become his main occupation; he prefers their love to any friendship, their friendship to that of men. Women inspire his books, feminine figures people them; the fact is that he writes for them in large part. "I take my chance of being read in 1900 by the souls I love, the Mme Rolands, the Mélanie Guilberts. . . ." They were the very substance of his life. How did they come to have that preferment?

This tender friend of women does not believe in the feminine mystery, precisely because he loves them as they really are; no essence defines woman once for all; to him the idea of "the eternal feminine" seems pedantic and ridiculous. "Pedants have for two thousand years reiterated

"Stendhal or the Romantic of Reality." From *The Second Sex* by Simone de Beauvoir (New York, 1952), pp. 238-248. Copyright 1952 by Alfred A. Knopf, Inc. Reprinted by permission of Alfred A. Knopf, Inc., and Johnathan Cape Ltd., London.

the notion that women have a more lively spirit, men more solidity; that women have more delicacy in their ideas and men greater power of attention. A Paris idler who once took a walk in the Versailles Gardens concluded that, judging from all he saw, the trees grow ready trimmed." The differences to be noted between men and women reflect the difference in their situations. Why, for instance, should women not be more romantic than their lovers? "A woman occupied in embroidering, dull work that uses only the hands, dreams of her lover; whereas this lover, riding in the open with his squadron, is put under arrest if he makes a wrong move." Similarly, women are accused of lacking judgment. "Women prefer the emotions to reason, and it is quite simple: since according to our stupid customs they are not charged with any family responsibility, *reason is never useful to them.* . . . Let your wife run your business affairs with the farmers on two of your pieces of property, and I wager that the accounts will be kept better than if you did it yourself." If but a few feminine geniuses are found in history, it is because society deprives them of all means for expressing themselves. "All geniuses who are born *women* are lost to the public welfare; once fate gives them means to make themselves known, you will see them achieve the most difficult attainments."

The worst handicap they have is the besotting education imposed upon them; the oppressor always strives to dwarf the oppressed; man intentionally deprives women of their opportunities. "We leave idle in women qualities of great brilliance that could be rich in benefit for themselves and for us." At ten the little girl is quicker and more clever than her brother; at twenty the young fellow is a man of wit and the young girl "a great awkward idiot, shy and afraid of a spider"; the blame is to be laid on her training. Women should be given just as much instruction as boys. Antifeminists raise the objection that cultivated and intelligent women are monsters, but the whole trouble is that they are still exceptional; if all of them could have access to culture as naturally as men, they would profit by it as naturally. After they have been thus injured, they are subjected to laws contrary to nature: married against their feelings, they are expected to be faithful, and divorce, if resorted to, is itself held a matter of reproach, like misconduct. A great many women are doomed to idleness, when there is no happiness apart from work. This state of affairs makes Stendhal indignant, and he sees in it the source of all the faults for which women are reproached. They are not angels, nor demons, nor sphinxes: merely human beings reduced to semislavery by the imbecile ways of society.

It is precisely because they are oppressed that the best of them avoid the defects that disfigure their oppressors; they are in themselves neither inferior nor superior to man; but by a curious reversal their unhappy situation favors them. It is well known how Stendhal hated serious-mindedness: money, honors, rank, power seemed to him the most melancholy of idols; the vast majority of men sell themselves for profit; the pedant, the man of consequence, the bourgeois, the husband—all smother within them every spark of life and truth; larded with ready-made ideas and acquired sentiments and conformable to social routines, their personalitites contain nothing but emptiness; a world peopled by these soulless creatures is a desert of ennui. There are many women, unfortunately, who wallow in the same dismal swamps; these are dolls with "narrow and Parisian ideas," or often hypocritical devotees. Stendhal experiences "a mortal disgust for respectable women and their indispensable hypocrisy"; they bring to their frivolous occupations the same seriousness that makes their husbands stiff with affectation; stupid from bad education, envious, vain, gossipy, worthless through idleness, cold, dry, pretentious, malicious, they populate Paris and the provinces; we see them swarming behind the noble figure of a Mme de Rênal, a Mme de Chasteller. The one Stendhal has painted with the most malevolent care is without doubt Mme Grandet, in whom he has set forth the exact negative of a Mme Roland, a Métilde. Beautiful but expressionless, scornful and without charm, she is formidable in her "celebrated virtue" but knows not the true modesty that comes from the soul; filled with admiration for herself, puffed up with her own importance, she can only copy the outer semblance of grandeur; fundamentally she is vulgar and base; "she has no character . . . she bores me," thinks M. Leuwen. "Perfectly reasonable, careful for the success of her plans," her whole ambition is to make her husband a cabinet minister; "her spirit is arid"; prudent, a conformist, she has always kept away from love, she is incapable of a generous act; when passion breaks out in that dry soul, there is burning but no illumination.

This picture need only be reversed to show clearly what Stendhal asks of women: it is first of all not to permit themselves to be caught in the snares of seriousness; and because of the fact that the things supposed to be of importance are out of their range, women run less risk than men of getting lost in them; they have better chances of preserving that naturalness, that naïveté, that generosity which Stendhal puts above all other merit. What he likes in them is what today we call their authenticity: that is the common trait in all the women he loved or lovingly invented; all are free and true beings. Some of them flaunt their freedom most conspicuously: Angela Pietragrua, "strumpet sublime, in the Italian manner, *à la* Lucretia Borgia," and Mme Azur, "strumpet *à la* Du Barry . . . one of the least vain and frivolous Frenchwomen I have met," scoff openly at social conventions. Lamiel laughs at customs, mores, laws; the Sanseverina joins ardently in intrigue and does not hesitate at crime. Others are raised above the vulgar by their vigor of spirit: such is Menta, and another is Mathilde de La Mole, who criticizes, disparages, and scorns the society around her and wants to be distinguished from it. With others, again, liberty assumes a quite negative aspect; the remarkable thing in Mme de Chasteller is her attitude of detachment from everything secondary; submissive to the will of her father and even to his opinions, she none the less disputes bourgeois values by the indifference which she is reproached for as childishness and which is the source of her insouciant gaiety. Clélia Conti also is distinguished for her reserve; balls and other usual amusements of young girls leave her cold; she always seems distant "whether through scorn for what is around her, or through regret for some absent chimera"; she passes judgment on the world, she is indignant at its baseness.

But it is in Mme de Rênal that independence of soul is most deeply hidden; she is herself unaware that she is not fully resigned to her lot; it is her extreme delicacy, her lively sensitivity, that show her repugnance for the vulgarity of the people around her; she is without hypocrisy; she has preserved a generous heart, capable of violent emotions, and she has a flair for happiness. The heat of this fire which is smoldering within her can hardly be felt from outside, but a breath would be enough to set her all ablaze.

These women are, quite simply, *alive;* they know that the source of true values is not in external things but in human hearts. This gives its charm to the world they live in: they banish ennui by the simple fact of their presence, with their dreams, their desires, their pleasures, their emotions, their ingenuities. The Sanseverina, that "active soul," dreads ennui more than death. To stagnate in ennui "is to keep from dying, she said, not to live"; she is "always impassioned over something, always in action, and gay, too." Thoughtless, childish or profound, gay or grave, daring or secretive, they all reject the heavy sleep in which humanity is mired. And these women who have been able to maintain their liberty— empty as it has been—will rise through passion to heroism once they find an objective worthy of them; their spiritual power, their energy, suggest the fierce purity of total dedication.

But liberty alone could hardly give them so many romantic attributes: pure liberty gives rise rather to esteem than to emotion; what touches the feelings is the effort to reach liberty through the obstructive forces that beat it down. It is the more moving in women in that the struggle is more difficult. Victory over mere external coercion is enough to delight Stendhal; in his *Chroniques italiennes* he immures his heroines deep within convents, he shuts them up in the palaces of jealous husbands. Thus they have to invent a thousand ruses to rejoin their lovers; secret doors, rope ladders, bloodstained chests, abductions, seclusions, assassinations, outbursts of passion and disobedience are treated with the most intelligent ingenuity; death and impending tortures add excitement to the audacities of the mad souls he depicts for us. Even in his maturer work Stendhal remains sensitive to this obvious romanticism: it is the outward manifestation of what springs from the heart; they can be no more distinguished from each other than a mouth can be separated from its smile. Clélia invents love anew when she invents the alphabet that enables her to correspond with Fabrice. The Sanseverina is described for us as "an always sincere soul who never acted with prudence, who abandoned herself wholly to the impression of the moment"; it is when she plots, when she poisons the prince, and when she floods Parma that this soul is revealed to us: she is herself no more than the sublime and mad escapade she has chosen to live. The ladder that Mathilde de La Mole sets against her windowsill is no mere theatrical prop: it is, in tangible form, her proud imprudence, her taste for the extraordinary, her provocative courage. The qualities of these souls would not be displayed were they not surrounded by such inimical powers as prison walls, a ruler's will, a family's severity.

But the most difficult constraints to overcome are those which each person encounters within himself: here the adventure of liberty is most dubious, most poignant, most pungent. Clearly Stendhal's sympathy for his heroines is the greater the more closely they are confined. To be sure, he likes the strumpets, sublime or not, who have trampled upon the conventions once for all; but he cherishes Métilde more tenderly, held back as she is by her scruples and her modesty. Lucien Leuwen enjoys being with that free spirit Mme de Hocquincourt; but he passionately loves the chaste, reserved, and hesitant Mme de Chasteller; he admires the headstrong soul of the Sanseverina, who flinches at nothing; but he prefers Clélia to her, and it is the young girl who wins Fabrice's heart. And Mme de Rênal, fettered by her pride, her prejudices, and her ignorance, is of all the women created by Stendhal perhaps the one who most astounds him. He frequently locates his heroines in a provincial, limited environment, under the control of a husband or an imbecile father; he is pleased to make them uncultured and even full of false notions. Mme de Rênal and Mme de Chasteller are both obstinately legitimist; the former is timid and without experience; the latter has a brilliant intelligence but does not appreciate its value; thus they are not responsible for their mistakes, but rather they are as much the victims of them as of institutions and the mores; and it is from error that the romantic blossoms forth, as poetry from frustration.

A clear-headed person who decides upon his acts in full knowledge of the situation is to be curtly approved or blamed; whereas one admires with fear, pity, irony, love, the courage and the stratagems of a generous heart trying to make its way in the shadows. It is because women are baffled that we see flourishing in them such useless and charming virtues as their modesty, their pride, their extreme delicacy; in a sense these are faults, for they give rise to deception, oversensitiveness, fits of anger;

but they are sufficiently accounted for by the situation in which women are placed. Women are led to take pride in little things or at least in "things of merely sentimental value" because all the things "regarded as important" are out of their reach. Their modesty results from their dependent condition: because they are forbidden to show their capabilities in action, they call in question their very being. It seems to them that the perception of others, especially that of their lover, reveals them truly as they are: they fear this and try to escape from it. A real regard for value is expressed in their flights, their hesitations, their revolts, and even in their lies; and this is what makes them worthy of respect; but it is expressed awkwardly, even in bad faith; and this is what makes them touching and even mildly comic. It is when liberty is taken in its own snares and cheats against itself that it is most deeply human and therefore to Stendhal most engaging.

Stendhal's women are touching when their hearts set them unforeseen problems: no law, no recipe, no reasoning, no example from without can any longer guide them; they have to decide for themselves, alone. This forlornness is the high point of freedom. Célia was brought up in an atmosphere of liberal ideas, she is lucid and reasonable; but opinions acquired from others, true or false, are of no avail in a moral conflict. Mme de Rênal loves Julien in spite of her morality, and Clélia saves Fabrice against her better judgment: there is in the two cases the same going beyond all recognized values. This hardihood is what arouses Stendhal's enthusiasm; but it is the more moving in that it scarcely dares to avow itself, and on this account it is more natural, more spontaneous, more authentic. In Mme de Rênal audacity is hidden under innocence: not knowing about love, she is unable to recognize it and so yields to it without resistance; it would seem that because of having lived in the dark she is defenseless against the flashing light of passion; she receives it, dazzled, whether it is against heaven and hell or not. When this flame dies down, she falls back into the shadows where husbands and priests are in control. She has no confidence in her own judgment, but whatever is clearly present overwhelms her; as soon as she finds Julien again, she gives him her soul once more. Her remorse and the letter that her confessor wrests from her show to what lengths this ardent and sincere soul had to go in order to escape from the prison where society shut her away and attain to the heaven of happiness.

In Clélia the conflict is more clearly conscious; she hesitates between her loyalty to her father and her amorous pity; she tries to think of arguments. The triumph of the values Stendhal believes in seems to him the more magnificent in that it is regarded as a defeat by the victims of a hypocritical civilization; and he is delighted to see them using trickery and bad faith to make the truth of passion and happiness prevail over the lies they believe in. Thus Clélia is at once laughable and deeply affecting

when she promises the Madonna not to *see* Fabrice any more and then
for two years accepts his kisses and embraces on condition that she keep
her eyes shut!

With the same tender irony Stendhal considers Mme de Chasteller's
hesitancies and Mathilde de La Mole's incoherencies; so many detours,
reversals, scruples, hidden victories and defeats in order to arrive at
certain simple and legitimate ends! All this is for him the most ravishing
of comedies. There is drollery in these dramas because the actress is at
once judge and culprit, because she is her own dupe, because she imposes
roundabout ways upon herself when she need only decree that the Gordian
knot be cut. But nevertheless these inner struggles reveal all the most
worthy solicitude that could torture a noble soul: the actress wants to
retain her self-respect; she puts her approbation of herself above that of
others and thus becomes herself an absolute. These echoless, solitary debates are graver than a cabinet crisis; when Mme de Chasteller asks herself whether she is or is not going to respond to Lucien Leuwen's love, she
is making a decision concerning herself and also the world. Can one, she
asks, have confidence in others? Can one rely on one's own heart? What
is the worth of love and human pledges? Is it foolish or generous to believe and to love?

Such interrogations put in question the very meaning of life, the life
of each and of all. The so-called serious man is really futile, because he
accepts ready-made justifications for his life; whereas a passionate and
profound woman revises established values from moment to moment.
She knows the constant tension of unsupported freedom; it puts her in
constant danger: she can win or lose all in an instant. It is the anxious
assumption of this risk that gives her story the colors of a heroic adventure.
And the stakes are the highest there are: the very meaning of existence,
this existence which is each one's portion, his only portion. Mina de
Vanghel's escapade can in a sense seem absurd; but it involves a whole
scheme of ethics. "Was her life a miscalculation? Her happiness had
lasted eight months. Hers was a soul too ardent to be contented with the
reality of life." Mathilde de La Mole is less sincere than Clélia or Mme
de Chasteller; she regulates her actions according to the idea of herself
which she has built up, not according to the clear actuality of love, of
happiness: would it be more haughty and grand to save oneself than to
be lost, to humiliate oneself before one's beloved than to resist him? She
also is alone in the midst of her doubts, and she is risking that self-respect
which means more to her than life. It is the ardent quest for valid reasons
for living, the search through the darkness of ignorance, of prejudices, of
frauds, in the shifting and feverish light of passion, it is the infinite risk
of happiness or death, of grandeur or shame, that gives glory to these
women's lives.

Woman is of course unaware of the seductiveness she spreads around her; to contemplate herself, to act the personage, is always an inauthentic attitude; Mme Grandet, comparing herself with Mme Roland, proves by the act that she is not like her. If Mathilde de La Mole remains engaging, it is because she gets herself involved in her comedies and because she is frequently the prey of her heart just when she thinks she is in control of it; she touches our feelings to the degree that she escapes her own will. But the purest heroines are quite unselfconscious. Mme de Rênal is unaware of her elegance, as Mme de Chasteller is of her intelligence. In this lies one of the deep joys of the lover, with whom both reader and author identify themselves; he is the witness through whom these secret riches come to light; he is alone in admiring that vivacity which Mme de Rênal's glances spread abroad, that "lively, mercurial, profound spirit" which Mme de Chasteller's entourage fails to appreciate; and even if others appreciate the Sanseverina's mind, he is the one who penetrates farthest into her soul.

Before woman, man tastes the pleasure of contemplation; he is enraptured with her as with a landscape or a painting; she sings in his heart and tints the sky. This revelation reveals him to himself: it is impossible to comprehend the delicacy of women, their sensitiveness, their ardor, without becoming a delicate, sensitive, and ardent soul; feminine sentiments create a world of nuances, of requirements the discovery of which enriches the lover: in the company of Mme de Rênal, Julien becomes a different person from that ambitious man he had resolved to be, he makes a new choice. If a man has only a superficial desire for a woman, he will find it amusing to seduce her. But true love really transfigures his life. "Love such as Werther's opens the soul . . . to sentiment and to the enjoyment of the *beautiful* under whatever form it presents itself, however ill-clothed. It brings happiness even without wealth. . . ." "It is a new aim in life to which everything is related and which changes the face of everything. Love-passion flings all nature with its sublimities before a man's eyes like a novelty just invented yesterday." Love breaks the everyday routine, drives ennui away, the ennui in which Stendhal sees such deep evil because it is the lack of any reason for living or dying; the lover has an aim and that is enough to turn each day into an adventure: what a pleasure for Stendhal to spend three days hidden in Menta's cave! Rope ladders, bloodstained caskets, and the like express in his novels this taste for the extraordinary. Love— that is to say, woman—makes apparent the true ends of existence: beauty, happiness, fresh sensations, and a new world. It tears out a man's soul and thereby gives him possession of it; the lover feels the same tension, knows the same risks as his mistress, and proves himself more authentically than in his professional career. When Julien hesitates at the foot of a ladder placed by Mathilde, he puts in question his entire destiny:

in that moment his true measure is taken. It is through women, under their influence, in reaction to their behavior, that Julien, Fabrice, Lucien work out their apprenticeship in dealing with the world and themselves. Test, reward, judge, friend—woman truly is in Stendhal what Hegel was for a moment tempted to make of her: that other consciousness which in reciprocal recognition gives to the other subject the same truth that she receives from him. Two who know each other in love make a happy couple, defying time and the universe; such a couple is sufficient unto itself, it realizes the absolute.

But all this presupposes that woman is not pure alterity: she is subject in her own right. Stendhal never limits himself to describing his heroines as functions of his heroes: he gives them a destiny of their own. He has attempted a still rarer enterprise, one that I believe no novelist has before undertaken: he has projected himself into a female character. He does not hover over Lamiel like Marivaux over Marianne or Richardson over Clarissa Harlowe; he assumes her destiny just as he had assumed Julien's. On this account Lamiel's outline remains somewhat speculative, but it is singularly significant. Stendhal has raised all imaginable obstacles about the young girl: she is a poor peasant, ignorant, coarsely raised by people imbued with all the prejudices; but she clears from her path all moral barriers once she understands the full meaning of the little words: "that's silly." Her new freedom of mind allows her in her own fashion to act upon all the impulses of her curiosity, her ambition, her gaiety. Before so stout a heart, material obstacles could not but be smoothed away, and her only problem will be to shape a destiny worthy of her in a mediocre world. She must find fulfillment in crime and death; but this is also Julien's lot. There is no place for great souls in society as it exists. And men and women are in the same boat.

It is noteworthy that Stendhal should be at once so deeply romantic and so decidedly feministic; usually feminists are rational minds who in all matters take a universal point of view; but Stendhal demands woman's emancipation not only in the name of liberty in general but also in the name of individual happiness. Love, he believes, will have nothing to lose; on the contrary, it will be the more true as woman, being man's equal, is able to understand him the more completely. No doubt certain qualities admired in women will disappear; but their worth comes from the freedom they express. This will be manifested under other forms, and the romantic will not vanish from the world. Two separate beings, in different circumstances, face to face in freedom and seeking justification of their existence through one another, will always live an adventure full of risk and promise. Stendhal puts his trust in truth. To depart from it means a living death; but where it shines forth, there shine forth also beauty, happiness, love, and a joy that carries its own justification. That is why he rejects the mystifications of the serious, as he rejects the false poetry of the myths. Human reality suffices him. Woman according to him is simply a human being: nor could any shape of dreams be more enrapturing.

Stendhal,
Analyst or Amorist?

by Victor Brombert

"Ahi! tanto amò la non amante amata"
—Tasso

De l'Amour—what title could be more alluring, more filled with promise? Many eager readers, in search of erotic thrills or bedroom memoirs, have, no doubt, leafed through these pages, only to be left dismally frustrated by the results of their exploration. For what they found in this book that pretends to treat the enticing subject of love "simply, reasonably and mathematically" was both much less and much more than what they had set out to discover. Certainly Stendhal is not a Casanova nor a marquis de Sade. He is even less a Darles de Montigny or a Vivant-Denon, although if he had read the latter's *Point de lendemain,* he might conceivably have shared Sainte-Beuve's appreciation of this unusually delicate and sensitive example of *ars erotica.* But *De l'Amour* is nothing of the sort; it is not even the scientific treatise with which the preface explicitly threatens the reader. To state the case quite bluntly: this uneven book does not correspond to anything the reader may reasonably expect; it merely satisfies the selfish needs of a thirty-seven year old adolescent, self-conscious, unsuccessful in his amorous enterprises and very much in need of idealizing an experience that fate, his own clumsiness and the untimely *accès de vertu* of a Milanese lady have relegated to the realm of the intangible. *De l'Amour* is simultaneously a *plaidoyer,* a self-administered therapeutic treatment and a Stendhalian *Vita Nuova.*

What is true of *De l'Amour* is in many ways true also of Stendhal's fictional work. The thirty-seven year old adolescent has grown and matured into a forty-seven year old adolescent. At fifty-five, he will still be the same, forever carrying the imaginative battle against his self-

"Stendhal, Analyst or Amorist?" From *Yale French Studies,* No. 11 (Summer 1953), pp. 39-48. Copyright 1953 by *Yale French Studies.* Reprinted by permission of *Yale French Studies.*

consciousness to the very outposts of his sensibility. André Gide once flippantly remarked that of ten moments of joy, Stendhal owed nine to satisfied vanity. There is much in Stendhal's work that seems to uphold this unflattering view, although his particular brand of *egotism* stems not so much from a desire to impress the outside world, as from an inner compulsion to live up to self-imposed standards.

Love is of course the central theme of his work, as it had been the "grande et unique affaire" of his life. Yet the entire literary output of this man so devoid of *cant*, so shockingly frank at times, so unwilling to flirt with either bourgeois conventionality or metaphysical subtleties, is—erotically speaking—as disappointing as *De l'Amour*. No morbid curiosity assails his soul. To be sure, zealous Freudians have ascribed great importance to Stendhal's confession of his physical love for his mother and of his early jealousy of his father. "I wanted to cover my mother with kisses, and also that she should have no clothes on," he remembers having wished at the age of seven. There is also the somewhat daring chapter on "Fiascos" in *De l'Amour*, which, coupled with the pathetic handicap of one of his heroes (Octave in *Armance*) has led some gleeful tongues and no less gleeful pens to the conclusion that Stendhal was sexually impotent—a conclusion most categorically refuted by competent and well-informed witnesses. In this respect, Stendhal was assuredly quite healthy.

It is significant that Mario Praz, in his painstaking comparative study of erotic and morbid sensibility in nineteenth-century literature, has exiled Stendhal to a few minor footnotes. Sainte-Beuve's assertion that Sade and Byron had been the great inspirers of his contemporaries— that their work provides a key to the hidden recesses of contemporary novels—simply does not apply to Stendhal. In spite of a frequently cynical and even sometimes obscene correspondence with Prosper Mérimée (I refer in particular to the letter of December 23, 1826, concerning *Armance*), Stendhal's work displays none of the more turbulent and "sinful" currents that pervade the bulk of Romantic literature, or at least that part not sufficiently chaste for anthology and class-room consumption.

Stendhal had read, of course, and even enjoyed many of the books that sowed the seeds of the Romantic frenzy. He knew the "roman noir" and recommended some of the more outstanding examples to his sister Pauline. But unlike Balzac who fed on the monstrous tales of the turn of the century, Stendhal remained impermeable to these influences. Few writers, indeed, have so persistently avoided the literary clichés of their time. Nor are there many who lend themselves so well as he to negative definitions. His unconsciously stubborn rejection of all currents not suited to his artistic and psychological needs is cause for us to know him even better by what he hated than by what he liked. But his stubbornness which to some may appear as a limitation is also our guarantee of his authenticity. Stendhal never professed to be more profound, more evil, more obsessed by the devil than he really was. Mental as well as physical aphrodisiacs were distasteful to him. He would not have found palatable the Rimbaldian "dérèglement des sens." Stendhal is thus a disappointment to those who, like Mario Praz, are held in spell by Chateaubriand's voluptuous meditations on death, Shelley's strident exaltation of Medusan beauty, Flaubert's wild dreams of exotic tortures, the Goncourts' taste for the *faisandé* or Swinburne's imaginary orgies. No epicurean pain ever appealed to Stendhal. Even his exoticism is not of an erotic nature (as it is with Mérimée, Flaubert, or Théophile Gautier). No fatal women —no Cleopatras or Salomes—strut through his fictions. No fatal men, "majestic though in ruin," appear on his stage. He would have noticed nothing diabolical in the smile of Mona Lisa. He may have been fascinated by cloisters and by cloistered women (usually they are cloistered more by their pride and timidity than by actual walls), but his cloisters never conceal perverse demons. He may have sung and praised the pleasures of revenge, but even the passionate Sanseverina does not indulge in murder as in one of the fine arts. No regenerate prostitutes, no persecuted innocent virgins, no vampires people his imagination. Even man's supposedly inherent sense of guilt is so absent in Stendhal that nowhere do we find a quest for expiation.

If attraction to violence be indicative of an erotic imagination, as it seems to be with novelists such as Flaubert, Zola, and, in our own day, Hemingway and Malraux, a good "case" could no doubt also be made of Stendhal. Quite assuredly, this poet of energy and of Renaissance vendettas had a taste for prolonged hatreds, dark plots, romantic crimes and solemn executions. It is a well-known fact that Stendhal was an assiduous collector of crime stories. With tongue in cheek, he warned his English readers (*Courrier anglais,* December 24, 1828) against the "disgusting details" and "sanguinary horrors" of these accounts. Nevertheless, the *Gazette des Tribunaux* supplied the basic plot for the *Rouge et le noir.* What is less well known is that Stendhal's library, at the time of his death, contained three volumes each of the *Causes célèbres, Chroniques du crime, Cour d'assises,* and *Palais de justice.* While in Italy, he acquired manuscripts concerning "tragic stories" (a real museum of horror), and later wrote the *Chroniques italiennes.* The very names of Vittoria Accoramboni and of Beatrice Cenci bring to mind a climate of bloodshed and cruelty. Vittoria is killed while the murderer, twisting and turning his dagger in every direction, asks his panting victim whether he is reaching her heart; Beatrice is put to the question *ad torturam capillorum,* an apparent refinement of the infamous *tratta di corda* used by the Inquisitors. Yet, surprisingly enough, what remains with the reader, what lingers in his imagination, is not the violence, but the courage and the generosity of the protagonists. By social ethics, Julien Sorel, Fabrice del Dongo, the duchess Sanseverina, the Carbonaro patriot-bandit Ferrante Palla—all are criminals. Pistols and poison are more frequently the instruments of passionate revenge than of devotion to a noble cause. But this distinction is purely theoretical. Nobility, in the Stendhalian universe, is bestowed on any compelling emotion. Only petty crimes remain unredeemable. For what really captures his imagination is not the crime, and even less the punishment, but the *élan* (essentially sign and symptom of life and health) that goes into the crime and transforms it into an eloquent expression of man's dignity.

Paradoxical though it may seem, this dabbler in criminology was in fact as repulsed by violence as he was by obscenity. Writing about the church of Santo Stefano Rotondo (*Promenades dans Rome*), he expresses strong disgust for the scenes of martyrdom by Pomarancio and Tempesta. A saint whose head is crushed between two millstones, whose eyes are driven out of their sockets—this kind of *réalité atroce,* suggests Stendhal, can only appeal to a vulgar mind. (Stendhal's contemptuous expression is "âme commune.") He was appalled by Hugo's *Han d'Islande;* in an article published in the *New Monthly Magazine* (*Courrier anglais,* April 1, 1823), he accuses the author of this literally bloodthirsty and blood-drunk hero of having given birth to a "monstrous foetus."

But it is Stendhal's own work that best attests to his deep-seated reluctance to indulge in any mysticism of the senses. The Italian chronicle that most fascinated him, together with the story of Accoramboni and Cenci, was undoubtedly the account of the youth of Paul III and of the dissolute life of Vannozza Farnese (largely a legendary creature). This pamphlet—the *Origine delle grandezze della famiglia Farnese*—which reveals the Renaissance mores at their crudest, was one of the main sources of the *Chartreuse de Parme.* We need hardly go to the novel, however, to notice the deep transformation which this story underwent. Already in an early free translation—or adaptation—of the account can we measure the metamorphosis imposed by Stendhal's mind. The "lascivious" Vannozza becomes an "aimable volcan d'idées nouvelles" (she will eventually grow into a duchess of Sanseverina). The rape of a defenseless young lady by the unscrupulous future pope is translated, as though by magic, into a gallant and idyllic adventure story, while awaiting to be further transformed into Fabrice's sentimental escapade with the very beautiful—and very willing—young Marietta. Never did Stendhal have at his disposal a document in which the sins of the flesh were more cynically exposed. Yet never did he more obstinately transform brutality into elegance, and evil deeds into an unquenching zest for life.

And even Stendhal's *Cenci,* with all its incest, parricide, and torture, seems chaste if compared with Shelley's dramatic version. While Shelley details old Cenci's "delight in sensual luxury," his pleasure at hearing his victims' groans, his "wicked laughter round the eyes," Stendhal only vaguely suggests the action that takes place between the Roman Don Juan (as he calls him) and his daughter. "Flesh," "pollution," "putrefying limbs," "agony," "leprous stains"—not only Shelley's terms, but the very climate of his play would have been distasteful to him. Against Shelley's satanic Cenci who exclaims

> I do not feel as if I were a man,
> But like a fiend appointed to chastise
> The offences of some unremembered world

Stendhal opposes a *man* who merely wants to "étonner ses contemporains."

As to *sex* in Stendhal's novels (and are they not all tales of adultery and of seduction!), it is nearly altogether refined out of existence. Stendhal's *pudeur* colors his very style. Here, at the beginning of the *Rouge,* is the first description of Madame de Rênal:

> . . . aux yeux d'un Parisien, cette grâce naïve, pleine d'innocence et de vivacité, serait même allée jusqu'à rappeler des idées de douce volupté. Si elle eût appris ce genre de succès, Mme de Rênal en eût été bien honteuse.

In these two conditional sentences, any reader of the *Rouge* can recognize the typically Stendhalian manner of describing in depth by means of allusions and hypotheses. We have scarcely seen Madame de Rênal, and already we penetrate into her intimacy. We observe qualities of which she herself is not aware. We foresee reactions that are still lost in the unpatterned chaos of possibilities. The presentational method is that of the omniscient writer. But the use of the conditional form permits the author to shade very delicately the implicit suggestion of eroticism in this passage. The first sentence alludes to the feminine charm of Madame de Rênal; the second establishes the authenticity of her modesty. But all is thinned out, and, as it were, enveloped by a chaste though transparent veil. The "real" personage is observed by an "imaginary" one (the Parisian), and this game, this appreciation by means of an imaginary dramatic form provides the illusion of action. It is a hypothetical approach, so dear to Stendhal. But this approach is in fact as little concerned with Madame de Rênal's charm as it is with her modesty. What really matters is that the "Stendhalian" conditional form corresponds to his type of imagination and echoes his creative process. His novels—as well as his autobiographic writings—denote the same effort to reconcile memory and imagination, to force an agreement between what was and what *might have* been. A certain speculative quality characterizes all his works.

The bedroom scenes are no less chaste. And this is not only because Stendhal evades the issue, but because the minds of the heroes are actually centered *elsewhere*. Julien Sorel, on his first visit to Madame de Rênal, could hardly be accused of nurturing lascivious thoughts! All he knows is the self-imposed challenge and the timidity he so clumsily combats. The scene is above all comic: beginning with Julien's disappointment at hearing Monsieur de Rênal snore (even the last pretext for not going has vanished), and ending with Julien's exclamation of disillusionment: "n'est-ce que ça?"

Only one other *nuit d'amour* with Madame de Rênal is depicted. It is also the last. Julien, after fourteen months at the theological seminary, is about to leave the province for Paris. Comedy has given way to tenderness. The intervening months had seen their love take on the "physiognomy of crime." Appropriately then, the scene begins on a note of remorse and recrimination. But soon the two lovers join in tender reminiscences. Madame de Rênal weakens and is about to relapse. This relapse is beautifully conveyed by the simplest artistic means: imperceptible transitions from the active to the passive voice, as well as from the personal pronoun *elle* to the indefinite pronoun *on* (same device during the famous garden scene at the beginning of the novel!). But this relapse marks above all a strategic victory for Julien. It is not physical pleasure he seeks or finds, but, as Stendhal himself explains, "les voluptés de l'orgueil." For this young man who jumps from Madame de Rênal's window may have the agility of Chérubin; the caresses his soul requires are of a more sophisticated nature.

There are two other bedroom episodes (in book II of the novel)—this time the partner being the extravagant Mathilde de La Mole, who summons Julien to her room in the most romantic manner. Needless to say that here again Julien is hardly guilty of carnal desire. All our hero can think of as he climbs up the moonlit ladder (pistol in hand!) is his fear and his compulsion to live up to this new challenge. There is not even a snoring husband whom he may hope to awaken: only the faint hope that Mathilde herself may put him off. But even this does not materialize and the whole scene ends in mutual embarrassment.

As to the last in this series of apparent parodies of love scenes, it begins very appropriately with a real exhibition of Julien's acrobatic talents. He again chooses to enter his mistress' room through the window. But this time things are carried one step further: Julien, filled with "superhuman force," twists one of the links of the chain to which the ladder is attached. All this is described very minutely. But when it comes to Julien's reward, when finally Mathilde throws herself ecstatically into his arms, Stendhal withdraws behind a line of dots. . . .

This romantic paraphernalia which clutters the stage at the most inopportune moments, this silence behind which the author bashfully conceals himself, this *escamotage,* or juggling away, of sex are characteristic of Stendhal. In his later novels, he shows himself even more reserved. There is one two-and-a-half line exception, however: it is when Clélia Conti, the gaoler's daughter, rushes to the rescue of the beloved prisoner (her "husband" as she calls him):

> Elle était si belle, à demi vêtue et dans cet état d'extrême passion, que Fabrice ne put résister à un mouvement presqu'involontaire. Aucune résistance ne fut opposée.
>
> *(Chartreuse,* chapter XXV)

But "passion" is of course an ambiguous term: it applies more to Clélia's will to save Fabrice than to any concrete physical desire. Clélia is above all heroically inspired. (She, too, it should be noted, is filled with a "supernatural strength"!) Moreover, the love-making is so rapid, so sweeping and the circumstances are so unreal (in a prison cell, with poisoned food on a table nearby) that the "involuntary movement" of Fabrice is more of the nature of a symbolic gesture which lends the scene a clearly stylized air. Never has physical action been more convincingly translated into a *mood* than in this brief passage. Rhythm has replaced depiction. Love has been sublimated into a miraculous literary choreography!

This tendency to substitute mood and stylized movement for lengthy verbal accounts becomes even more evident as this most tender and lyrical of all of Stendhal's love stories draws to a close. Comedy and pathos intermingle—as in *opera buffa* for which he always had a clear predilection—during the Princess of Parma's reception, when Fabrice, turning his face away from Clélia who is now married to the marquis of Crescenzi, cries bitterly, while listening simultaneously to a famous aria of Cimarosa and to the endless chatter of a monk. But when, on some dark night a well-known voice rings out to him "Di quà amico del cuore," and a well-known hand guides him into a secret room, pathos and comedy give way to enchantment; we have entered a world of magic—a word in which a single gesture can be indefinitely prolonged and in which a sentence can echo forever. All has been brought to completion. The characters can now die; the novel can now come to an abrupt end.

To be sure, much remains untouched. Whether due to self-consciousness or to an esthetic compulsion, this constant elusion from the realities of physical love—this avoiding of what in fact may be a difficult subject—limits the scope of Stendhal's novels and may disappoint some of his readers. Woman's sensuality transformed after surrender, tenderness persisting and transformed after shared physical experiences, the eventual death of love—all these are subjects totally neglected by Stendhal. It is worth noting, however, that the poetry of his novels proceeds directly from unsatiated desire embellished by regret. It is above all the poetry of renouncement. And this renouncement is all the more total as all has been consummated. It is when Stendhal's heroes are granted that which secretly they had renounced from the very start, that they turn aside from this gift with the greatest sense of self-denial. That is the meaning of the recurring prison-symbol. That is also the meaning of Julien's attempt on his mistress' life, of Clélia's premature death and of Fabrice's retirement to the charterhouse. This, too, had already been the meaning of Octave's lyrical death by poison on the ship carrying him toward Greece (*Armance*) —although in that early novel Stendhal had not yet found what Eliot would call the "objective correlative."

II

How then are we to account for Stendhal's originality in his treatment of the love theme? Sex is juggled away; the plot itself is stylized. Does Stendhal's fame as a "specialist" in this field rest solely on his acute penetration into the involved mechanism of love's parturition and birth? To be sure, even such an early fictional attempt as *Ernestine ou la naissance de l'amour* not only conveys the pet theory of the seven stages of love, but rivals in charm many an exquisite scene of Marivaux. No one would deny that the account of crystallization, a term launched by Stendhal, provides a most enchanting metaphor. Even Proust, that most poetic of theoricians, is duly indebted to Stendhal. Swann's "malady" for Odette is in many ways Stendhal transposed into a minor key. Nor should Stendhal's conception of jealousy as a real passion be underrated. Being a person who liked to hang on desperately to the very memories that tortured him, Stendhal found no doubt some bitter compensation in dragging his fictional characters through crises of self-deprecation. Taine, however, at the time he was collecting materials for his work on *The Will,* carried matters a step too far when he decided to use Mosca's jealousy as a prop for his own theories. Critics will thus forever be tempted to ask of writers—and of novelists in particular—to be psychologists and "painters of the soul." Yet no demand could be more unfair, even though Stendhal himself fancied that he was above all a first-class anatomist of the human heart.

The fact is, of course, that Stendhal's vision of love is not only limited, but strictly unscientific. "Analysis" is but one of the many masks he wore to protect his lyricism and to dissimulate his chronic self-consciousness. The real masters of this pseudo-*idéologue* are not Helvétius, Condillac, and Destutt de Tracy, but rather Rousseau, Corneille, and Tasso. Even Racine is too obsessed by the demon of self-destructive lucidity really to appeal to that most willfully blind among escape-seekers. Stendhal at the age of fifty—though weighed down by cascades of flesh that required armchairs made to order—was still able to soar high and trace the shadows of "high romance." Exiled to Civitavecchia, the old consul still "sympathized"—as he used to, at the age of ten, when he first discovered Ariosto in the translation of the count of Tressan—"with all that is of tale of love, of forests (the woods and their vast silence), of generosity." Those familiar with Italian studies on Stendhal may recall Pietro-Paolo Trompeo's suggestive essay "L'Ariostesco Stendhal" (*La Ruota*, April and September 1940). But if the prophecies and the landscape in the *Chartreuse* summon up remembrances of *Orlando*, the tenderness of the author and his lyric participation in the very lives of his fictional creatures remind us of Tasso. "Il Tassesco Stendhal" could indeed be the title of some still unwritten study that would show in some detail how Stendhal's characters hold a view of love that would not have been out of place in some idealized Ferrara of Alphonso II.[1] As we leaf through Stendhal's autobiographical and fictional writings, we are constantly reminded of the advice given by Dafne to a shy and recalcitrant Sylvia in *Aminta:*

> Forse, se tu gustassi anco una volta
> La millesima parte de le gioie
> Che gusta un core amato rïamando,
> Diresti, ripentita, sospirando:
> Perduto é tutto il tempo
> Che in amar non si spende.

All of Stendhal's works seem to carry this message. And though Stendhal himself, and most of his characters, may have tried in vain to find this requiting heart ("amato rïamando"), they are nevertheless convinced that the only time not wasted was that employed in the service of love. Better to die of love like Salviati (in *De l'Amour*), than never to acquire that nobility of feeling that comes with failure and that permits one to rejoice even in despair. The Stendhalian heroes all learn to smile the hard way.

If Stendhal had to choose between Valmont and Werther, he would choose Werther. So at least he affirms. Certainly he uses his full powers as omnipotent author to maintain his fictional characters in a state of frustration. He constantly places them in situations where they fail in their amorous enterprises either as a result of their clumsiness or because they are blind to the true feelings of their partner. Lucien Leuwen thus never realizes that Madame de Chasteller's apparent coldness toward him is only a symptom of her imminent surrender. This chronic blindness with which Stendhal curses his most cherished heroes stems undoubtedly from an unconscious need for self-justification. A quest for an imaginary compensation lies unquestionably at the root of the sarcasms he so generously

---

[1] It is noteworthy that, according to Stendhal, the ideal region for love is Sorrento, "la patrie de Tasse" (*De l'Amour*, I, chap. XXIV).

lavishes on all the unsuccessful lovers in his novels. To be sure, their inability to achieve victory is also a sign of their moral distinction. But the irony with which he accompanies their self-deprecation goes beyond the simple problem of praise or blame. When Stendhal accuses Lucien of utter stupidity, he inevitably evokes sufferings with which he is but too familiar. But this *dédoublement* always presents itself in the shape of an apparent contradiction: he reprimands, but indirectly he also consoles himself. From his omniscient vantage point, he can overcome his hero's humility and embarrassment. He can meet them with his mockery, but also with his dream of compensation. He can exploit the ignorance of his hero, and thus, behind his back, turn defeat into victory. The clumsier Lucien is, the more he deprecates himself. The more he deprecates himself, the greater his clumsiness and his timidity, the better also his chances of success. By a strange twist of the imagination, blindness and dejection become the very condition of victory. A strange victory indeed, of which the hero may never reap the fruits, but which the author savors to the fullest.

This ability to toy with his own imagination and feelings, this habit of glorifying self-deception (in spite of his professed contempt for dupery), makes it difficult, in the last analysis, to assess properly the function of love in his novels. Certainly, the powers at work are not those of scientific curiosity, but of moral and poetic synthesis. Love constantly marks a *dépassement,* a going beyond the contingencies of the flesh and of daily life. It is the dignity-bestowing force that animates all his work. But this dynamism, which expresses itself most frequently through the baffling romantic irony so typical of Stendhal, also marks a very real challenge to life. Love, in the Stendhalian universe, assumes the proportions of a vast allegory of escape—an escape rendered tragic by the awareness on the part of the reader that it is *without real hope* that Stendhal repeatedly sets sail for the regions of dream. If he loves his heroes more perhaps than any other novelist, it is not because he identifies himself with them, but precisely because he gives them the *right* to be blind. Not indefinitely, it should be added. They, too, learn as he has learned, first not to believe, and then to delude themselves voluntarily and smile in the face of failure. But there is courage in that smile.

Chronology of Important Dates

1783	Birth of Henri Beyle (Stendhal) in Grenoble.
1796-1799	Studies at the École Centrale in Grenoble.
1799-1802	Arrival in Paris. Protected by his relative Pierre Daru, he obtains a commission in the army and leaves for Italy. Sojourn in Milan as Second Lieutenant. At the end of 1801 he returns to Paris and soon resigns from the army.
1802-1806	Formative years in Paris. Henri Beyle reads Helvetius, Cabanis, Destutt de Tracy (the *Idéologues*), studies acting, and plans to become a playwright. He follows an actress to Marseille.
1806-1814	Pierre Daru, now chief of the army commissary, obtains for Beyle an important administrative position in the army. Stationed in Germany. Becomes Auditeur au Conseil d'État. Occasionally back in Paris where he leads the life of a dandy. Participates in the retreat from Moscow (1812), is Indendant in Sagan. In 1814, helps organize the military defense of the Dauphiné.
1814-1821	Life as a dilettante in Milan. Frequents groups of Italian liberals, and enjoys Italian art and music. Begins a *Vie de Napoléon*. Unrequited love for Métilde Dembowski. Politically suspect, is forced to leave Milan.
1815	*Vies de Haydn, Mozart et Métastase.*
1817	*Histoire de la peinture en Italie* and *Rome, Naples et Florence.*
1821-1830	Literary and worldly life in Paris. Financial difficulties. Trips to England and contributions to English publications. Polemics about Romanticism. Some important love affairs.
1822	*De l'Amour.*
1823	*Racine et Shakespeare,* part I; *Vie de Rossini.*
1825	*Racine et Shakespeare,* part II.
1827	His first novel, *Armance.*
1829	*Promenades dans Rome.*
1830	*Le Rouge et le noir.*

1831-1836	Stendhal is consul in Civitavecchia. Writes his autobiographical *Souvenirs d'égotisme,* and *Vie de Henry Brulard,* as well as the uncompleted novel *Lucien Leuwen* (all of them published posthumously).
1836-1839	Long leave in Paris. Begins a new *Vie de Napoléon*. A productive period.
1837-1839	*Chroniques italiennes.*
1838	*Mémoires d'un touriste.*
1839	*La Chartreuse de Parme.*
1839-1841	Back in Civitavecchia. Begins *Lamiel* (unfinished novel).
1841	Return to Paris.
1842	Dies in Paris.

Notes on the Editor and Contributors

VICTOR BROMBERT, the editor of this volume, is the author of *Stendhal et la voie oblique* and of many articles on Stendhal. He is also the author of a book on T. S. Eliot, and has recently published *The Intellectual Hero: Studies in the French Novel, 1880-1955*. He teaches at Yale.

ERICH AUERBACH, distinguished humanist, is the author of *Mimesis*, a masterful study of the representation of reality in Western literature. A great medieval scholar, Erich Auerbach extended his curiosity and knowledge to many periods. At the time of his death in 1957, he was Sterling Professor of Romance Philology at Yale.

SIMONE DE BEAUVOIR, first lady of French Existentialism, occupies a key position in French intellectual life. Widely known for her novels and essays, she is perhaps most familiar to the American public for her challenging book *The Second Sex*, from which the essay on Stendhal has been taken.

LÉON BLUM, famous French socialist leader and statesman, was also a refined essayist and literary critic. His book on Stendhal, though written several decades ago, has paved the way for much of the later criticism and has remained strikingly fresh.

RAYMOND GIRAUD, a specialist of nineteenth-century French literature, has written on Stendhal, Balzac, and Flaubert. His *Unheroic Hero* is a vigorous and original study of the "bourgeois" in the nineteenth-century novel. He is currently preparing a study of "l'art pour l'art" movement. He teaches at Stanford University.

IRVING HOWE, well known as literary critic and as author of *Politics and the Novel*, has also written significant studies on Faulkner and Sherwood Anderson. A frequent reviewer for the *New Republic, Partisan Review*, and other publications, Irving Howe teaches at Stanford University.

JUDD D. HUBERT teaches French literature at the University of California. His studies on Baudelaire, Racine, and Molière, as well as his many distinguished articles, are well known to scholars in his field.

JEAN PRÉVOST, essayist, novelist, and literary critic, was one of the outstanding young intellectuals of his generation. Killed by the Germans during the Occupation of France, he was not allowed to fulfill all of his great promise. His work on Stendhal, many other writings, as well as his courage, will not be forgotten.

JEAN-PIERRE RICHARD published his remarkable book of criticism *Littérature et sensation* in 1954. He has since published another volume, *Poésie et profondeur*. Disciple of Georges Poulet and other phenomenological critics, Jean-Pierre Richard has applied to literary criticism his keen psychological and philosophical insights.

JEAN STAROBINSKI, a brilliant critic and scholar whose studies of Montesquieu and Rousseau have won wide acclaim, is one of the outstanding figures of the new generation of critics. His remarkable essay on Stendhal is part of *L'Œil vivant,* a volume which also deals with Corneille, Racine, and Jean-Jacques Rousseau. Jean Starobinski is Professor at the University of Geneva, Switzerland.

MARTIN TURNELL is a distinguished English critic who has written extensively on French literature. Among his better known works are *The Classical Moment* and *The Novel in France*. His love for Stendhal is of long standing, and he has recently devoted a new study to him in *The Art of French Fiction*. Martin Turnell has also written books on Baudelaire and Jacques Rivière.

Bibliography

Adams, Robert M. *Stendhal: Notes on a Novelist*. New York: Noonday Press, 1959. A brilliant and challenging book that bridges biography and literary criticism in an original fashion.

Arbelet, Paul. *La Jeunesse de Stendhal*. Paris: E. Champion, 1919. An admirably thorough and entertaining study of Stendhal's youth.

Bardèche, Maurice. *Stendhal, romancier*. Paris: Editions de la Table Ronde, 1947. A mature and extremely intelligent general discussion of Stendhal as novelist, marred occasionally by a biased political perspective.

Billy, André. *Ce cher Stendhal* . . . Paris: Flammarion, 1958. A quick-paced, well documented biography.

Blin, Georges. *Stendhal et les problèmes du roman* and *Stendhal et les problèmes de la personnalité*. Paris: J. Corti, 1954 and 1958. Thorough and often profound studies of Stendhal's art and of the complexities of his personality.

Blum, Léon. *Stendhal et le Beylisme*. Paris: A. Michel, 1930. A very elegant general study, with emphasis on biography and on the typical heroes of Stendhal.

Brombert, Victor. *Stendhal et la voie oblique*. Paris and New Haven: Presses Universitaires de France and Yale University Press, 1954. An analysis of Stendhal's irony and of the patterns of his sensibility as revealed in his novels.

Dutourd, Jean. *The Man of Sensibility*. New York: Simon and Schuster, Inc., 1961. A very unconventional, very "Stendhalian" meditation on Stendhal and on many general problems of interest to the writer.

Levin, Harry. *Toward Stendhal*. Murray, Utah (Pharos No. 3), 1945. A brilliant and well informed essay.

del Litto, Vittorio. *La Vie intellectuelle de Stendhal*. Paris: Presses Universitaires de France, 1959. A fine scholarly study of the genesis and evolution of Stendhal's idea during his formative years.

Martineau, Henri. *Le Coeur de Stendhal*. 2 vols. Paris: A. Michel, 1952, 1953. The best biography of Stendhal by the greatest Stendhal authority.

Prévost, Jean. *La Création chez Stendhal*. Paris: Mercure de France, 1951. An extremely suggestive study of Stendhal's writings, with emphasis on problems of style and literary technique.

TWENTIETH CENTURY VIEWS

The aim of this series is to present the best in contemporary critical opinion on major authors, providing a twentieth century perspective on their changing status in an era of profound revaluation.

Maynard Mack, *Series Editor*
Yale University

OTHER VOLUMES IN THIS SERIES

PROUST, edited by René Girard

T. S. ELIOT, edited by Hugh Kenner

CAMUS, edited by Germaine Brée

ROBERT FROST, edited by James M. Cox

WHITMAN, edited by Roy Harvey Pearce

SINCLAIR LEWIS, edited by Mark Schorer

HEMINGWAY, edited by Robert P. Weeks

FIELDING, edited by Ronald Paulson

THOREAU, edited by Sherman Paul